NATIONALISM AND THE MULTINATION STATE

D0760058

WITHDRAWN

THE CERI SERIES IN COMPARATIVE POLITICS AND INTERNATIONAL STUDIES

Series editor, Christophe Jaffrelot

The series consists of original manuscripts and translations of noteworthy manuscripts and publications in the social sciences emanating from the foremost French researchers.

The focus of the series is the transformation of politics and society by transnational and domestic factors—globalisation, migration and religion. States are more permeable to external influence than ever before and this phenomenon is accelerating processes of social and political change the world over. In seeking to understand and interpret these transformations, this series gives priority to social trends from below as much as to the interventions of state and nonstate actors.

ALAIN DIECKHOFF

Nationalism and the Multination State

Translated by
CYNTHIA SCHOCH

OXFORD
UNIVERSITY PRESS

Oxford University Press is a department of the
University of Oxford. It furthers the University's objective
of excellence in research, scholarship, and education
by publishing worldwide.

Oxford   New York

Auckland   Cape Town   Dar es Salaam   Hong Kong   Karachi
Kuala Lumpur   Madrid   Melbourne   Mexico City   Nairobi
New Delhi   Shanghai   Taipei   Toronto

With offices in

Argentina   Austria   Brazil   Chile   Czech Republic   France   Greece
Guatemala   Hungary   Italy   Japan   Poland   Portugal   Singapore
South Korea   Switzerland   Thailand   Turkey   Ukraine   Vietnam

Oxford is a registered trade mark of Oxford University Press
in the UK and certain other countries.

Published in the United States of America by
Oxford University Press
198 Madison Avenue, New York, NY 10016

Library of Congress Cataloging-in-Publication Data is available
Alain Dieckhoff.
Nationalism and the Multination State.
ISBN: 9780190607913

Printed in India on acid-free paper

For Milena

"Milena, what a rich, heavy name!
almost too full to be lifted!"

Franz KAFKA

To the memory of Ernest Gellner (1925–1995),
who was able to take nationalism seriously
from an intellectual standpoint
without ever departing from true humanism

CONTENTS

FOREWORD

Throughout the Cold War, national issues, which had been so preponderant in the interwar period, receded into the background, dwarfed by the bipolar ideological confrontation that was tearing the world in two. Nationalism probably had not vanished from the political horizon during that time, national liberation movements having provided the impetus for decolonization. But the specifically national character of these movements tended to be masked by Marxist-leaning rhetoric and buried under an internationalism of convenience.[1] From China to Yugoslavia and Cuba, this strategy of dissimulation proved crucial for Third World communists and was also adopted by other anti-colonial leaders such as Nasser in Egypt and the supporters of the Syrian Baath Party. These leaders eagerly combined a fervent nationalism with an equally vibrant "Arab socialism" whose primary objective was essentially to nationalize the economy. The Cold War thus unfolded under the banner of a euphemized form of nationalism.

The fall of the Berlin Wall unleashed a dramatic transformation. The abrupt end of the ideological and military struggle between the "socialist camp" and the "free world" reopened the national question on the European continent, as the Baltic states reasserted their independence and Germany promptly began the process of reunification. Elsewhere, in Yugoslavia as well as the Caucasus, confrontations between nationalisms took a violent turn. The air was suddenly filled with talk of the revenge of nations and the awakening of nationalisms. The prevailing discourse—often carrying alarmist undertones—saw this return of repressed nationalism as insufferably archaic.

This assessment was obviously over-simplistic, primarily because it is part of a teleological, linear notion of progress according to which nationalism will necessarily be surpassed by universalistic ideals—liberal democracy and communism alike. This longstanding belief was irrevocably disproven by the unparalleled exacerbation of nationalisms throughout the twentieth century. That does not mean that nationalism is eternal. However, it clearly must not be discarded too quickly, as it has been by a large number of inveterate rationalists in both the liberal and the socialist camps.

Viewing nationalism merely as a primitive form of tribalism astray in the modern world obscures the reality that its persistence, contrary to the opinion of its zealous critics, is due to the fact that nationalism is a key configuration of modernity, even if it sometimes takes on appalling forms. As an ideology and a movement, nationalism has left a deep mark on the history of the past two centuries, for better and for worse. Any survey of the history of the notion must imperatively take into account its true multiplicity.

Nationalism is a complex sociological object that cannot be reduced to its most extremist, hysterical or homicidal expressions. Focusing on these more salient manifestations (with their strong xenophobic and racist components) inevitably leads to disqualifying nationalism outright, thereby making it impossible to gain a grasp on its true driving forces. It is unlikely that nationalism would stir such passion if it were a wholly negative phenomenon. In fact, it has often served a liberating function by enabling peoples to assert their historical, cultural and social specificities.

It would be difficult to deny that engagement in national struggles was an absolutely necessary step for the Polish, Jewish or Irish peoples, just to name a few. Whether oppressed, persecuted or massacred, the only means by which they were able to overcome their existential vulnerability was to pursue nationalism to its logical conclusion by building a state whose sovereignty could provide them the collective security that they so ardently sought. Arguments that discredit nationalism too hastily should thus be avoided. In the words of Jewish historian Simon Dubnow, who nevertheless lost his life to an outbreak of nationalist hatred, "Are Kossuth's or Garibaldi's nationalist ideals reprehensible because chauvinists such as Schönerer and Wolf or Drumont and Rochefort also acted in the name of nationalism?"[2] A century later, his admonition could be rephrased without any loss of impact: "Are the nationalist ideals of Lech Walesa in Poland or Ibrahim Rugova in Kosovo reprehensible because populist demagogues such as Gábor Vona of Hungary's Jobbik party and Jean-Marie Le Pen of France's National Front proclaim themselves nationalists?"

Because nationalism is such a complex configuration that includes excessive forms as well as liberal variants and is fundamentally polysemic, constructing a general theory of nationalism is hazardous. There have nevertheless been some commendable attempts.[3] I personally will not venture in this direction, preferring to focus on a more narrowly defined phenomenon: the universalization of nationalism. Association of the two terms might appear surprising at first, in that nationalism is a principle typically used to defend particularism. This ideology for mobilizing specificity has expanded phenomenally in the past two centuries, however—at first in Europe, then gradually spreading to other continents. The club of initially European nation-states has subsequently become worldwide, and although proletarian internationalism remains a dream, the universalization of nationalism has become a reality, continuing to produce a cascade of effects.

My longstanding acquaintance with the Middle East, and particularly with Israel/Palestine, "the holy land of antagonistic nationalisms," has certainly contributed to nourishing sensitivity to the question of national identities, their crystallization and their development in both ideological and practical terms. All of my previous work has revolved around these topics in one way or another. The present book thus represents in many ways the extension of an abiding intellectual interest, albeit with a new scope, because it is grounded in a comparative approach primarily focused on Europe and North America.

The objective of the book is to suggest avenues for reflection on dissociative nationalisms; in other words on "nationalitarian"[4] movements at work within a constituted state that demand political autonomy or even independence, in the name of a human group described as a "nation" and sharing certain specific characteristics, such as history, culture, language, shared past, or territory.

This peripheral, breakaway nationalism is the most active form of contemporary nationalism, from Quebec to the Balkans, via Catalonia, Flanders and Corsica. This is certainly not to suggest that the centralist, unitary nationalism forcefully proclaimed by strands of the populist extreme right—the National Front and the Austrian "Liberal" Party, for example—have disappeared. But while these nationalisms fit by definition within existing state frameworks, breakaway nationalisms strive to create new political spaces, and in that sense, they help to give new impetus to the spread of nationalism.

I will endeavor to present what I believe are the driving forces behind this phenomenon and to analyze how they have manifested themselves, before examining, in the book's second part, how states can respond.

PART ONE

THE CALL OF NATIONALISM

1

NATIONALISM AND GLOBALIZATION

In the course of the 1990s, new countries enhanced the world map, most of which had no previous political existence. From Uzbekistan, Moldova and Slovenia to Eritrea, no fewer than twenty new states came into being. And even this tally, which takes only internationally recognized entities into account, offers a fragmented image of a much deeper trend in national claims.

In one instance, a Flemish minister-president demanded the establishment of confederalism in Belgium, which is considered by some analysts to be the final stage before the country breaks up. In another, Scottish First Minister Alex Salmond obstinately fought for Scotland's independence and in September 2014 called an independence referendum.[1] Elsewhere, Quebecois[2] sovereignists continue to campaign for the independence of the "Belle Province" despite the failure of a second referendum in 1995. Beyond the West, there are equally remarkable examples of nationalist dynamics, including Turkish and Iraqi Kurdistan and Indian Punjab, where Sikhs are struggling to establish Khalistan (the land of the pure) as an independent state.

Such examples of nationalist fervor are often seen as regressive and anachronistic. They are described as regressive because by privileging individual identities, nationalism compromises political citizenship as the supreme form of allegiance transcending individual attachments. Charges of anachronism stem from the fact that these expressions of nationalism run counter to a globalization process frequently perceived as a harbinger of the true human condition, leveling differences. However, further discussion is warranted of the vision that sees the expansion of foreign trade, the increase in global communications and the spread of a standardized mass culture as leading to the dilution of national specificities and the gradual breakdown of barriers between peoples.

This optimistic appraisal of globalization is essentially shared by neo-Marxists and neo-liberals alike. While neo-Marxists complain about the social costs of economic globalization, they persist in thinking that "National differences and antagonism between peoples are vanishing every day, owing to the development of the bourgeoisie, to freedom of commerce, to the world market, to uniformity in the mode of production and in the conditions of life corresponding thereto."[3] On the other hand, liberals observe matters from a functionalist perspective that views the emergence of a globalized market economy as a means of fostering interdependence and interactions and of creating a truly international community based on shared interests. Still, reality obstinately resists such rosy forecasts, and borders, far from being abolished, have proliferated even as globalization advances. How can this paradox be explained?[4]

Similarity Sharpens Difference

We can begin to address this question by narrowing its scope and pointing out that globalization is relative. In fact, in two respects it is only partial. First, while a growing share of trade takes place in the "world economy," the movement of goods still takes place primarily within each country's borders. Second, the internationalization of trade and capital primarily affects developed countries and some "emerging economies," bypassing entire segments of the Third World. Globalization actually operates within a network of large metropolises in which trade activities are concentrated, while vast areas—such as the African continent and the "internal peripheries" of rich countries—are wholly neglected.[5]

Because globalization remains fragmentary, it is currently unable to create a uniform, truly global social space and so lastingly to diminish national particularism. Nevertheless, for proponents of a homogenizing globalization, this state of affairs is not necessarily permanent. In the long run, the consolidation of the global economy will be accompanied by the retreat of nation-states and the decline of both nations and nationalism, which will no longer play more than "subordinate, and often rather minor roles."[6] In other words, in this view, the march of world history will eventually overcome nationalism.

This line of reasoning awakens a degree of skepticism, however. Even if one accepts the argument that globalization is still in its early stages and is too underdeveloped to dampen nationalist demands, what then explains the concomitance between the gradual deepening of globalization and the upsurge in claims to nationhood?

Eric Hobsbawm and other analysts have attempted to discern a hidden dialectic behind appearances. They view the various manifestations of nationalist fervor in the late twentieth century as the swan song of nationalism rather than its apotheosis. Far from demonstrating the vitality of the phenomenon, this period allegedly proves that it has run out of steam. Thus, before breathing its last, nationalism shines in all its glory one last time. This conception eludes verification and, as a "ruse of history," ultimately explains very little.

It would seem to be more accurate to limit the scope of the globalization/ fragmentation paradox by circumscribing the causal relationship between these two phenomena. The appearance of a myriad of new states in the 1990s in fact owes little to economic globalization and its social and cultural corollaries. On the contrary, it was countries sidelined by the capitalist economy, the "true socialist" countries, that experienced national implosions. The disintegration of the Soviet Union, Czechoslovakia and Yugoslavia was above all the consequence of the crumbling of authoritarian federal systems, or even, in the case of the USSR, of a veritable empire.

Does this mean that the relationship between globalization and the surge in nationalist movements is purely coincidental? I do not believe that this is the case. Indeed, there are observable interactions between them. Whereas the breakup of the USSR and the other two federations can be explained largely by political factors, in developed countries, the persistence and deepening of nationalist claims are sustained by globalization, the newest and most decisive phase of modernization. Again, this is not what is behind the Flemish, Catalan or Basque nationalisms which, having emerged in the nineteenth century, are the products of a specific socio-historic context and in particular of a certain type of relationship to the state. On the other hand, the strong support they enjoy today is partly explained by the rise of globalization, which, through a demonstration effect, exerts a catalyzing influence on nationalism.

In its current phase, globalization is a twofold process. On the one hand, economic globalization, the growing role of international organizations, the emergence of global issues such as the environment, the spread of a universal, standardized—and to a large extent Americanized—culture and the universalization of certain principles such as human rights and democracy have brought about a global civilization. Although it clearly does not yet span the entire planet, this global culture undeniably exists in certain places.

People from different societies inhabiting the four corners of the planet currently share certain common traits, including consumer habits, cultural references and values. The civilizing process, to borrow Norbert Elias' expression, demonstrably leads to a convergence of lifestyles, conceptions and representations. On the other hand, however, these intersections themselves generate powerful symbolic differentiations that tend to be expressed particularly through national or ethnic identity claims. In other words, the paradox of nationalism in the early twenty-first century, which is most clearly noticeable in the West, the center of the global civilization, resides precisely in this tension: that nationalism is becoming strongest at a time when people have more and more in common.[7]

Two examples suffice to illustrate this trend. Modernization in the province of Quebec once lagged behind English-speaking Canada. It was probably not as sudden and belated as some have argued, citing the 1960s as the critical period for Quebec's supposedly abrupt transition from a rural, agricultural society to an urban, industrial society. Although its modernization was more gradual than this, spanning the entire first half of the century, it undeniably experienced phenomenal acceleration after the Liberal Party came to power in the province in 1960. This period marked the beginning of the "Quiet Revolution" during which the provincial government became the agent of emancipation for the Quebecois and society became rapidly secularized. This period of profound social change gradually erased the disparities between anglophones and francophones. In fact, the indicators all point to a startling convergence of the two communities.

Whereas francophones made up large segments of the working class in the early twentieth century, they subsequently experienced a considerable rise in social status in terms of both income and occupation. Today, levels of urbanization and consumer practices are virtually identical. The same observation can be made with respect to behavior, as Quebec aligned itself with the rest of Canada in manifesting a drastic reduction in religious practice and birth rates and a significant increase in divorce rates. Attitudes toward civil liberties and ethics are now found to be very similar.[8] Yet it was when francophones were growing closer to anglophones that francophones founded the Parti Québécois. This political party came to power in Quebec in 1976 and twice has sought to make Quebec a sovereign state. In 1970, 34% of francophones defined themselves as Canadians and 21% as Quebecois; twenty years later, these figures were 9% and 59% respectively.

A similar duality can be observed in Spain. Catalonia and the Basque Country spearheaded industrialization in the nineteenth century, leading to the rapid modernization of social structures, accompanied by the rise of the proletariat and major industrialists. Castile, on the other hand, remained a traditional society in which a small landed aristocracy dominated the peasant majority. This contrast between peripheries at the vanguard of economic development and social change and a highly conservative political center began to soften under the Franco-era technocracy of the 1960s and continued to diminish after democracy was established. There again, the gap also closed in terms of lifestyles and value systems among the various nationalities that make up the Spanish nation. And yet, while in 1979 28.3% of the Basque population declared that they felt solely or primarily Spanish, only 21.6% agreed with the same statement in 1991, a figure that had dropped to 8.5% by 2007. A similar but even more striking trend was observable among Catalans: 37.5% identified themselves as Spanish in 1979, 19% in 1994, and 12.6% in 2010.

These examples clearly challenge the validity of the nation-building theory promoted by the political scientist Karl Deutsch. Deutsch contended that modernization—the principal indicators of which are urbanization, industrialization, mass education and the development of communications—gives rise to an intensification of exchanges. Increased social mobility then gradually leads to deeper and deeper national integration, sweeping away former local or regional allegiances.[9] Some scholars have argued that the webs of interdependence become so dense that they could have a corrosive effect on nations, eventually leading to the formation of a single world state.[10]

This correlation has not been borne out. Although increased interactions do indeed produce growing similarity- and therefore, to some extent, national (Spanish, Canadian) or even supranational (European) assimilation—they do nothing to dampen parallel tendencies toward differentiation. Any argument to the contrary entails confusion between socio-cultural proximity and identity convergence. The adoption of similar habits, behaviors and values does not suffice to bring about a common identity. The convergence of attitudes and values probably does not spontaneously generate a desire for national distinction. Bavarians, Saxons and Hessians are not about to engage in a process of separation to re-establish the kingdoms and principalities of yore simply because they share a standardized German identity. But conversely, similarity, far from eroding identity distinctions, frequently helps to strengthen them.

The Logics behind the Nationalist Paradox

How can this peculiar dialectic between resemblance and difference be explained? There have been some attempts to elucidate this mystery based on

Freud's notion of the "narcissism of minor differences." Individuals—and peoples—appear to attach ever-greater importance to their differences as those differences become smaller.[11] In other words, the symbolic importance attributed to dissimilarities becomes more intense as real disparities diminish. While this psychological compensatory mechanism undoubtedly plays a role, it cannot explain everything. Reducing the nationalitarian process to its purely psychological effects is tantamount to considering it as an artificial phenomenon that can be overcome using willpower, which is manifestly false.

An anthropological approach may shed light on this question. As Claude Lévi-Strauss noted, "Forces working in contrary directions operate simultaneously in human societies, some being conducive to the preservation and even the accentuation of particularism, while others tend to promote convergence and affinity."[12] The first tendency is sustained by isolation, but also by proximity, which prompts a desire to distinguish oneself, to assert oneself by highlighting differences with others; the second is fostered by geographic contiguity, exchange and contact. Proximity thus works simultaneously in two opposite directions, both towards closeness and eventually homogenization, and towards diversification and fragmentation. "In the inter-relations of human societies," there is "an *optimum* degree of diversity, which they cannot surpass but which they can also not fall short of without incurring risks."[13] If they surpass the diversity threshold, they become caught up in a process of infinite fragmentation that would strip them of even the faintest traces of cohesion. And if they fall short of the threshold, they completely lose their specificity, blending into a kind of shapeless social magma. The convergence/divergence dialectic is precisely what maintains the differential gap between societies that is critical to their survival.

The anthropological perspective described above clearly coincides with the sociological intuitions of Alexis de Tocqueville, the French historian, who foresaw the advent of a global civilization. Democracy, a political regime that promotes equality among individuals, as well as the economic modernity it accompanies, stimulates the spread of similar ways of acting, thinking and feeling. By contrast to the Middle Ages, an era of total fragmentation, Tocqueville envisioned the opposite tendency taking shape in modern times: "Peoples seem to march toward unity. Intellectual bonds unite the most distant parts of the land [sic] and men cannot remain strangers to one another for a single day."[14] Paradoxically, however, this growing similitude heightens a need for distinction. As Tocqueville phrased it, "When ... conditions differ little, the least advantages gain importance. As each sees a million people around him who possess [advantages] that are wholly alike or analogous, pride becomes demanding and jealous; it becomes attached to pittances and defends them stubbornly."[15] The aristocratic principle of distinction thus creeps into the very heart of egalitarian democracy, manifesting itself at both the individual and group levels. At the collective level, it is expressed through different spheres of belonging, such as religious communities and associations, but is primarily focused on a national reference point, the only political framework considered to be legitimate, because it is based on the ultimate democratic passion: equality.

This insight in turn contributes to an understanding of the resurgence of national claims in Europe and in the developed world, in precisely those regions where the standardization process caused by modernity is strongest. Nationalist movements in Scotland and Flanders are not anachronistic manifestations, but instead represent hallmarks of modernity. They are neither remnants of a past that is slipping away nor some primitive after-effect, but preface the future of contemporary societies.

The history of recent centuries demonstrates, moreover, that periods experiencing a significant increase in exchanges have always been unambiguously correlated with increased momentum in nationalist claims. The invention of the printing press, which provoked unparalleled dissemination of knowledge, the development of maritime trade and the discovery of the New World gave rise to a more open perspective on the world. At the same time, however, various European national communities were increasingly asserting themselves and distancing themselves from each other in both religious and linguistic terms (which in fact often overlapped). Spain completed the *Reconquista* and, in the process, its early political and cultural nationalization. France and England came out of the Hundred Years War with far more pronounced national specificities. Elsewhere, nascent Protestantism and the promotion of vernacular languages (Luther translated the Bible into German), as well as the establishment of state churches, fostered the development of national sentiment. This effervescence in turn led to the establishment of the first state system, which was formally recognized in 1648 in the Peace of Westphalia.

Two centuries later, the industrial revolution brought in tow a phenomenal increase of communications and the accelerated movement of goods and capital. As the world shrank, new states such as Serbia, Greece, Romania and Bulgaria nevertheless came into being within the Ottoman Empire, and, after the First World War, the ruins of the Austro-Hungarian Empire and, to a lesser extent, the Russian Empire (the Baltic states, Finland). The gradual rise of mass society in the interwar period and rapid technological development later contributed to the globalization of certain problems, including war; this was also accompanied by a "counter-shock" phenomenon in which dozens of colonized countries took control of their political destinies, transforming the community of nations, hitherto essentially European, into a truly international community. Today, economic globalization, the standardization of cultural production based on the American model, the spread of the market economy, the propagation of the democratic model and the development of a communication society appear to be ushering in a fourth phase in this identity quest that will once again find expression in nationalist demands.

History thus cruelly belies the naïve view that the multiplication of social and economic exchanges and the development of information and travel should necessarily contribute to the elimination of political, religious and community barriers. In his day, the historian Carlton Hayes had already denounced the misguided optimism of those who were "convinced that the Industrial Revolution is fundamentally anti-nationalist, that what nationalist effects it has had during the past [nineteenth] century have been incidental and temporary, and that in the long run it must generate increasingly such economic and material forces as will bring peoples into vital interdependence and thereby supplant nationalism with internationalism and cosmopolitanism."[16]

In fact, globalization has helped, mostly involuntarily, to maintain the logics of identity. First, in their phase of imperialist expansion, European nations directly propagated political concepts—democracy, nation, self-determination—that subjugated peoples later appropriated and turned against the colonizers in order to develop their own projects of collective emancipation. Second, in a more subtle way, Europe's expansion in Asia and Africa helped spread universal norms, both in affairs of state via colonial administrations and in the religious domain through the Christian missions, while also contributing to the proliferation of ethnic particularisms by formalizing previously loose dividing lines between populations. As Jean-François Bayart has shown, colonization manufactured ethnicity both to facilitate bureaucratic control over the "natives" and to preserve the African pseudo-authenticity that it actually endeavored to create.[17]

There is every reason to believe that the present acceleration of globalization will serve to maintain this phenomenon of particularization by providing it with additional ways of manifesting itself. As groups are increasingly open to the world, they tend to withdraw into themselves.

The Alliance between Nationalism and Capitalism

The process of modernity is paradoxical: it breaks down existing barriers while constantly creating new ones. Nothing better illustrates this extraordinary contradiction than the transformations that have taken place in our relationships to space. In some respects, the phenomenal development of modern communications ultimately leads to the annihilation of space through time.[18] Technology has harnessed both its contours and its expanse. This has not only made the world smaller, but it has downgraded the role of the state, whose claim to exclusive control of the national territory is jeopardized. The loss of absolute control, in particular over borders, weakens the sovereign capacity of the state. This challenge to state power, however, has not brought about a world without borders but has instead fostered withdrawal into ever-smaller spaces. As distance becomes effaced by denser and faster communications, real physical locations gain in importance. Neighborhoods, cities and regions form a web of local spaces reinforced by globalization itself, to the detriment of the abstract notion of state territoriality.[19]

This phenomenon is linked to the dynamics of capitalism. As Karl Marx noted with remarkable accuracy, capitalism seeks the universal development of the forces of production, a sustained increase in wealth and the intensification of trade; the creation of a world market is its ultimate goal. This objective requires perpetual upheaval of the conditions for producing capital. By virtue of this principle, "capital drives behind barriers and national prejudices... It is destructive towards and constantly revolutionizes it, tearing down all the barriers which hem in the development of the forces of production."[20] Even if, by nature, capitalism resembles Kronos devouring his children, it nevertheless constantly confronts and must overcome specific conditions of production— natural (related to geography or climate) and social (anthropological or historical). Not only does capitalism thus constantly encounter limits inherent to its nature, but its continued development also requires the perpetual creation of new bases for expansion. Special economic zones, tax havens and free trade zones are all examples of new spaces that are critical to the true globalization of capitalism.

The investment strategies of economic actors consequently target nation-states less than they do region-states. These are economic zones with fuzzy boundaries that can be entirely subsumed under a given state (the Kansai region around the Japanese city of Osaka, or the German state of Baden-Württemberg), or may straddle several states, as in the "growth triangle" of Singapore, Johor (Malaysia) and Batam (Indonesia).[21] Many investors now

11

perceive such regions as operational units in the global economy because their fairly small size provides sufficient density while also forcing them constantly to adapt to changes in international competition. With a small domestic market, regions have no other choice than to have open economies fully integrated into world trade.[22] To attract foreign capital, the economic and political elites of these region-states have every interest in promoting their regional assets and distancing themselves from oversight by the political center. Their inclusion in the world economy ensures them direct access to resources, which allows them at least partially to do without a national market, while strengthening an independent economic base.

Although this situation has no direct political implications for many region-states (such as Sao Paulo or Tokyo), it unquestionably gives those with a strong "identity differential," such as Catalonia and Flanders, additional resources for their national identity strategies.[23] In Flanders, for instance, a wide array of assets is promoted in order to attract foreign companies to the area: modern infrastructure, qualified labor and a strong work ethic, for instance. Such arguments obviously persuaded a number of international businesses, including Mazda, Volvo, Philip Morris and Pioneer, to establish themselves in the north of Belgium rather than in Wallonia. Globalization thus acts as a positive factor in national identity strategies. The existence of identity markers, particularly language, is not a prerequisite for political mobilization, however, as exemplified by the Northern League in Italy.

This movement, founded by Umberto Bossi, managed to become a major political player in northern Italy (and especially the northeast) by advocating economic nationalism based on denunciations of the tentacular, inefficient and parasitic state bureaucracy. Small business owners, who form much of the League's social base, are not holdovers from a bygone era but instead operate in the most dynamic and innovative sectors of the economy. They are tempted by the separation of northern from southern Italy (either through federalization or outright independence) in the interest of efficiency. Economic modernity thus feeds nationalist protest, even if superficial observation could give the impression that Leaguism is archaic and backward.

In mid-September 1996, Bossi announced Padania's (the Po Valley) independence, after initiating a northern march to the sea from the source of the River Po to Venice. This was in some ways pointlessly grandiloquent and even downright grotesque. Yet it would be an error to simply smile at the flags bearing a six-point star and activists clad in green shirts waving banknotes bearing Bossi's effigy. By this ceremonial, the *Senatur* was simply seeking to endow Leaguism with the symbols associated with nationhood. He had a dual objective: to mask the economic utilitarianism underlying the movement's secessionist tendencies and to generate a sense of unity in Padania, a region historically divided into rival kingdoms, dukedoms and republics.

Clearly, the ebbs and flows of claims to national identity are more tortuous than ingenuous interpreters of globalization might think, considering nationalist forces as a steamroller that can flatten out differences without encountering resistance. This is due to the structural contradiction inherent in modernization. It is not meant to spontaneously create a world without borders any more than it is naturally inclined to exacerbate differences. It just happens to be doing both.

In its early phase, modernization historically had a homogenizing influence, but it was often partial and unanticipated. In the nineteenth century, industrialization brought about major migratory flows inside countries in which populations moved from their native provinces and traditional occupations to settle in capitals and other areas experiencing industrial expansion. These internal migrations generally had an assimilative effect, transforming Auvergnats and Bretons into Frenchmen, and Slovaks and Moravians into Austrians. The results of modernization were vastly different, however, when population movements were confined to a single region.

Intra-regional migration led to the abandonment of local micro-identities, in favor not of national (state) identities, but of regional identities. The industrial boom in Catalonia in the last quarter of the nineteenth century prompted rural dwellers, from the border along the Pyrenees in the north to Valencia in the south, to move to Barcelona. Sharing a spoken language in Barcelona, they experienced for the first time the vague sensation of forming one and the same human community. Their village identities were gradually supplanted by a Catalan identity that early nationalist political organizations energetically promoted. In this context, the migration from the 1920s of populations from other regions of Spain, far from toning down an awareness of Catalan specificity, only stimulated it. Although modest at first, these flows took on enormous proportions under Franco's rule, with the arrival of 1.5 million people (particularly from Andalusia) between 1951 and 1975 in a region with a population of only 3.5 million in the early 1950s. This massive influx reinforced the sense of urgency among Catalan organizations to vigorously defend their Catalan-ness.

Modernization thus indeed appears to be a powerful factor in national consciousness building, because it underscores the common features within a group as well as features that distinguish one group from the next.[24] One important question remains to be explored: Why does culture play such an important discriminating role in this strategy of differentiation?

2

THE NATION AS A COMMUNITY OF CULTURE

Human societies are societies of culture. In that regard, their world differs radically from the animal world.[1] As culture is the foundation of life in society, it performs an essential function in the shaping of collective identities. This is true as much for social classes as it is for "social groups" (women, homosexuals, etc.), and as much for ethnic minorities as for territorialized national groups. While political mobilizations in the name of the nation—the central configuration of modernity—have naturally had to "make do" with culture, the forms this interaction takes are complex and warrant detailed examination.

The Shaping of Cultures

Cultures, in the anthropological sense, are clearly not entities possessed with a timeless and permanent substance. They are not organic units with hermetic boundaries but are instead constantly being shaped, fashioned and reworked through ongoing processes of borrowing and exchange. Yet each one has a certain specific configuration that makes it possible to identify and distinguish it from its neighbors. Without this minimal internal coherence, cultural diversity would be unthinkable.

Claude Lévi-Strauss emphasized this extraordinary variety by pointing out the existence of thousands of human cultures, whereas "races" were counted in digits. We could add that cultures are also far more numerous than political regimes, which can be counted on two hands. Since cultures exist in such abundance, they breed specificity, which is conducive to underscoring differences and thus apt to promote particularism. Furthermore, cultural diversification is constantly sustained by the historical process itself.

Every culture lives and prospers through contact with others. Such numerous ties are necessary to its enrichment, for without them, closed in on itself, it could only fall into decay. Yet the coalition of cultures inevitably prompts mutual readjustments, even a leveling out that could eventually lead to the emergence of a homogenous world civilization. This possibility is countered by new aspirations for diversification that in return reintroduce other differential gaps between cultures. The process does not imply the perpetual, static or exact reproduction of cultures. On the contrary, throughout historical evolution, some cultures die out, others appear, and most of them evolve through constant reconfiguration. However, cultural diversity itself is perpetually reinvigorated because it is a requisite for mankind's survival.[2]

Cultures have also gained visibility. The use of the concept of culture as a synonym for education and the shaping of the mind is in fact contemporaneous with two major phenomena dating from the second half of the eighteenth century: the emergence of the individual as an autonomous subject and the advent of the nation as a collective subject. Culture became a recognized category of thought at the very moment when societies were undergoing a radical organizational transformation: the hierarchical order of social groups was replaced by a collection of individuals sharing equal rights within a national community. This Copernican revolution radically altered the place occupied by culture, as Ernest Gellner ably demonstrated.

In agrarian societies, opposite the ruling strata (warriors, bureaucrats and especially clerics), who alone possessed high culture, the peasant masses remained closed off in rural communities that were shut in on themselves and within which internal distinctions were so strong that they did not even share a common popular culture. Industrial society radically altered this order of things. Division of labor required greater social mobility, which took the form of a standardized education, and thus the spread of a common culture, in particular a written and spoken language.[3] The function of culture changed meaning: while in pre-modern societies it was a way of signifying differences in status, it henceforth underscored similarities among members of a given social unit and served to consolidate a new form of community: the nation. Culture has in fact moved the differentiation axis. Whereas in traditional society it replicated the rigid social boundary between ruling strata and peasant masses along a horizontal line, it now establishes lines of national separation along a vertical axis.

The multiple facets and meanings of culture—customs, habits, memories, beliefs—make it particularly attractive to nationalist actors. Their strategies can draw on a wide variety of registers depending on the moment. Thus, the creation of Belgium in 1830 was the product of a political rift with the Netherlands that coincided with a religious divide dating back more than two centuries: the Catholic south stood against the Calvinist north. Catholicism was central in structuring Belgian identity, to such an extent that even the emergence of a strong secular movement can only be understood as a reaction to the omnipresent influence Catholicism had acquired since the sixteenth-century Counter-Reformation in the then Spanish Netherlands. Yet this religious factor gradually lost its relevance, and the linguistic divide between French and Dutch speakers, originally quite secondary, gained in importance through the efforts of nationalist entrepreneurs, to the point of awakening separatist temptations. Today language has totally overtaken religion as an identity resource.

The same resource, moreover, can be used in completely opposite perspectives, depending on the actors' intentions. This is true, for instance, of language in the former Yugoslavia. In the nineteenth century, linguistic reformers deliberately forged a language common to Croats and Serbs based on a central dialect, to emphasize the "Illyrian identity" of the South Slavs. This identity was specifically meant to transcend religious differences and eclipse divergent historical trajectories. With the breakup of the Yugoslav federation, the Croatian authorities started hunting down "Serbisms," which they attempted to replace with "purely Croatian" words. Linguistic dissociation was encouraged, the better to reinforce Croatia's political separation from its Serbian neighbors.

Plainly, the malleability of culture makes it a suitable instrument to wield in a wide variety of strategies. And this culture need not be high culture, sustained by scholars, or even a folk culture striving for recognition. It can be a culture in the limited sense, as for the Northern League in Italy, which rebelled against Rome's centralism to defend the entrepreneurial culture of the "white areas" in the northeast and the work ethic of small business owners and craftsmen in that region. Due to its highly plural nature, culture is extremely useful for highlighting particularism, especially when it is the only immediately available resource to perform the task of national differentiation.

For peoples who had never had their own political entity, such as the Estonians and the Latvians, or who were deprived of it through centuries of oppression, as in Bulgaria and Lithuania, only through culture could they assert their individuality. But even in such cases, an internal coherence had to be found for a culture originally far less cohesive than one might have thought. Linguistically, for instance, the "national language" often did not exist. It had to be created from various dialects, and this was not always an easy task. The first attempt to standardize the Slovak language, undertaken in the late eighteenth century, failed because its advocates had opted for the western variant, which was understood by too few speakers. It was not until the middle of the nineteenth century, with the adoption of the dialect of central Slovakia under the impetus of Ludovit Stúr, that Slovak became a unified literary language.

In another vein, folklorists undertook a remarkable effort to collect popular songs, poems and folktales and publish them in numerous anthologies to prove the vivacity and unity of the Slovene, Ukrainian and Finnish cultures. This foundational research by cultural entrepreneurs who forge a national culture by piecing disparate elements together into a system was the initial and *sine qua non* condition for commencing national mobilization.[4]

Political Uses of Culture

Once the cultural bedrock has thus been formed, it has a dual strategic function. It must first of all "prove" the existence of a people by conferring upon it a semblance of "primordial" unity. Despite its political subjection, the people in question is endowed with its own specificity. At the same time, culture also offers a means to challenge the political order to which the people is subjected. Culture thus serves as "an ideal foundation to every tribunal undertaking"[5] by standing in opposition to the universal pretentions of empires or states, in the name of the particularisms the people claim. Appealing to culture should eventually make it easier to cast off political subordination.

By insisting on cultural specificities, even if this means accentuating them, nationalist leaders seek above all else to distinguish their people as far as possible from others, so as to give full legitimacy to their aspirations for political independence. As such, promoting Ukrainian, Bulgarian or Latvian culture fits into the process of forging an identity and protesting against the imperial order of the Habsburgs, the Osmanlis and the Romanovs. In the same manner, Third World national liberation movements' exaltation of Black, Arab or South Asian cultures sought to renew with a past frequently denigrated by colonialism, while at the same time distancing themselves from the West, a process essential to their political success.

Frantz Fanon emphasized just how indispensable the reappropriation of an "indigenous" culture was to the success of the anti-colonial struggle: "This passionate quest for a national culture prior to the colonial era can be justified by the colonized intellectuals' shared interest in stepping back and taking a hard look at the Western culture in which they risk becoming ensnared."[6] We should not, however, mistake the reasons for successful reference to "national culture." This success is not because the standard-bearers of nationalism have rediscovered some sort of original, intact and virgin identity, even if such is their claim. Their aspiration to restore lost purity is in fact largely illusory, given that cultures are always forged through borrowing from other cultures, hybridization and infinite recombinations. Even so, despite its chimerical nature, this "return to the culture of origin" indeed fosters multifaceted identity-based mobilization, as it encourages rejection of the dominant culture and restores dignity to the dominated. In other words, reference to a so-called national culture is probably rooted in myth, but this in no way detracts from its unquestionable social effectiveness.

This paradox stems from the fact that culture thus used reflects the moral ideal of authenticity identified by Charles Taylor.[7] This ideal, a specific feature of the modern era, implies that each person affirms "an original way of being human" through his or her life choices. The ethics of authenticity do not, however, imply blind loyalty to a joint cultural legacy, as a hasty interpretation might lead one to believe. It "means being true to my own originality," which implies expressing one's freedom.

But being true to oneself necessarily fits into a historical and social background. It is therefore not entirely undefined. What we are cannot be separated from where we are from: identity is always localized. It is particularly dependent on the cultural context, which in the modern era is essentially shaped by the national framework. This explains most people's sincere attachment to this familiar space. The increase of migratory flows should not make us lose sight of the fact that the immense majority continue to live within their national environment and do not seek to change it.

Such loyalty is probably instrumental to some degree: it is easier to move within a society in which one has been socialized since childhood than to start a new life in a different environment and learn the rules by which it functions. Yet it would be wrong to interpret such loyalty solely in terms of ulterior motives. It is also the manifestation of the ideal of authenticity that prompts an individual—all else being equal—to remain in his own cultural universe rather than to join another.

Even in a Europe destined, according to some, to become "postnational," this remains overwhelmingly the case. Although European Community (EC) members have guaranteed right of residence throughout the entire Union territory, only 1.5 per cent of EC nationals live in a country other than their own. It would be a distortion to reduce this tendency to nervous withdrawal into one's self. The danger probably exists, but in general the individual propensity to prefer one's familiar cultural sphere is not synonymous with confinement; it could well be the essential condition for fulfillment. The full exercise of individual rights is facilitated in an accessible, comprehensible, cultural environment that can be mastered, rather than in an unfamiliar cultural framework where the rules governing it are a mystery.[8] Once again, this in no way implies that an individual cannot become accustomed to another cultural universe. On the contrary, migrations prove that such adaptation is perfectly possible, even if the adjustment required often carries a social or psychological cost that can be hard to bear. The rational choices an individual is bound to make will, however, undoubtedly be easier if they are made within a cultural universe of which he has a deep understanding.[9]

The importance of culture does not, however, imply that it has not been used in different ways in various national mobilization processes.

Culture has been resorted to all the more as it is expected to make up for a strong "national deficiency." This was particularly true of the "small nations" of Eastern Europe mentioned previously and that Engels called "peoples without history." They suffered from a compound deficiency: political (lack of political unity), social (lack of local ruling elites) and cultural (lack of high culture).[10] The case of the Slovaks well illustrates this triple deficit. Integrated into the Hungarian Kingdom, dominated politically by the Hungarian nobility, deprived of an entrepreneurial class that was German and Jewish, they could not even take pride in an ancient literary tradition. In this desolate landscape, the formation of a national culture remained the easiest task and in any event was an essential prerequisite to the production of indigenous political and economic elites and the achievement of political independence.

However, while "small nations" invested heavily in culture, they were not the only ones to do so. To remain within the context of nineteenth-century Europe, cultural nationalism was a reality in each and every case. It was present in emerging nations that suffered from far more limited "structural deficits" than the "peoples without a history." Let us take two examples. Nineteenth-century Hungary had only two sources of frustration. Unlike the peasant nations of Eastern Europe, it presented the image of a complete society: rural masses at its base, nobility at the top, and between the two the clergy, the gentry and an emerging middle class. This social completeness was hampered, however, by the country's political subjection to Habsburg Austria and by the cultural predominance of Latin (as well as German, to a lesser extent), which prevented the emergence of a national literature in Hungarian, until the late eighteenth century. Then, a host of poets such as Kazinczy and Vitéz lent it expression, giving Hungarian literature a shine that ushered it into the pantheon of great European writing.

Germany offers another example. At the end of the eighteenth century, its most crippling deficit was political. The Holy Roman Empire of the German Nation was merely a loose association of more than 300 territorial states and 1500 imperial duchies. The little southern territory of Swabia alone was divided into ninety-two duchies and imperial cities. There again, culture played a decisive role in establishing among the Germans a sense of historical unity that could raise them above their political fragmentation. Unlike in "small nations," in late-eighteenth-century Germany, cultural entrepreneurs had a high culture immediately available to them, with two major assets: a language and a national myth.

By translating the Bible into German, Luther gave the language of the people extraordinary legitimacy and national literature a decisive boost. At the same time, humanist historians were able to trace a line of descent between the Germanic tribes and the late medieval Germans thanks to the rediscovery of Tacitus' *Germania*. The name of Arminius, chieftain of the Cherusci tribe who fought against Rome's domination, was Germanized as Hermann. He became the central figure of the German national myth and came to embody the Germans' ethical superiority despite their chronic political weakness.[11] This budding national consciousness was given decisive impetus by Herder, the *Sturm und Drang* poets and later the Romantics, who made culture the repository of the people's national genius. Schiller had sensed the extent to which this cultural overdevelopment harbored virtues able to compensate for political weakness when he declared, "While the political Empire has tottered, the spiritual realm has become all the firmer and richer." Effervescence in all artistic domains (literature, theater, music and painting) gave rise to a sense of shared cultural community among the elites that would prove highly valuable in the ensuing phase of political mobilization when it came time to constitute a unified German state.

Territorialized nations deprived of political sovereignty were not the only ones to resort to culture. It was also used by national minorities—in other words, ethnic groups living in a given country while having a cultural attachment to a neighboring nation. Until 1945, this was the case for a multitude of groups scattered among several countries but able to appeal to the protection of a "mother-nation": Hungarians, Germans, Ruthenians, and so on. Among these minorities, cultural undertakings played a decisive role as they facilitated the preservation of the group's collective identity and its transnational nature.

Lastly, with a similar concern to create a bond of solidarity across borders, diaspora communities in past centuries constantly promoted culture as the unifying cement. The publication of newspapers and books in Yiddish and Hebrew strengthened a sense of unity within a dispersed Jewish world. In the eighteenth century, the profusion of titles in Greek printed all over Europe, from Venice to Vienna to Saint Petersburg, as well as in the eastern Mediterranean, from Jerusalem to Aleppo to Istanbul, helped to stimulate Hellenic identity.

The Intelligentsia, the Voice of Nationalism

Culture could not have fulfilled its dual strategic function of attestation and contestation had it not been forcefully embodied by a particular social class keen to promote it, namely the intelligentsia. Most research on the expansion of nationalism in the nineteenth century has shown the extent to which this was the driving force behind claims to nationhood. The intelligentsia owed this vital awakening function to its intermediary role. The product of a more open educational system, the intelligentsia emerged in a phase of social transition from an agrarian and feudal society to an industrial and national society and found itself doubly alienated, both from the overall society in which it moved and from traditional elites within its group of belonging. It was therefore the perfect agent to translate modernity into the people's language. Modernity, hitherto transmitted by a language used internationally (such as French in the eighteenth century), was now conveyed via a codified and standardized language of the people, all the more valued as the people were supposedly the repository of the unadulterated authenticity extolled by Romanticism.

Nationalism is closely linked to the emergence of modern society and the increase in contacts—through the escalation of exchanges and migration—between worlds previously unknown to each other. In nineteenth-century Central Europe, industrialization thus prompted the migration of a fraction of Slavic peasant peoples to the major urban centers, where the German culture predominated. At the same time, for the small Slavic elites, social promotion involved their incorporation into German-speaking universities. Such acculturation was to a large extent successful, but there also remained malaise, even resentment, among a fraction of the educated class, sustained by the scorn with which their original culture was regarded. Some members of the intelligentsia were simply not prepared to pay the price of their social advancement with the eviction, even extinction, of their cultural universe. In reaction, the scorned culture was promoted by a host of folklorists, historians, musicians and writers. Such defense movements are without a doubt largely selfless undertakings, motivated by a thirst for dignity and promoted by nationalist intellectuals full of generous ardor.[12] However, these "pure" intentions do not rule out individual strategic calculations that the intelligentsia defends, both against other social strata within the same people and against the intelligentsias of other peoples.

Internally, the new class that is spawned by the spread of education and which enjoys direct access to knowledge is likely to enter into competition with two types of keepers of high culture: clerics and the acculturated nobility. The hieratic caste monopolizing access to sacred culture is opposed by members of the intelligentsia in the name of popular culture, to which they have lent the systematic expression it was lacking. This strategy enables them to enlist the support of a segment of the population, understandably pleased to see the prestige of their traditional culture enhanced, as it was hitherto scorned as primitive. This competitive and power-seeking rationale explains the structural opposition that secular nationalisms have encountered among peoples previously defined mainly by their religion—even when that religion has played an essential role in preserving the collective particularism that subsequently facilitated the enterprise of national mobilization.

Within an Ottoman Empire that recognized only religious differences, the Ecumenical Patriarch of Constantinople, who exercised his authority over the entire Christian *millet*[13] excepting the Armenians, did not look favorably on the emergence of Greek nationalism. First, he was extremely suspicious of its inclination toward Antiquity, extolling polytheistic Ancient Greece and thus instituting a myth of origins prior to that of Christianity, which was associated with the appearance of the Byzantine Church. Second, the high clergy correctly perceived that a reterritorialization of the Greeks at the tip of the Balkan peninsula would reduce its influence over the Orthodox world and even its control over the Greeks. This is indeed what happened after Greece won its independence, when the Church of Greece proclaimed its autonomy from the patriarchate, which also lost its remaining authority over certain non-Greek orthodoxies, such as the Romanian Orthodox Church.

The position of the Catholic Church leaders in Austria-Hungary was hardly different. Out of both loyalty to the Habsburgs and fear of establishing national demarcation lines among the "Catholic people," throughout the nineteenth century the bishops were generally very reserved with regard to national movements led by an intelligentsia guilty of two crimes which often went hand in hand: representing a certain modernity and being Protestant (in Slovakia as well as Hungary). The position of the rural Catholic clergy was different, however. Sharing the same condition as their parishioners, village priests were not insensitive to nationalist rhetoric and often even stood in for a virtually non-existent intelligentsia (for instance, in Slovenia and Slovakia). Their involvement was not, however, by virtue of their calling, but as representatives of a plebeian culture with popular Catholicism at its core.

The Church hierarchs were not the only ones against whom the intelligentsia rose up in the name of national culture. The nobility was also subjected to a full-scale attack. Thus the "enlightened middle class," a social group composed of well-educated civil servants, professors, doctors, writers and so on, expended considerable effort to propagate a high German culture, at the expense of the French culture that was widespread among the noble elite. This educated middle class, "by dissociating themselves from the cultural hegemony of France on the continent ... became more keenly aware of their own national identity."[14] Behind the rejection of a foreign cultural influence lurked a social struggle to lead society, a battle for power that the intelligentsia ended up winning.

However, the struggle of the new educated class is not confined to clerical and/or nobiliary elites of one's own people. It is waged even more against rival intelligentsias of other peoples. Educated individuals' social ascension does not only carry a heavy social and symbolic price (transplantation to cities far from the native soil, giving up the mother tongue). They also usually face competition from other national groups. This situation then prompts the intelligentsia to create a specific national space in which, as managers of their own culture, they can eliminate or at least reduce the influence of rival groups.

The destiny of Austria-Hungary fully substantiates this hypothesis. The creation of independent states from the ruins of Kakania opened immediate career opportunities for the Slavic intelligentsia, in its own bureaucracy; until then, competition had been fierce in a state apparatus dominated by German speakers. On the contrary, if social mobility is favored by the central power and offers real economic and social advantages, the intelligentsia only has a residual interest in employing a strategy of dissociation, even if the price for social advancement is total acculturation.

The failure of the Occitan movement for autonomy in southern France can be explained at least in part by the success of the Parisian political center's strategy of co-opting the southern elites. The south—and particularly the southwest, a hotbed of radicalism—supplied the Third Republic with many of the leaders the new regime needed, thus making any inclination toward secessionism less than appealing. Frédéric Mistral's Félibrige, a literary movement promoting the renaissance of the Occitan language, could not hope to attract the lawyers and professors who largely peopled the republic's institutions. Only the downgraded nobility and the Catholic bourgeoisie, nostalgic for the old order, were enthralled by a rhetoric defending the cultural specificity of the Occitan community, blended with a backward-looking idealization of rural life.

Motivated Involvement

Today as yesterday, the intelligentsia continues to be a driving force of nationalism because it has an objective interest in defending the culture it is responsible for and in helping it to thrive. Yet an oversimplistic explanation should be avoided. Nationalism does not exert the same attraction over all intellectuals. Some, following Jürgen Habermas, have taken the route of postnationalism, looking beyond the nation.[15] There is no doubt, however, that the cohort of organic intellectuals defending nationalism remains impressive.

For instance, in 1992, the nationalist manifesto proclaiming Catalonia's sovereign right to self-determination was signed by a battalion of authors, artists and academics similar to the one that a century earlier had put their names to the Bases de Manresa, a political program which explicitly demanded autonomy for Catalonia for the first time. Aside from the remarkable permanence of historians', philosophers' and poets' "national structuring" role, it is also worth emphasizing the conversion of many erstwhile internationalists to fervent nationalism.

In 1950s Quebec, stuck in its clerical traditionalism, intellectuals at political journal *Cité Libre*, foremost among them Pierre Elliott Trudeau—Canada's prime minister from 1968 to 1984 excluding a nine-month hiatus—embarked on a salutary challenge to social immobilism. The butt of their criticism was hardly limited to the narrow-minded and backward-looking nationalism that held French Canadian society in its grip. It involved a wholesale rejection of nationalism, considered a pernicious and negative ideology.[16] Categorical anti-nationalism, however, did not last long.

Fairly quickly, in the 1960s, a number of intellectuals attempted an original synthesis: while continuing to denounce the traditional nationalism of their elders, instead of calling for national reference to be discarded, they advocated its modernization through respect for a pluralistic society and openness to the world. The Quebecois society that, in the space of a few years, shook off the secular control of the Church and conservative elites embodied this *aggiornamento* of nationalism, which made it possible to broaden its social base. The left, which had hitherto been fiercely anti-nationalist due to the tight equation between nationalism and traditionalism, saw the light and converted *en masse* to the renewed nationalism represented by the Parti Québécois. It became perfectly compatible to be leftist and nationalist, the precise synthesis for which most Third World national liberation movements had strived.

This itinerary is less tortuous than it might at first seem. While support for Third World liberation struggles had indeed always been orchestrated by calling on internationalist principles (the fight against colonialism and imperialism), the mobilizing capacity of these struggles on the ground could largely be ascribed to the national self-determination they were supposed to lead to. Through a mimicking effect, a portion of the Quebecois elite soon borrowed the nationalist logic for their own society that they had seen at work in Algeria and Vietnam.

Just as the intelligentsia's involvement in nationalist struggles partly corresponds to logics of interests, the reception and circulation of nationalist ideology among the masses is not devoid of materialistic motives either.

The power of the reference to culture can be explained in such cases not by its ability to create a national imaginary, but by its social resonance and its political implications. Cultural demands are in fact often the vehicle for very specific demands and expectations. The example of Belgium serves to illustrate this point. Its independence in 1830 through the joint action of the liberal middle class allied with the landed aristocracy and the Catholic clergy led to the establishment of a constitutional monarchy that guaranteed fundamental political rights within the framework of a nation-state somewhat akin to the French model.[17]

The Belgian state was nevertheless primarily associated from the start with a particular culture, the French culture. French became the dominant language of the political leadership, even though almost 60 per cent of the kingdom's citizens spoke Flemish dialects. If French enjoyed a monopoly from the start despite Belgium's linguistic heterogeneity, it was due to the fact that it was the language of the voting bourgeoisie leading the new country in Wallonia and in Flanders, where the elite had been profoundly Gallicized. In the northern part of the country, only the lower social classes (peasants, workers, the lower middle class) remained loyal to Flemish. Because this linguistic divide overlapped with a social demarcation and an asymmetrical access to the political center, the cultural battle for the defense of Flemish was necessarily also a fight for social and political equality.

This link was not immediately perceived by the first Flemish nationalists (Hendrik Conscience, Jean-Baptist David), who confined themselves to a literary celebration of the popular language,[18] but it was very quickly underlined by their successors. The growing Gallicization of the Flemish civil service, due to the nomination of Walloon bureaucrats with whom the popular classes could not communicate, fostered a growing social frustration on which the Flemish movement capitalized from the 1860s. To halt the Gallicization of Flemish society, the government resorted to two measures.

The first was parliamentary. By cultivating a certain influence among liberal and Catholic deputies, the Flemish nationalist movement succeeded in 1873 in having a series of linguistic laws passed officializing the use of Dutch in the public administration of Flanders. This incomplete legislative device only moderately slowed the process of Gallicization. The Flemish movement then undertook a much more ambitious project—Dutch-only schooling in Flanders. This goal, which was progressively attained between 1883 and 1932, was only marginally cultural. In reality, imposing one language from primary school to university fulfilled a dual objective—distancing the Gallicized elites and fostering the social advancement of the Dutch-speaking popular classes. In other words, the aim was to "nationalize" the Flemings within their own cultural space where they no longer had anything to fear from the competition of French-speakers, who had until then benefited from the privileged status of the French language, occupying many posts in Flemish bureaucracy and private companies.

The Flemish case is no doubt particularly eloquent, but it is not unique. In Quebec as well, the linguistic divide had very obvious social implications, to the point that there was what could be described as a cultural division of labor in the 1950s. The English-speaking middle class, concentrated in the western part of Montreal, controlled the province's economy while the francophones made up most of the working class and farming community. By encouraging from the 1960s the use of French in business and the workplace through legislative mechanisms, successive Quebec governments expanded job opportunities for French speakers, thus contributing to their social advancement. This affirmative action, which enabled francophones to work in their own language, led to the emergence of a francophone business class that has partially replaced the English-speaking businessmen.

These two examples confirm Ernest Gellner's hypothesis linking the emergence of nationalism with an inadequate system of communication. When language acts as a barrier to communication by preventing, or at least hampering, the social advancement of the members of the group who speak it, they are driven to create a protective niche, within which they are assured of social mobility, by starting down the road of cultural and then political nationalism.[19] It is in fact clear that reference to culture is only rarely an end in itself: it inevitably comes down to politics. Consequently, the dichotomy between two conceptions of the nation, one political, the other cultural, requires considerable qualification.

Deconstructing an Illusion

One type of nation is presented as the result of the free association of citizens. It is a rational and voluntary political construction. This contractual, elective, civic nation is the French model of nationhood, conceptualized by the Enlightenment philosophers and achieved by the Great Revolution. In contrast, the other type of nation is presented as the concretization of a cultural community, the expression of a sense of identity, the reflection of a natural order. This ascriptive, organic and ultimately ethnic nation is the German model of the nation, nurtured by romanticism and embodied by the Second and then Third Reich.

This dichotomy was spawned in very particular historical circumstances, in the 1870s, revolving around the Alsace-Moselle issue. German historians (Mommsen, Strauss) justified the incorporation of the Alsatians into the Reich on the basis of their Germanic culture. Their French counterparts (Renan, Fustel de Coulanges) countered the claim by arguing the right of the Alsatians to remain French if such was their political choice.[20] Although this distinction appeared in a specific controversial context, it met with tremendous intellectual success. After Friedrich Meinecke popularized it by contrasting the cultural nation (*Kulturnation*) and the political nation (*Staatsnation*),[21] it was taken up by a host of analysts.

Hans Kohn, the American political scientist of German descent, played a considerable role in generalizing this dichotomy. It is thus worth quoting him at some length:

> Outside the Western world... nationalism arose not only later, but also generally at a more backward stage of social and political development... This rising nationalism found its first expression in the cultural field... Each new nationalism looked for its

justification and its differentiation to the heritage of its own past, and extolled the primitive and ancient depth and peculiarities of its traditions in contrast to Western rationalism and to universal standards... While Western nationalism was, in its origin, connected with the concepts of individual liberty and rational cosmopolitanism current in the eighteenth century, the later nationalism in Central and Eastern Europe and in Asia easily tended towards a contrary development.[22]

Over the years, variants of this theory have been developed by a number of scholars: the political nationalism born in the wake of the French Revolution around a long-established and powerful state is said to contrast with an organic nationalism nourished by language and history that has prospered in countries devoid of a state, such as Italy or Poland and, generally speaking, throughout the Third World.[23] This binary typology still ultimately rests on the distinction between the "Western" nation (Great Britain, France, the United States), gathering together free and equal citizens, and the "Eastern" nation (Germany, Eastern Europe, Third World), a community of origin united by a shared cultural heritage. This conceptual opposition should, however, be handled with great care.[24]

First, such a general opposition has limited heuristic value. It views things from so far away that it rigidifies the terms of the comparison, at the risk of succumbing to the pitfalls of overdrawn culturalism. The danger is then to "reduce the alternative between the two ideas of the national simply to two culturally determined understandings of collective identity: one French, the other German."[25] An obvious oversimplification, for it overlooks another German philosophical tradition, which, with Hegel and his followers, assigned great importance to political bonds, while neglecting ideological currents in France that stressed the importance of a cultural bond to cement national ties (Barrès, Maurras).

Furthermore, such a dichotomy takes no account of the diversity of national trajectories. It is risky to say the least to lump together under the category "Eastern nationalism," with its culture dominant, the case of both "small nations," where culture indeed represented a decisive catalyst at the outset, and politically fragmented nations such as Italy and Germany, which had a very rich high culture. To describe India as a country where nationalism was primarily expressed through cultural claims is simply preposterous. The Indian National Congress party founded in 1885, which represented the struggle for independence, defended political and territorial nationalism from the very start and certainly did not revel in the worship of cultural specificity.

The sharpness of the contrast can be softened if, following French anthropologist Louis Dumont, the French and German are perceived as subcultures, two variants of the same modern ideology characterized by the rise of individualism. In that case, Herder's holism need not be perceived as the negation of individualism but the transfer of the individualist principle to the collective level, cultures being perceived as collective individuals that should be respected in their fundamental diversity.[26] In keeping with this dialectical approach, national differences can fit within the same ideological configuration yet be expressed through contrasting modes of identification: while in Germany the mode is cultural, it is primarily political in France. This dissimilarity only has meaning with respect to ideological representations (and in their legal manifestations, particularly citizenship rights). It does not imply a radical contrast in the ways national entities are consolidated from a sociological standpoint. In fact, even though the interaction between the political and the cultural occurs in different ways and at different paces, it is nevertheless essential to the success of all modern nationalisms.

Furthermore, "Eastern nationalism" itself shows internal lines of division. Though for some forty years the shared experience of communism lent the "other" Europe ideological unity, this recent past should not obscure the significant cleavage between Central Europe on the one hand and Eastern Europe, including the Balkans, on the other.

"Middle" Europe (Poland, Croatia, Hungary, Bohemia) experienced a hybrid socio-political development in which archaic features coexisted with modern characteristics. This originality set it radically apart from Eastern Europe, the latter having been subjected to imperial autocracies (Russia, the Ottoman Empire) that hampered endogenous economic and social progress, as the historian Jenó Szúcs has shown.[27] As a result, the processes of national mobilization were different.

In Central Europe, Estate societies, in which the nobility had a pivotal position (with the exception of the Czech lands), the king had to deal with Estate assemblies, the Diets. There was already a political representation of "the nation" in medieval times, even if the nobility alone claimed to embody it. Thus, in the Habsburg Empire, under the aegis of an aristocracy anxious to protect its liberties and privileges, Hungary was still able to keep real autonomy which was only suppressed for twenty years after the failure of the 1848–9 revolution. The early Hungarian nationalists could fight the centralist propensities of Vienna by invoking the constitutional particularism of the country, and even a genuine state tradition going back to the year 1000 (the coronation of Saint Stephen). In other words, they had political arguments at their disposal in order to further their claims to nationhood. Recourse to cultural nationalism was thus more marginal.

The emergence of an abundant national literature written in Hungarian instead of Latin very probably strengthened the feeling of national unity. Glorification of the Hungarian language in the face of the Germanization threat bore testimony, in the purest Romantic tradition, to the greatness of the Magyar nation. But behind the defense of a language whose deep linguistic originality facilitated demarcation from its Slav surroundings lurked an intransigent political commitment, as illustrated by the active part taken by the great Hungarian poets (Petöfi, Vörösmarty, Arany) in the aborted 1848 Revolution. The twelve-point program drafted by Kossuth was moreover presented symbolically under the triple heading "liberty, equality, fraternity." The objective of the popular uprising was clearly the full restoration of political sovereignty to the Hungarian nation (convening of a national assembly, respect for public liberties), not the obsessive safeguarding of a cultural specificity.[28] The Hungarian example can be applied, with some nuances, to all of the other Central European countries that had a state tradition: specifically political demands were clearly dominant while cultural claims were, so to speak, auxiliary.

The picture looks noticeably different when examining the small peasant peoples of Eastern Europe, who never enjoyed an independent political framework and were subsumed for centuries into imperial structures.[29]

Unlike "historical nations" (Czech, Hungarian, etc.), their counterparts to the east did not have immediately available political resources, which explains a remarkably heavy cultural investment. Yet this was in no way an end in itself. Once the folktales were collected, the language standardized, the historical narratives rewritten, this "cultural unity" created a social bond that was liable to solidify politically. The interpretative framework proposed by Czech historian Miroslav Hroch, who identified three stages in national revival, is fully convincing in this regard. Once the intelligentsia completes the task of cultural reform, political agitation then begins with the impetus of an active minority of patriots who strive to spread the sense of belonging to one and the same national entity among the popular strata. In the third phase, agitation leads to the reception of nationalism among the masses who form a movement to achieve independence.[30] A return to cultural roots was thus a necessary step to politicizing nationalism, and not an outcome.

3

CULTURE, A STATE AFFAIR

The state itself does not escape concerns of a cultural order. Far from being a neutral actor that organizes an anonymous group of citizens, the national project that it represents cannot dispense with reference to culture. The example of Belgium provides a telling illustration of this point. Language became an essential issue for the Flemish movement simply because the central state administration was itself the guardian of a (French) culture that it fully intended to propagate and impose on all its citizens, particularly through the education system. Up until the 1870s, the dominant bourgeoisie obstinately tried to use the centralized state, which it controlled, to Gallicize the entire society. This undertaking failed not through lack of political will but due to the weakness of a state torn between Catholics and liberals, and to early resistance from the Flemish movement.

What motivates the state to standardize culture in this way? As Ernest Gellner pointed out, it is certainly, at least in part, due to a structural necessity of industrial society, requiring a standardized education and hence a nationwide educational system under state control that disseminates the same culture across the entire national territory.[1] Despite the pertinence of this functional need for education, the state's ambition to instill a common culture remains a fundamentally political goal, often preceding industrialization and tied in with both its mode of construction and the fact of granting the nation sovereignty.

The State, a Highly Enterprising Cultural Actor

The emergence of the first modern states (France, Spain, England) in the fourteenth and fifteenth centuries was in effect characterized by a dual phenomenon. First, the king reinforced his power over his lords as well as the Church, asserted his prerogatives in military, judicial and fiscal affairs and gradually set up a bureaucracy. Consolidation of the political foundation went hand in hand with the start of cultural integration, which would take two forms: linguistic and religious. In Spain, this process emerged with particular force in 1492 alone. That year saw the ultimate unification of the kingdom with the conquest of Grenada—the final episode of the *Reconquista*—the expulsion of the Jews, followed later by that of the Moors, and the publication of Antonio de Nebrija's Castilian grammar. Political unity and cultural unity were for the Catholic Kings two sides of the same coin.

The political and the cultural realms were similarly intertwined in England and France, although the process occurred over a longer period of time. In England, unification of the state was difficult, the king being forced to compromise with the barons and burghers. From the beginning of the fourteenth century, however, the English language, to which Chaucer's *Canterbury Tales* had given considerable luster, was the ferment of specificity for a budding national consciousness. Crown officials went to great lengths to spread the use of the vernacular language in administrative decrees. This linguistic zeal had an indisputable strategic objective: "to affirm the linguistic identity of the English in opposition to the French."[2] English translations of the Bible, by John Wycliff and then William Tyndale, which would serve as the basis for the King James Bible, also encouraged the formation of an independent cultural environment, reinforcing the geographical insularity of the British Isles. Finally, the religious schism that occurred under Henry VIII, with the establishment of Anglicanism as the state religion, marked the final stage of England's cultural nationalization.

In France, the gradual assertion of royal authority went together with the resolve to make the French language the sole medium of state communication. With the Ordinance of Villers-Cotterêts (1539), Francis I prescribed the use of French for judicial decisions and legislative acts at the same time as Pierre de Ronsard, Joachim du Bellay, Henri Estienne and others were extolling the eminence of the French language. State defense of the language continued throughout the Classical period, with the creation of the French Academy (1634) and the compilation of the official dictionary (1694). At the same time, although Henry IV had demonstrated a spirit of tolerance that was unique in Europe by granting Protestants religious freedom, royal absolutism was later consolidated by Louis XIV. The revocation of the Edict of Nantes was an attempt to make state unity congruent with confessional unity. The aspiration for cultural unity was backed by an extension of state control. Nevertheless, there was a limit: the Bourbons' objective was to promote French as the language of the state as well as of high culture, without seeking to standardize the country using authoritarian methods. That the peasants of Anjou or Burgundy continued to speak *patois*, or that the people of Roussillon or Navarre spoke Catalan or Basque, posed no threat to a power in which the rural masses and the urban plebeians had no license to participate.

This indifference with regard to France's linguistic plurality vanished with the French Revolution. As sovereignty was supposed to reside within the nation, the body politic could no longer abide social, religious, regional or any other cleavages that had existed under the Ancien Régime. It had to reflect the Republic's image: one and indivisible. Abbé Grégoire conducted a study in 1792, the title of which was a policy statement in itself: "Report on the Need and Means to Annihilate *Patois* and Universalize the Use of the French Language." Barère, who presided over the Convention during the King's trial, having praised French as "the most beautiful language of Europe, whose role it is to convey to the world the most subtle thoughts on liberty," also declared relentless war against local languages in the name of consolidating national unity. The concern for Gallicization satisfied a frenetic need for uniformity induced by revolutionary egalitarianism, which Benjamin Constant identified with remarkable perspicuity: "The same code of law, the same measures, the same regulations, and, if they could contrive it gradually, the same language, this is what it proclaimed to be the perfect form of social organization."[3]

The spread of the French language and the confinement of regional tongues to an increasingly narrow circle of speakers met a dual objective. One was functional. If all citizens could speak and read French, they would be the direct recipients of the revolutionary ideology radiating from Paris.

The other aim was purely political. It was to create among the French the sense of belonging to the same imagined community: the French nation. As Benedict Anderson brilliantly showed, reading the same newspapers distributed out of Paris was precisely meant to instill in each reader a sense of communion, with dozens of thousands of other readers absorbed at the same moment in deciphering the same lines.[4] The revolutionaries, caught up in more urgent tasks, never had the time to impose the French language in Corsica or the Basque Country. The Third Republic proved to be more effective in that regard.

By the time the republican regime arrived, France remained a country of multiple facets, with a great variety of customs, traditions and languages. As this extreme diversity flagrantly contradicted the credo of republican unity, it became imperative to turn this credo into a social reality. It is therefore hardly surprising that when opportunistic republicans came to power in 1879, they immediately began to implement an extremely ambitious educational policy, under the aegis of Jules Ferry. As they consolidated political institutions, the new elites also laid the foundations for a national education system that was to shape citizens who were won over to republican ideals and hitherto partook of the same culture; in other words, French culture.

For the peasants who made up the overwhelming majority of the French population, the nation as a collection of citizens remained an abstraction, an empty slogan. This notion had to be converted into a living reality, a true community. More than a daily plebiscite, the nation was to become a living reality experienced on an everyday basis. Cultural (and especially linguistic) homogenization was therefore indispensable, so that each person could directly experience the intimate feeling of belonging to the same national entity. The nationalization of the mind could only come through a formidable effort of inculcation undertaken by the state via its educational system. The state became the zealous propagator of the "official culture" and tireless dispenser of the "beautiful mother tongue."

It was impossible for the founders of the Third Republic to accept that one could be a French citizen while maintaining a different "primary culture," be it Basque, Breton or Catalan. Local particularisms were denigrated as archaic regionalisms. They were combated and relegated forcibly to the private sphere, which, in the long term, inevitably lead to their gradual extinction. Without reliable means of transmission (schools, newspapers, social institutions), these cultures were condemned, if not to disappear, at least to become folklorized and increasingly marginalized. It would probably be an exaggeration, as Jean-François Chanet points out in a fine book, to speak of "cultural genocide" regarding the Third Republic's educational policy.[5] The Republic's troops of schoolteachers could—often out of pragmatism, at times out of personal inclination—show a degree of tolerance toward *patois* and regional tongues.

The fact remains that they were caught up in a system where everything was done to promote the French language through the official monopoly of French in schools and the devaluation of regional languages, which were associated with clericalism and anti-modernism. Certain social processes, such as increased internal migration (the Auvergnats and the Bretons, for instance), were clearly a powerful medium for Gallicization. In the provinces, however, the decline of regional languages would have been far more limited if the Republic itself had not implemented a brand of linguistic nationalism in which the "nationalization" of the Bretons, Alsatians and Provençals involved a genuine campaign of deculturalization.[6]

It is moreover disturbing to note that these populations at the fringes of the national territory were considered domestic immigrants, invited to become part of a civilization that was not their own. Significantly, in language instruction, French was treated as a foreign language in the "peripheral provinces." Bretons and Basques were dealt with no differently than the "external immigrants" (Italians or Russian Jews) that France had begun to bring in at the same time: civic integration in both cases involved cultural assimilation.

Another striking similarity: even if they were citizens, the Basques, Flemings and Corsicans, for instance, were not treated much differently from the Arabs and Vietnamese that France was in the process of colonizing.[7] Many government officials sent from Paris treated the "natives" with incredible condescension and did not hesitate to compare Brittany or the Landes to lands that should be subject to intense colonization, like the Mitidja plain in Algeria. It is probably mere coincidence that one man, Jules Ferry, was both a driving force in France's colonial policy and the instigator of a colossal educational undertaking that, *inter alia*, was supposed to anchor the French peripheries firmly to the center. In both cases was manifest the same duty to civilize "backward populations."

Once again, the contrast between an essentially political French conception of the nation and a more cultural German conception shows obvious limits. The French republic consolidated its political foundation by engaging in a huge operation of cultural normalization. Even though it was basically ideological in nature, the republican scheme could not fail to establish the nation through an intense cultural endeavor, so as to create a primary bond of solidarity among citizens.

The situation is similar in monarchies, often, moreover, patterned on France, which under absolutism had rationalized the functioning of the state even prior to inventing the modern nation-state.

South of the Pyrenees, the Bourbons endeavored to reform government structures after their victory in the War of the Spanish Succession by working toward greater centralization. For the Catalans, who had been defeated militarily, this policy was embodied by the Nueva Planta decree (1716), which abolished its specific governmental institutions (Generalitat, assemblies), fiscal independence, currency and so on. There again, the center in Madrid asserted itself politically through an attempt at cultural homogenization. The process of castilianization of course preceded the abolition of Catalonia's political autonomy. It had begun in the sixteenth century, the Golden Age during which Spain experienced extraordinary artistic efflorescence and Castilian came to dominate as the language of culture adopted by Church, noble and urban elites. Castile's dynamism led to its culture's diffusion in a ripple effect throughout the peninsula.

However, even if the influence of Castilian literature, fostered by the development of the printing press, predated French-style monarchic centralization, the French model nevertheless gave official castilianization a considerable boost. A host of laws imposed the use of Spanish before the courts, in bookkeeping and in education. In 1801, even theatrical performances in Catalan were expressly banned.[8] This state policy contributed to the dissociation of the Castilian high culture, which the social elites in Catalonia possessed, from a robust popular Catalan culture. However, the policy was unable to achieve its ultimate objective of cultural homogenization.

This failure can be ascribed to the weakness of the Spanish state in the nineteenth century. It lacked the means to pursue its centralizing impulses. Thus, unlike France where Jules Ferry had instituted a primary education that was secular, tuition-free, and mandatory—which presupposed a considerable effort on the part of the public authorities—Spain's budget for education remained chronically lacking and thus did not make it possible to extend instruction to the general population. Castilianization could therefore only be partial. It was further hampered by the fact that while the center remained dominant from Madrid, it lagged behind economically, while the Basque and Catalonian peripheries were spearheading capitalist innovation.

While the Spanish monarchy was too weak to accomplish cultural integration, after the Act of Union joining Ireland to Great Britain in 1800, the British crown managed to develop a school system in the former in which teaching was in English, even when 50% of the population spoke Gaelic. Acculturation was achieved, as a century later only 12% of the population, confined to the western fringes of Ireland, remained faithful to this old Celtic language.

While anglicization was undeniably a success, how can the accompanying rise of Irish nationalism be explained? The answer once again lies in the stagnation of social mobility.

Even though, as of 1831, the Catholics had begun to be integrated in the education system in large numbers (at least in primary school), their opportunities for social advancement were seriously limited. Most of the private sector was in the hands of the Protestants, and Catholics were barred from entering the senior ranks of the British administration in Ireland by an implicit religious barrier that reserved such jobs for Protestants. While language was no longer a demarcation line between the dominated majority and the dominating minority, the religious cleavage persisted. There lies a major difference between late-nineteenth-century France and Great Britain: intense linguistic assimilation was compensated in secular France by real possibilities of upward social mobility, whereas in the United Kingdom, with its system of privileges, such possibilities were considerably limited. An identity marker such as religion thus became available for mobilization in a strategy of nationalist protest.

The National Grounding of Democracy

Whether a failure or a success, the cultural assimilation policies conducted by different nation-states nevertheless demonstrate one thing: to bind together a people into a national community, the political association created by civic allegiance has always proven to be insufficient. Political ties, the only legal basis for membership in the nation, must be replicated in reality by social ties based on a common culture with a national language at its epicenter.

This phenomenon of communalization accompanied the emergence and expansion of democracy. Just as economic liberalism postulates the existence of a free market in which rational individuals partake, modern democracy posits the existence of isomorphic individuals. It is based on a convention—the formal equality of individuals—constantly belied by their actual inequality (of knowledge, money, etc.). Democracy does not recognize constituent groups (social classes, religious or ethnic communities) but only individuals who collectively hold sovereignty. Yet while democracy is based on horizontal legitimacy, unlike the vertical legitimacy of monarchy, it is not without a horizon: it is bound by a highly determined socio-political space formed by given historic societies.

Democratic universalism could not have escaped such demarcation except in a scenario where it could have been achieved instantly across the entire planet, under the aegis of a world government. In reality, modern democracy developed in various societies that had previously experienced different historical trajectories. Its very advent presupposed the prior existence of a national framework. No one is a world citizen. We are all French, American,

Japanese citizens and so on. To be deprived of a homeland is not the highest achievement of humanity but the radical denial of it. Deprived of a political community, stateless people are those "people who had indeed lost all other qualities and specific relationships—except that they were still human."[9]

Human rights are inseparable from the rights of the citizen, and these are realized within a given political nation that is distinct from others. This polity excludes foreigners—except in the case of naturalization—precisely because they are part of another polity. Expression of the general will is up to a nation's citizens alone—and even then, not to all nationals, because minors, those declared incompetent and for a long time women are or were excluded from the universality of citizenship. Already the French Revolution, after an initial phase exalting human fraternity, reconsidered its universalist pretensions by adopting retaliatory measures against foreigners after the motherland was declared to be in danger in 1792. The revolutionaries' generous proclamations came at the expense of those who believed in them. The American Thomas Paine, although elected to the Convention, was thrown in prison during the Terror; the Germans Adam Lux and Anacharsis Cloots, who declared themselves "ambassadors of the human race," were guillotined as foreign agents. Even the Great Revolution proved to be incapable of imagining a form of citizenship that was not national.

Extension of the democratic principle throughout the nineteenth century subsequently went along with the reinforcement of what Gérard Noiriel has called the social construction of national identities, in other words the state-supervised demarcation of respective national entities.[10] Democracy became acceptable as a mode of regulating interests and conflicts from the moment that the formal equality between the peasant in the Lauragais, the fisherman from Cancale and the nobleman from the Dauphiné was realized within a "higher" community considered united by national ties. This political rationale, which associates democratic fulfillment with a national framework, had already been clearly set forth by Rousseau.

The nation as he conceived it is not an impersonal structure, but a collective entity of which the leaders must preserve the "national physiognomy." In his *Constitutional Project for Corsica*, Rousseau wrote, "The first rule to be followed is the principle of national character; for each people has, or ought to have, a national character; if it did not, we should have to start by giving it one."[11] This cardinal pronouncement, far from lapsing into some sort of national substantialism, lays down a golden rule: free political institutions presuppose a people that is equally so; in other words, a people that can invoke or adopt a specific "national form" in order to legitimate its aspirations to independence. This national specificity should be cultivated through a patriotic education in order not to dissolve. To the Poles, he urged, "At twenty, a Pole ought not to be a man of any other sort; he ought to be a Pole."[12] Implementing democracy thus does not rule out preserving the nation's collective identity. Rather, it requires it.

Some might object that Rousseau, sometimes presented as a champion of totalitarianism with his theory of the general will, is not the best guide for pondering the link between democracy and nation. In that case, we can turn to an individualistic and liberal thinker such as John Stuart Mill.

In *Considerations on Representative Government*, he wrote, "Free institutions are next to impossible in a country made up of different nationalities. Among a people without fellow-feeling, especially if they read and speak different languages, the united public opinion necessary to the working of representative government cannot exist." The smooth functioning of democracy requires that "boundaries of governments should coincide in the main with those of nationalities."[13] Political allegiance among citizens thus calls for the existence of a common national sentiment that may be based on a number of different elements: ties of lineage, language, religion, geography and, most importantly political antecedents (national history, memories in common, shared pride and humiliations). We once again come back to the same observation: even if political democracy is legally founded on abstract principles, it in fact takes root in historical cultural entities. Citizens do not exist within an abstract humanity. They are formed in a particular society, with its concrete history, memory and culture.

The Impossibility of State Neutrality

The state's cultural tropism requires all the more attentive examination as it contradicts a cardinal principle of liberalism: the state's neutrality toward ethno-cultural values and identities. For the philosopher John Rawls, the implementation of distributive justice, which is the basis for regulating democracy, thus assumes that a "veil of ignorance" is thrown over individuals' personal attachments, be they social, ethnic or other.[14] The state should thus be blind to differences, which supposes that it values no particular identity over another and that it is not founded on any comprehensive religious, moral or other doctrine.

Philosophically, this liberal purism can be justified on a hypothetical basis, as in Rawls, but it must be admitted that historically it does not hold water, for no state is culturally neutral, as Will Kymlicka has convincingly demonstrated. "There is no way to have a complete 'separation of state and ethnicity.' In various ways, the ideal of 'benign neglect' is a myth. Government decisions on languages, internal boundaries, public holidays, and state symbols unavoidably involve recognizing, accommodating, and supporting the needs and identities of particular ethnic and national groups."[15] By opting for an official language—which will almost always be that of the majority or dominant group—the state associates itself with a culture, if not exclusively, at least primarily.

Although western countries have become largely secularized, the legal day of rest remains Sunday and many official holidays are Christian holy days. There is nothing scandalous about this in itself, but it simply proves that the state's perfect neutrality is an illusion. Only the members of the French Convention tried to sever the French state from society's Christian roots by undertaking a huge effort of de-christianization, manifested among other things by the institution of the revolutionary calendar with the proclamation of the Republic, and replacing Sunday with Decadi.[16] The return to the Gregorian calendar under the Empire proved the vanity of trying to establish a political order that was totally disconnected from the cultural substratum. Nevertheless, the nature of the link between state and culture is highly variable. In some cases, it will be robust, in others rather loose, but it will always subsist in one form or the other.

There are extreme cases, such as South Africa under apartheid, when the state was totally mobilized around a two-pronged ideological undertaking. On the one hand, the state, ruled by the National Party, promoted racial segregation, distinguishing whites from non-whites on the basis of racial criteria. The aim of this policy was to preserve the political superiority of the whites as well as to defend "the purity of the White race and Western civilization." The obsession with purity was epitomized in its most scandalous form in the legal ban against mixed marriages and sexual intercourse between people of different races. But the state was also involved in defending a specific culture, the Afrikaner culture, which the government attempted to propagate through the educational system among the English-speaking population, and then in the 1970s among the blacks.[17] Unable to achieve the "Afrikanerization" of the whites, the authorities strove to transmit the culture of the *volk Afrikaner* (its history, language and religion) via a specific school system separate from that of the English-speakers.

South Africa carried cultural identitarianism to the extreme, the absurd, and the unacceptable by coupling it with a racial classification. But the phenomenon can be detected in more or less explicit forms in many other parts of the world. There are any number of ethnic states, exclusively or primarily associated with a group and hence the culture it represents. Such states frequently have an authoritarian form of government, such as the Ethiopian Empire dominated by the Amharas, or Myanmar governed by the Burmese, with the Kachin, Karen, Chin, Kayah, Shan and Mon minorities in a clearly subordinate position. Democratic countries themselves, however, are not always exempt from ethnicity.

In ethnic democracies,[18] political equality among citizens is guaranteed, whatever their origin, but the state itself belongs to the "main people," so to speak, and not to the citizenry as a whole. Israel offers the most flagrant example of an ethnic democracy: as a Jewish state that has set itself the mission of gathering together the Jews scattered throughout the world, it is necessarily Jewish in nature. This is evident in its national symbolism (flag bearing the star of David, seven-arm candelabra as the state's emblem), the officially recognized role of religion in the public arena, citizenship rights, the granting of public aid and so on.[19]

Israel is anything but a neutral liberal state. It explicitly defends particular values, as the former president of the Supreme Court, Aharon Barak, solemnly proclaimed:

> A Jewish state is a state whose history is bound up with the history of the Jewish people, whose principal language is Hebrew, and whose main holidays reflect its national mission. [...] A 'Jewish state' is a state that fosters Jewish culture, Jewish education, and love of the Jewish people. A 'Jewish state' is a state whose values are the values of freedom, justice, righteousness and peace within the Jewish heritage. A 'Jewish state' is a state whose values are drawn from its religious tradition, in which the Bible is the most basic of its books and the prophets of Israel are the foundation of its morality. A 'Jewish state' is a state in which Hebrew jurisprudence fulfills an important role, and in which matters of marriage and divorce of Jews are determined according to the rules of the Torah.[20]

Defense of a particular collective identity in a democratic environment is not specific to Israel. Croatia thus defines itself constitutionally as "the national state of the Croatian nation and the state of the members of autochthonous national minorities... who are citizens." The very wording, by making a distinction between two categories of citizens, clearly emphasizes that the state is exclusively that of the Croatian nation. This special link is accentuated, here again, by symbolism (coat of arms showing the medieval chessboard with twenty-five white and red squares, and Latin lettering) and by certain provisions, such as the state's particular responsibility for protecting Croatians living in foreign countries.[21]

As for Greece's constitution, adopted in 1975 "in the name of the Holy and Consubstantial and Indivisible Trinity," it declares, "the prevailing religion in Greece is that of the Eastern Orthodox Church of Christ," thereby showing that orthodoxy is one with Greekness. The Church is a pillar of Greek society and in this regard has a strong presence in public life: catechism in school, religious wedding ceremonies, civil servant status of popes and so on. As in Judaism, religion has a very strong ethnic dimension that even the state means to defend. In the early 1990s, left and right joined forces unanimously to maintain the mention of religion on identity cards, which was finally removed in 2001 in the wake of repeated injunctions from the European Union.

Germany also combines full recognition of representative democracy with an ethnic foundation that is clearly manifest in the citizenship law of 1913, which grants German citizenship to any person of German stock who comes to settle in the Federal Republic. Even if they have been living in Transylvania since the thirteenth century, they remain *Aussiedler*, in other words German émigrés who thus have the right of return to the country. On the other hand, the 7.3 million Turkish, Italian and Greek immigrants, even if they settled in Germany many years ago, remain foreigners (*Ausländer*). Until recently, they could only become part of the German nation in small numbers.[22] Although the new reform of the nationality code does not call into question the state's association with a form of "transnational Germanness" that applies to Saxons and Swabs of Romania as well as to Germans of Russia, it is decidedly innovative in that it introduces *jus soli* for children of foreign nationals and facilitates naturalization.[23] While the state has not renounced its ethnic underpinnings, it has nevertheless chosen to ease them considerably.

Even though they are not ethnic states in the strict sense of the term, Muslim states are similar in many respects. While a certain number of them may profess to be secular (Turkey, Senegal, Niger, etc.), many proclaim Islam the state religion, even the religion of the state. In the first case (Egypt, Syria), Islam is granted special status; in the second, it is plainly the official religion of the state (Saudi Arabia, Iran, Pakistan). *Sharia* is the sole or main source of law. Even if other religions are tolerated, in many Muslim countries the state is in the service of Islam. It should at least be its guardian, or even, as in Saudi Arabia, work actively to propagate it through true proselytism. Islam is a framework for collective identification that the state has the job of preserving. In an obviously different form, as they are secular and highly individualist states, Scandinavia offers examples of countries in which the Lutheran Church, a genuine national institution, has long been an integral part of the state apparatus. In these countries of great denominational homogeneity, religious ties are largely congruent with the national bond.[24]

Very well, one might say, but don't the United States and France offer counter-examples of states with a republican form of government in which only political citizenship matters? Doesn't the secularism at their base ensure a healthy impartiality? Is not the integration of immigrants facilitated by *jus soli*?

France/United States: Underneath Politics Lies Culture

Being based on the preeminence of the political contract, these two states could at first be assumed to be at the head of nations in the purely political sense. Yet upon closer scrutiny, the picture appears more nuanced.

Following a meticulous study on American identity, torn between openness and rejection of everything foreign, between praise of diversity and an aspiration to blend by assimilation, Denis Lacorne concluded that the United States nation is "civic by inclusion and ethnic by exclusion."[25] At the outset, the United States was fundamentally multicultural. Established on the principle of tolerance, it admitted religious and cultural differences, those of the Dutch and the Germans remaining at first remarkably robust. In the wake of the Civil War (1861–5), a change came about with the emergence of a nativism that promoted race-based Protestant supremacy embraced by the social and political elites. Racial Anglo Saxonism manifested itself in a number of ways.

The most obvious was unquestionably the immigration laws passed between 1882 and 1924, inspired by social Darwinism and based on a cardinal axiom: to ensure the demographic and hence cultural predominance of the Anglo-Saxons by restricting the arrival of Slavic, Latin and Asian peoples. The same concern for preserving a white Anglo-Saxon Protestant United States was also evident in the federal government policy of incorporating the western territories into the United States.

Even though Mexico ceded Arizona and New Mexico to the United States in 1848, they did not enter the Union until the early twentieth century, once Spanish-speakers and Indian tribes had become a minority in relation to the English-speaking newcomers. Similarly, Hawaii did not achieve statehood until 1959, once the Polynesians had been reduced to a minority. As for the colonies ceded to the United States by Spain after its humiliating defeat in 1898 (Puerto Rico, Guam), because it proved difficult to put its natives in a demographic minority, they were given a hybrid status that offered the great advantage of avoiding giving the population the same rights as those enjoyed by citizens of the

Union. This policy of staggered incorporation was entirely deliberate, "the speed of entry into the Union being dependent on the racial quality of the candidate peoples and their real or imaginary degree of assimilation."[26]

The rise of nativism in the late nineteenth century brought about a campaign to Americanize immigrants, meaning primarily to anglicize them. The process was exceptionally brutal for Germans, whose particularly rich culture was nevertheless denounced as a mark of foreignness and who were deracinated due to the First World War. Political loyalty required their forced cultural assimilation: to be American also meant to speak English.[27] This ethno-cultural aspect of American identity was notably championed during a period when the federal state was being consolidated. It was also given expression in foreign policy through overt imperialism, as if the state needed to strengthen its base at the very moment it was flexing its muscles. The interventionist state required a more patriotic, less heterogeneous society. Such posturing inevitably calls forth a comparison with France under the Third Republic, which during the same period was involved in a process of international affirmation of the nation-state, accompanied by an internal effort of cultural homogenization.

Yet, with reference to the previous century, the trajectories of the United States and France diverged: the United States moved toward the open recognition of ethnicity in the wake of the civil rights movement in the 1960s. While until then the ethnic dimension of the American model was at least implicitly based on the primacy of the Anglo-Saxon reference, it was henceforth plural as well. The various ethnicities are all acknowledged as equally respectable and as having given rise to a vibrant multicultural society. This cultural pluralism, openly embraced despite the sometimes pernicious drifts of a multiculturalist ideology and nativist reactions, is in a way the ultimate confirmation of the United States' specific destiny as the "laboratory of a new humanity."

The evolution in France took a different path. The country is certainly more culturally hybridized than it was forty years ago, and this diversity has gained undeniable artistic visibility. This change is evidenced by immigrant cultures (raï and African music, etc.) as well as regional cultures (Corsican polyphony, Celtic music, etc.). The central government has also made concessions in the education system to include immigrant languages and cultures as well as regional languages.

The first breach in unilingualism was introduced by the Deixonne Law of 1951, which authorized the optional teaching of regional languages in schools, in regions where it was used. In the 1980s, a series of laws expanded opportunities to teach these languages in the course of elementary education as well as to include them on baccalaureate exams. CAPES teacher certification now exists for Breton, Basque, Catalan, Corsican, Occitan and Alsatian. Television channels have also parsimoniously allowed a few minutes of broadcasting in regional languages.[28] Slight progress has thus been made, but the apparent liberalism is mostly deceptive.

First of all, little incentive is provided for learning regional languages. Classes are usually optional in public schools (except for in bilingual classes, which enjoy a degree of success). As a result, only a small percentage of children are studying these languages: 3% of the school population learns Breton in primary school and 5% of middle school students learn Catalan. The situation is better for Corsican, given the special powers of the Corsican Assembly. The assessment is also more positive for Alsatian, although it is rarely taught in its own right. But it benefits considerably from the fact that the teaching of German, recognized as the literary expression of Alsatian dialects, is widespread in the school system from primary school up. These two examples clearly demonstrate that a regional culture remains more robust if it benefits from a system of protection: specific institutions and/or proximity to a major cultural language associated with a state. Otherwise, the language, surviving on life support, simply tries to escape a slow death.

Another handicap for the development of regional languages is that the state budgets earmarked for these educational structures are dwindling, and this limited support is offset only partly by the dynamism of non-governmental schooling associations (Diwan in Brittany, Calendretas in Occitania, Ikastolas in the Basque Country) and local government aids.

Lastly, the state has always refused to provide real legal guarantees for protecting these languages. Despite the persistent efforts of some lawmakers from areas with a strong local identity, no bill aiming to give regional cultures special status has managed to pass. On the contrary, two measures adopted in the 1990s clearly penalize regional languages.

In June 1992, during the debate over the Maastricht Treaty, a new paragraph was added to the Constitution to make French the official language of the Republic. This constitutional provision had a clearly stated aim: to avoid any untoward anglicization of public life in the context of a more integrated Europe. Yet it also satisfied a hidden agenda: to prevent regional languages from earning any sort of official recognition. The prohibitive scope of this paragraph was fully confirmed, as both the Council of State and the Constitutional Council used it to argue that it was impossible for France to ratify the European Charter for Regional or Minority Languages even though, after much prevarication and after having carefully chosen the thirty-nine commitments it made, the French government ultimately signed the text.

The Charter adopted by the Council of Europe in 1992 aimed to prevent the right to use a regional language from being purely hypothetical, by requesting that states take a series of measures to facilitate and foster their oral and written use in education, the media, cultural affairs and most importantly, in legal proceedings and relations with the administrative authorities and the public service. The Charter unquestionably gave regional languages relative visibility in the public arena, an unacceptable "heresy" in the eyes of the finicky guardians of France's republican shrine, for whom national unity requires using a single language.

The law of 4 August 1994 on the use of the French language was a step in the same direction. Defined as a "fundamental element of the personality and heritage of France," it recognizes French, barring specific exceptions, as the language used in teaching, the workplace, communication and the public service. This reaffirmation of French as the language of state authority underscores the extent to which the Republic indeed manifests a cultural engagement that is in harmony with its foundational unitary ideology.

Admittedly, in the opposite direction, the Parliament added the following provision to the July 2008 constitutional amendment on the modernization of institutions: "Regional languages are part of France's heritage." Article 75–1 of the Constitution of the Fifth Republic provides indisputable symbolic recognition, but its actual scope will remain limited as long as no specific legislation concerning the matter has been passed. A modification of the constitution alone does not create any particular obligations for the state or specific rights for regional language speakers.

The much-vaunted French exception cannot therefore be reduced to the invention of an entirely political nation. Rather, what is exceptional is that in order for this nation, legally founded solely on the bond of citizenship, to become a reality, the state, and only the state, has used the entire array of resources at its disposal: not only social and economic resources but cultural ones as well.

A formidable protecting power, the French state had a role probably unequalled in other latitudes when it came to creating the nation, particularly in its voluntaristic action in the shaping of a national culture. In concluding a collective study on the French nation, Pierre Nora writes, "No state has established so close a correspondence between the national state, its economy, its culture, its language and its society."[29] Culture has been at the heart of the republican political project, right alongside its economic and social aspects; this offers ultimate proof, if proof need be, that there has never been a national political project that was not also cultural.[30]

To conclude this examination, culture indeed appears basically dual. It has often been used as an opposition force against existing political structures. Such was the case in Eastern Europe in the nineteenth century when national movements that emerged from within autocratic empires made culture the repository of their collective identity, to legitimate their subsequent political activism and the formation of a state. But culture cannot be confined to this tribunal function. It also plays a major role in strategies to concretize a nation, stimulated by early modern monarchies in Western Europe and then perfected by nation-states. The arrival of the latter truly ushered in the age of nationalism, the essence of which is precisely, with the state's intercession, "the fusion of culture and polity."[31]

Culture is thus a political resource that all movements of national affirmation have used, whether to dispute or to legitimate the state order. It is time to surpass the excessively clear-cut opposition between the "Western" nation bringing together free and equal citizens and the "Eastern" model of a community of origin united by shared cultural heritage. Culture will most likely occupy a place that varies depending on whether it is mobilized against an existing state, or by the state itself to legitimate its own existence. However, although variations in tempo and tone can be identified according to historical configurations, there is no radical difference in nature providing irreducible contrast between two types of nationalism, one entirely political, the other cultural.

4

THE APPEAL OF NATIONALISM

Many have expressed alarm at the proliferation of nationalitarian demands, vaguely perceiving them to be following a trend of unstoppable growth that is difficult to hold in check. After the Catalans and the Flemings, whose national claims are already longstanding, the "Lombards" of northern Italy began to stir at about the time that the Scottish National Party, which campaigns for Scotland's independence, won an absolute majority in the Scottish Parliament in Edinburgh.

France is not exempt from surges of nationalitarianism in various forms. In its overseas territories, such movements have gained in popularity, particularly in New Caledonia, where the Kanak Socialist National Liberation Front fully intends to lead the island to independence after a vote on self-determination to be scheduled no later than 2018. Similarly, on a number of occasions, an openly pro-independence president has headed French Polynesia, which has enjoyed considerable autonomy since 2004. Nationalitarian claims in metropolitan France, although more subdued and marginal, have also grown frequent: in addition to the Basque Country and Corsica where they sometimes take a violent turn, they are also expressed with greater refinement through the defense of cultural identity in North Catalonia (eastern Pyrenees), in Alsace, in Brittany and in Occitania. This regionalist symphony has a new member: the Savoy League, designed on the model of the neighboring Lombardy League, which calls for the repeal of its annexation to France in 1860 to make Savoy a sovereign state.

Such profusion may indeed seem surprising, all the more so as it often brings an antiquated decorum into play. In the south, for Saint John's feast day, a huge bonfire is lit on Catalonia's highest summit, Mount Canigou, with firewood from various Catalonian cities, supposedly to underscore the unshakeable unity of Catalonian lands. To the east, the Savoy League distributes identity cards and license plates bearing the State of Savoy coat of arms. In western Flanders, the monumental Yser Tower inscribed with the initials AVV-VVK ("All for Flanders, Flanders for Christ") draws tens of thousands of Flemings in the month of August. While some come to honor the memory of Dutch-speaking Belgian soldiers who perished in the First World War, many unrepentant Flemish-speakers have turned this pilgrimage into a patriotic jamboree calling for the independence of Flanders amid a sea of flags and banners.

One might find these dramatizations disconcerting, or even ridiculous, but it would be a serious mistake simply to dismiss them with a wave of the hand as backward-looking folklore. They partake of a whole array of nationalist posturings that indicate the remarkable vitality of the principle of self-determination. For it is indeed the universalization of this principle in the course of the twentieth century that must serve as a starting point to explain the political mobilizations of nationalist actors, from Quebec to Ireland and all the way to Indian Punjab.

The Spread of Nationalism

Like the Lernean Hydra, whose heads grew back as fast as they were cut off, nationalism can only spring up again and again in new forms, because its core principle—self-determination—is by its very nature indestructible. To say that peoples should be able to freely dispose of themselves and organize their lives together is to put forward a generous proposal that immediately poses a major problem, and that is the "content" of peoplehood. Who are these peoples in the name of whom political actors claim to act and demand the right to self-determination? By what criteria can they be identified?

Any illusion of objectivism should immediately be dispelled: there is no canonical definition of a "people," even if the existence of certain shared attributes (history, culture, territorial location, community of destiny, etc.) makes it possible to outline some of its features. The multiform nature of a "people" thus considerably extends the right to self-determination: since it is a general principle, it can theoretically be claimed by all human groups that plead this quality. And in fact, for nearly two centuries now, the application of this right has become increasingly broad in scope.

The first to benefit from such emancipation, often at the end of a victorious war of liberation (Greece, Serbia, Italy), were "historic nations," in other words those that could boast of sufficient political institutionalization, however distant in the past. The independence of Latin American states from the Spanish and Portuguese empires during the first half of the nineteenth century was also a harbinger of decolonization, a new phenomenon that would lend self-determination enormous momentum after the Second World War. But prior to that, by virtue of the principle of nationalities outlined by President Wilson in 1918, a multitude of peoples on the European continent who had never had their own political entities were able to form a state.

This initial extension of the principle of self-determination showed that Wilsonian idealism could not be reserved solely for certain peoples. This despite the fact that the First World War victors considered that it was not intended to apply in Asia and Africa to peoples subjected to European colonization, or, in Europe, to "peripheral nations" (Catalans, Scots) that had been integrated into powerful states, sometimes for many centuries. However, as the principle of nationalities contained a general axiom, it was by definition universally applicable. The two exclusions mentioned above were necessarily temporary, dependent on the geopolitical context and socio-historic conditions. They could not be considered valid for all time.

The subjugated peoples of Africa and Asia took hold of this emancipating grammar and turned it against the colonial powers to lead many successful struggles for independence. Decolonization was a decisive qualitative step in the universalization of the right to self-determination, which by a boomerang effect ended up landing in Europe itself, first in the western part of the continent. The ethno-regionalism of the 1960s clearly borrowed its methods and vocabulary from Third World liberation movements that had managed to shake off the European yoke: advocacy of armed struggle, association between regionalist struggle and the fight against capitalism, critique of state imperialism that had brought "residual nations" to heel. Colonialism is certainly the one theme that clearly shows the common inspiration behind both the demands of Corsicans and Bretons and those of the FLN or the Vietminh.

The Occitan writer and activist Robert Lafont thus railed against the vassalization of France's regions by a suzerain Parisian center, regional underdevelopment and the authoritarian acculturation of peripheral ethnic groups, all signs of internal colonialism practiced by the French state.[1] Nowhere in Western Europe has the quest for self-determination, expressed with highly variable force and intensity depending on the case, ultimately led to the formation of a new state. It has partially been concretized, however, in Spain (considerable autonomy instituted in Catalonia and the Basque Country), in

Belgium (federalization of the state) and even in France, though to a lesser extent (special status for Corsica).

Yet there is no guarantee that the dynamics of self-determination will not produce more effects in the West, as the unexpected implosion of the communist system gave a new lease on life to the right of peoples to decide their own future. The crumbling of the Soviet Union and the breakup of the Czechoslovakian and Yugoslav federations gave a myriad of peoples expression through a state, in many cases for the first time. After destroying multinational and then colonial empires, the right to self-determination entered its third stage with "decommunization," thus breaking apart an ideological empire.[2]

Self-determination may yet come into a new phase of development in the West by undermining the classic nation-state and its pretention to reduce national attachments to political citizenship. This is all the more true since the Eastern European precedents have shown that the accession to independence of new "nations without history" (Slovaks, Slovenes, Macedonians, etc.) can occur peacefully by amicable agreement, the counter-example of the war in Bosnia notwithstanding. The velvet divorce between Czechs and Slovaks shows other stateless nations with a dense political history (Flanders, Catalonia) that state dissociation can be accomplished without trauma or violence and that full independence is not necessarily a pipe dream.

The latest contemporary expression attesting to the vigor of this principle of peoples' right to self-determination is in the mobilization of indigenous peoples, those first nations crushed by the steamroller of conquest and colonization and kept in a state of endemic economic and political marginalization. Across the five continents, Native Americans, Tuaregs, Australian Aboriginals and the Samis of northern Scandinavia amount to a population of 300 million individuals distributed over 5000 ethnic groups. There again, these peoples have chosen to act within their respective states and on the international stage, asserting their right to freely decide their future, which at the very least involves the right to cultural and even administrative autonomy and property rights to their traditional lands. While most of these peoples would settle for the recognition of their basic collective rights within existing states, some of them mean to go further, toward extensive, territory-based internal autonomy (such as the Inuit in Canada who, in 1999, were granted their own territory, Nunavut) or even independence (the Uighurs, a Turkic-Mongol people 7 million strong living in the Chinese province of Xinjiang).

This effervescence undeniably shows that the right to self-determination is far from losing its appeal. Will its universal scope ineluctably bring about the Balkanization of the planet into ever smaller and more inclusive states?

Nothing could be less certain. It is important to measure properly the immense distance between potential nationalisms and accomplished nationalisms, that is, those able to form a new and independent state. There are many distinguishing factors by which differential gaps between peoples can be identified. These include language, religion, shared historical experience and so on. Taking into account only the language factor, the staggering figure of 6,000 human groups can be counted. This number would only multiply if it were cross-referenced with the criterion of religion, for as the Swiss example eloquently demonstrates, the same language can be spoken by different denominational groups.

Yet, as Ernest Gellner has noted, even if we accept that 6,000 languages would identify as many different peoples, each with its own nationalist project, at least 90% of these nationalisms are still only potential.[3] This lack of political legitimacy has to do with a series of factors, not the least of which the smooth assimilation of a minority group into another that is larger and enjoys powerful socio-cultural prestige. This iron law of assimilation, which in the age of global communication is undergoing phenomenal acceleration, is likely to bring about the disappearance of half the languages currently in use by the end of the twenty-first century, proportionally reducing the capacity of linguistic nationalisms to emerge.

Other elements also prevent virtual nationalisms from materializing: geographic dispersion, failure to consolidate the myth of historical continuity, lack of an intelligentsia, etc. Unfulfillment is therefore great, and the overwhelming majority of nationalisms are merely potential. Yet even nationalisms that do emerge in deed and manage to engage a true political process are far from guaranteed of seeing their aspirations to self-determination realized.

The most serious obstacle has to do with the existence of an international order structured by the division into states. The latter jealously guard their prerogatives and are scarcely willing to relinquish any of their territorial sovereignty. Deployment of alternative nationalisms is thus considerably restricted by the 200 or so states that share the world and ensure that their territorial integrity is respected. The case of Africa vividly illustrates that even when an outcome seems certain, things can still fo wrong. Theoretically, this continent where, as is often repeated with some exaggeration, the borders drawn by the colonizers are arbitrary and artificial because they frequently split human groups, should have produced a number of irredentist and secessionist nationalisms. With over 1,900 languages and a few thousand ethnic groups,[4] it seemed to offer a fertile breeding ground. Yet, remarkably, despite exceptionally vicious conflicts, the borders handed down from colonization, for which the Organization of African Unity urged respect in 1964, have endured. All the states that acceded to independence did so in the context of a decolonizing nationalism that accompanied the liquidation of colonial empires. So-called regionalist nationalisms (Biafra in Nigeria, Katanga in Zaire) all failed in the face of state resistance with international backing. The only recent exception is the July 2011 independence of South Sudan, following a long liberation war waged by the southern population and a peace agreement between Khartoum and rebel troops, under the auspices of the United Nations.

There is little question that in a finite world, in which existing states enjoy strong legitimacy, the capacity of effective nationalisms to fulfill their aim of achieving full independence is slimmer than what the ethnic or religious differentiation potential might at first suggest. Kurds, Palestinians, Sikhs, Basques and many others measure each day just how hard it is to carry their nationalism to statehood in a world already saturated with states. This difficulty does not call into question the universal nature of the principle of self-determination, but clearly emphasizes that its realization is in no way a foregone conclusion. In each given situation, this will depend on propitious political conditions and a favorable historical context, such as those that facilitated the breakup of the USSR in 1991.

A Short Historical Digression

If the deployment of nationalisms into statehood is thus in many respects more constrained than one might at first suppose, the fact nevertheless remains that in this early twenty-first century, nationalism continues to enjoy considerable resonance. But, to focus on Western Europe, it does not strike a chord everywhere or with consistent intensity.

Why do "the Frisians, who have a separate language and live in a clearly delimited territory, not have a credible independence or even autonomist movement whereas the Lombards are so terribly restless?"[5] Why, in Northern Italy, spearhead of the country's political unity and its driving economic force, has the openly separatist Northern League gained a lasting foothold in the political landscape, whereas Sicily, where autonomism was vibrant for a long time, is now legitimist and in favor of maintaining Italy's territorial integrity? Why do Catalans and Basques demonstrate militant nationalism while Bretons and Occitans merely voice certain cultural demands? In other words, what accounts for the considerable differential in nationalist mobilization?

We might start by noting that in Western Europe, the areas of instability fairly clearly match the "conceptual map of Europe" drawn up by the social scientist Stein Rokkan in the 1970s, which isolated three peripheral areas: the Atlantic façade, basically corresponding to the "Celtic area" (Ireland, Brittany, Galicia); the continental periphery, in other words the Slavic belt at the intersection of Catholicism and Orthodoxy (from Poland to Croatia); and the urban axis of city-states that runs from Belgium in the north to Italy along the Rhine Valley.[6] These areas, located geographically on the fringe of states in the process of formation (France, England), are more conducive to developing claims for autonomy or even outright nationalisms, due to their peripheral situation.

The hypothesis is an attractive one and has the merit of setting the question of nationalism in its long-term geo-historical context.[7] It makes it possible to identify the points where nationalisms create tectonic dislocation and areas of nation-state structural weakness. This global approach nevertheless harbors an intrinsic limitation: it only imperfectly explains variations within a particular ensemble. Why did a vibrant nationalism develop in the interwar period in Flanders whereas Alsatian autonomism ultimately remained fairly muffled, even though the two regions are on the same city-state axis and belong to the same "Germanic" cultural space?

To account for this difference, it is essential to examine how states are formed. A rapid historical comparison shows that the Western Europe states that experience the staunchest protest movements are those where the political center has suffered from precarious institutionalization. Whether born in the nineteenth century (Belgium, Italy) or earlier (Spain), these states have been incapable of suppressing infra-state attachments in the long term.

Belgium, a young country, was not the product of a centuries-long historical evolution accompanied by the gradual crystallization of national sentiment. Its official inception in 1830–1 owed as much to European powers' desire to form a buffer state as to the revolutionary agitation in Brussels. The state, created by elites, remained weak in the face of various cleavages (religious, political, linguistic) running through society, and it proved unable to counter the gradual rise of the Flemish movement.

In Italy, national unification, achieved under the aegis of the kingdom of Piedmont-Sardinia with the military backing of Napoleon III, remained incomplete, crippled by the persistence of strong parochialism and equally assertive regionalism. In Spain, the Castilian center, weakened by chronic political instability, was unable to integrate its recalcitrant peripheries (the Basque Country, Catalonia), which moreover were at the forefront of the country's economic development.

Yet, while some degree of state weakness accounts for greater vibrancy of nationalitarian movements, the explanation remains incomplete. Some countries where the political center had been consolidated as far back as the Middle Ages had to face significant nationalitarian turbulence, whereas others that had followed a similar political path were only marginally affected by the phenomenon. Great Britain has struggled for two centuries with Irish nationalism which, after obtaining partial satisfaction with the creation of the Irish Free State in 1922, still continues to contest the British presence in Ulster. The United Kingdom also faces a nationalist current which, although in the minority in Wales, has a large following in Scotland, united with England since 1707.[8] Conversely, metropolitan France, whose state formation took a similar path, has experienced only mild bouts of regionalist fever. Although also situated along the Atlantic arc, Brittany has not seen the development of a nationalist movement the likes of which have been experienced by Ireland, Scotland and even Wales.

The Nationalism of Affluence

Some have attempted to seek points of convergence using an economic framework of interpretation. In the 1970s, a time when a certain Marxist doctrine prevailed, many saw in the emergence of nationalitarian claims in the Western European peripheries the expression of political protest emanating from groups rebelling against their economic subordination to a "predatory" center. It was very much in vogue to analyze such unequal development in terms of internal colonialism.[9]

This paradigm was founded on the following idea: when the economic activity of a region with strong cultural specificity is subordinated to the center, it becomes an internal colony. To put an end to this situation of dependency, local elites can exploit their identity distinction to support nationalist mobilization. The model linking division of labor and cultural fault lines has the advantage of coherence but the drawback of being largely disproved by facts. It may fit the case of Ireland where the Protestant/Catholic dichotomy coincided with a social division between landowners and peasants, but it is at odds with many other examples. Thus the early nationalist stirrings in Catalonia, the Basque Country and Scotland in the last quarter of the nineteenth century emerged in prosperous regions where the Industrial Revolution had taken root, not in economically devastated areas. This observation still holds true over a century later.

Currently, the salient phenomenon is indeed the brazen vitality of national-isms in affluent regions (Catalonia, Flanders, Northern Italy). While the initial historical context differs considerably in these areas—Flanders having been sidelined within the Belgian state formed in 1830 whereas Lombardy became the economic hub of Italy, whose unity had been achieved by neigh-boring Piedmont—they are all characterized today by their remarkable mod-ernization. Whether these regions have long since spearheaded their country's industrialization (such as Catalonia in Spain) or if they've achieved a more recent economic boom (Flanders, Scotland), they are ahead of other, more economically depressed areas whose survival largely depends on the central state's redistributive intervention. The state thus appears both useless and parasitic, tapping part of the wealth produced in a prosperous region to spread it over less privileged areas which nevertheless still lag behind economically (Wallonia, Mezzogiorno). The idea that the region would be much better off relying on its own strengths ends up gaining popularity.

There is indisputably a form of economic selfishness in such self-interested nationalism, but it is nevertheless motivated by rational choice. This dimen-sion is too often overlooked, many commentators preferring to emphasize the irrational nature of nationalist commitments. However, voters who throw their support behind nationalitarian groups are no more unreasonable than their fellow citizens who vote for generalist parties. They, too, calculate the benefits and expect advantages from their party choice. In Belgium, voting for Flemish nationalist parties (Vlaams Belang, the New Flemish Alliance) amounts to demanding the end of social transfers from an economically healthy Flanders to a Wallonia suffering from total industrial collapse. Opting for the Scottish National Party also indicates a desire to see North Sea oil revenue benefit the Scottish alone and not the entire United Kingdom. These attitudes can be morally criticized for their manifest insensitivity and their refusal to show solidarity with their fellow citizens, but they are not absurd. They arise from what are indeed rational considerations.[10]

The true impact of the economic argument should nevertheless be properly gauged. While economic considerations may foster nationalist mobilization, they are never the sole driving force. There is an interaction between the two, but the economic sphere does not ultimately determine the political. Thus, although from 1967 to 1987 the Palestinians in the West Bank and the Gaza Strip derived individual benefits from their forced integration into the Israeli economy in terms of jobs and standard of living, at no time did these objective advantages lead to an ebb in Palestinian nationalism. On the contrary, the uneven but real improvement in the Palestinians' economic situation was clearly accompanied by an intensification of their political commitment.

This paradox has a fairly simple explanation: the accumulation of not only economic but also educational, cultural and other such resources gives actors greater autonomy, which enables them better to grasp the structural reality of power relations and makes their lack of control over their own destiny all the more unbearable. Ultimately, their national consciousness is honed in the process. Consequently, the perspective of collective emancipation justifies considerable sacrifice. Even if a future Palestinian state in the West Bank and the Gaza Strip, deprived of solid infrastructure, would have trouble getting by from an economic standpoint, this fact will in no way incite the Palestinians to dampen their nationalist mobilization. Their aspiration is rooted in a quest for political dignity that is worth considerable sacrifice. In answer to Ben-Gurion, who in 1934 suggested to a Palestinian that the Jews' arrival en masse was an economic blessing for the Arabs, Musa Alami made this scathing reply: "I would prefer that the country remain impoverished and barren for another hundred years until we ourselves are able to develop it on our own." Or to put it more figuratively, the struggle for national independence cannot be exchanged for a bowl of lentils.

Even if the economic context in which a given nationalism emerges is highly variable, once it has taken hold as a political reality, it will persist no matter how much economic conditions change. In the second half of the nineteenth century, Flemish nationalism emerged in a very poor agricultural region, whereas Wallonia was experiencing a remarkable industrial boom due to its coalmines. At the same time in Catalonia, the first nationalist organizations were appearing in a region where industrialization, especially in textiles, was developing steadily while the rest of Spain, except for the Basque Country, remained profoundly rural and cut off from the modern world. A century later, the fact is that nationalism has gained strength in both Catalonia, which has kept up its momentum, and in Flanders, where its prodigious economic success enabled it to catch up with and then surpass Wallonia. Yet nationalism, far from being numbed by economic development, has steadily made gains to the point that, in response, the Belgian state has now become fully federalized through successive reforms.

An initial conclusion can be drawn from this observation: economic improvement is not enough to dispel nationalism. On the contrary, when within the same political unit the growth differential of a region with a strong "identity profile" widens, its elites tend to want to maintain and even reinforce their region's enviable position and thus go even further in an autonomization strategy. This is what can be called the cumulative effect of nationalism: the increase in economic potential stimulates the desire to extend the capacity for action to other spheres, the first of them political. Moreover, the example of Catalonia shows that the accumulation of wealth during the twentieth century did not wear down the appeal of nationalism, any more than nationalism declined as the growth gap with the rest of Spain started to narrow, when the country began opening up to a modern capitalist economy in the 1960s.

Conversely, a close correlation between economic crisis and the rise of nationalism is difficult to establish. Although the Scottish National Party took 30% of the vote in 1974, it fell to 11% in 1983, and this during an ongoing economic crisis that was hitting Scotland with full force during Margaret Thatcher's premiership.

Economic conditions certainly influence the configuration of nationalisms, but more as a catalyst than as a trigger. Northern Italy offers an illustration of the insufficiency of the purely economic dimension.

The Northern League has since 1987 managed to carve out a place for itself in Italy's political landscape by mobilizing the most dynamic entrepreneurial forces in the northeast. Umberto Bossi's rhetoric, directed at the inefficiencies of a predatory state pursuing public fund transfers to the south which solely benefit clientelist networks, has held considerable sway over this "third Italy" subject to a disproportionate tax burden. The saber-rattling against "thieving Rome" and calls for a tax revolt plainly appealed to shopkeepers, craftsmen and business owners who expressed a protest vote through the League. However, it is highly unlikely that it will manage to represent the true separatist movement its leader aspires to, even if Bossi solemnly proclaimed the independence of "Padania," a neologism referring to Northern Italy along the River Po, from Piedmont to Lombardy and Friuli.

Such independence is of course only virtual, but it indicates a persistent determination to upset the political game by adopting an increasingly radical breakaway strategy. At first in favor of considerable autonomy within a federal Italy, the League's leader has since campaigned for the division of the country into three "federated republics" (Padania, Etruria, South), then advocated pure and simple secession. In the first decade of the 2000s, he came back to the idea of federalizing Italy, which ended up partially becoming a reality under the Berlusconi government with the law on fiscal federalism (2009), which granted fiscal autonomy to the various sub-state levels of governance (regions, provinces, townships, metropolitan areas). This zigzagging stance attests to the difficulty of truly giving shape to an independence strategy for Padania, for two reasons.

First, for many League supporters, the call for independence rests much more on tactical considerations than on real adherence to the idea. The independence theme, totally marginal in the early 1990s, has certainly gained some resonance since. In the mid-1990s, nearly a quarter of Northern Italians viewed independence as "a healthy and desirable solution."[11] Fifteen years later, 20% of Northern Italians declared they were in favor of dividing Italy into two entities.[12] This "separatist inclination," a marginal but nevertheless very real phenomenon, should be weighed carefully: does it truly express an authentic desire for secession, or is it the instinctive manifestation of protest against the workings of the state? For the non-wage-earning middle classes, the call for Northern Italy's independence in fact appears basically to be a threat waved at the central government so that it will reduce the tax burden and put in order public expenditure and one-way transfers to the south. As a result, "independence" is only marginally synonymous with separatism. It is more a call for wholesale reform of the state by injecting a large dose of federalism.

Furthermore, the identity deficit that plagues the League's project makes independence hardly an attractive option: the Padania cause does not kindle much enthusiasm. This was obvious on the occasion of the "declaration of independence": only 30,000 people gathered for Bossi in Venice while in Milan, Gianfranco Fini's National Alliance mobilized five times as many in defense of the country's national integrity. This failure demonstrates how difficult it is to lend credence to a "northern" nationalism based solely on economics. The invention of national symbols (a green and white flag, an anthem and a transitional constitution) has not been sufficient to mask the gaping void of the secessionist project in terms of identity content. And for good reason: the Padania to which Bossi made reference is no more homogeneous than Italy as a whole.

Until Risorgimento, the north of the peninsula was for centuries divided into rival kingdoms, republics and dukedoms, all under the heavy influence of neighboring countries such as France, Spain and Austria. There was no pre-existing political unity and scarcely a memory of shared history. Even economic cohesion was limited. The northeast's small businesses stand in contrast to the northwest's large industrial complexes. Of course, theoretically the League could instill a "Padanian" national consciousness by creating a specific mythology and forging trans-historical continuity. All nationalisms basically invent traditions and manufacture the past. The fact remains that, unlike

Flemish and Catalan nationalisms, which were able to position themselves within a long historical trajectory and a relatively coherent territory, "Padanism" obviously has real trouble overcoming the internal fragmentation of Northern Italy and legitimating its aspiration to independence.

Affluent regions wishing to take charge of their destiny by shaking off the yoke of the central state are not the only ones that endeavor to break the political pact. The breakup of a state can be precipitated by concern on the part of dominant elites to part ways with a region characterized by turbulent nationalism and economic sluggishness. Former Czechoslovakia is a case in point.

Initially, some Czech leaders did not hesitate to brandish the threat of separation, claiming it would irremediably impoverish Slovakia and thus believing that this would encourage Slovak leaders quickly back into line. Subsequently, as renegotiation of the federal pact got bogged down, the Czech leaders ended up finding more and more advantages in the breakup of Czechoslovakia in the name of economic rationality. Finally, the velvet divorce of 1993 enabled the more affluent Czechs to put an end to a costly redistribution policy from which the Slovaks benefited most, and to devote their resources solely to setting up a market economy. Some were close to thinking that splitting the state in two and putting an end to one-way transfers would be so costly for the Slovaks that they would bitterly regret becoming independent. This schadenfreude was not to be satisfied, for the simple reason that Slovakia, disproving all the experts' alarming predictions, has registered strong, steady economic growth since 1994.

Post-independence "economic punishment" thus did not occur, which may give others hope. The bankruptcy the federal government in Ottawa eternally predicts for Quebec to intimidate Quebecois lured by independence will not materialize any more than it did in Slovakia. The argument of economic impoverishment is in fact mainly strategic. It aims to frighten those in favor of political independence but afraid of paying dearly for it with a drop in their standard of living. However, while splitting up a state can of course generate economic costs, they are generally not as high as stalwart defenders of the political status quo may claim.

Again, economic rationality alone is not enough to explain nationalist dynamics. While economic factors may play an accelerating role, they only do so effectively if the society in question is highly differentiated and if it has a degree of unity lending it strong internal coherence that distinguishes it from its neighbors. Nationalism can only fully unfold within a global society.

A Complete Society

Quebec, Catalonia, the Basque Country, Scotland and Flanders share a significant sociological feature that explains the persistence of nationalism: these regions are global societies.[13] That is, these societies have a complete social structure, their own institutions, a specific territory and a particular culture. Due to the high density of these societies, their members situate themselves more with respect to the society in which they live than to the general state framework, in other words Canada, Spain, Great Britain or Belgium. For many citizens, the global society even becomes the primary, if not only, point of reference.

In this context, nationalism will necessarily maintain at least a constant critical mass. It may of course experience variations. Periods of relative ebbing may follow phases of expansion, possibly resulting in the global society's split from the state in which it was included and the formation of a separate state. While such a perspective is in no way inevitable, on the other hand it is doubtful that nationalism will ever entirely lose its appeal. In a global society, nationalism will not drop below a certain threshold. It will always remain a political force that must be taken into account.

A review of the main features of this type of society is in order. Its primary characteristic is its social completeness. As it includes all social categories (farmers, workers, employees, shopkeepers, etc.), a global society forms a largely autonomous unit. Its strong internal differentiation makes it a complete group. This in no way implies that no horizontal lines of cleavage exist (between, for instance, the propertied class and blue collars), but they are essentially contained within the global society. Moreover, they are secondary compared to the vertical dividing line between the global society and the neighboring social ensembles.

A second determining factor: such a society is linked to a particular culture, sufficiently rich and diversified to lend it a high degree of specificity. It is not a vague, residual, "weak" culture but indeed a societal culture, that is, "a culture which provides its members with meaningful ways of life across the full range of human activities, including social, educational, religious, recreational, and economic life, encompassing both public and private spheres."[14] This inclusive culture has a fairly large number of structured channels by which it is diffused (schools, media, institutions, associations, etc.). From this standpoint, Catalonia indubitably has a fully-fledged societal culture, distinct from that of Castile, present in its school and university system, its media output, its administration, the corporate world and so on. Conversely, Brittany has lost its societal culture, of which only shreds remain, despite the sustained efforts of a host of artists and educators to revive it. While a societal culture often means a particular language, this association is not necessary. For instance, although Scots and Gaelic are no longer in use in Scotland, the persistence of three institutions (the Presbyterian Church, an independent school system, a separate legal system), functioning within a territory established by the Treaty of York with England in 1237, are enough to give Scottish culture considerable density.[15]

Culture plays an essential role in integrating such societies. To borrow Gellner's expression, it institutes "a single overall orderliness" that differs immensely from the fragmentation into sub-units characteristic of structured societies in the past. As long as such a culture thus innervates a group, this group becomes a nation, whether or not it has a "political roof." It thus makes perfect sense to talk about "stateless nations,"[16] as long as within a given state entity there is a complete, distinct society that has its own culture.

This global society is at once civil and civic in that it comprises both an autonomous social space where individuals pursue their private interests and a specific political space in which they participate in governing public life.[17]

As a civil society, it is supported by two pillars: a network of voluntary associations and a network of businesses. Thus, to take only the Catalonian example, the remarkable density of cultural, sports and leisure associations, professional groupings, institutes and foundations contributes to the existence of a fully developed civil society that is more than simply a regional variant of Spanish civil society. It is worth noting that most of these global societies are located in traditionally Catholic areas, where over the centuries the Church developed a tight web of educational, social and cultural institutions. These institutions had a very strong presence, sometimes until recently, as in Quebec. In other cases, Church influence was very real but contested, as in Catalonia, where anarchism was a strong current in the interwar period. However, the pervasiveness of the Church was tangible in other cases. It sustained an intense sociability based on an ethos of solidarity that emphasized cooperation among social classes and mutual aid. It valued complementarity and cooperation between groups beyond the divergence of their short-term interests. Nationalism too aspires to this interclass perspective.

This common foundation explains why such societies, already characterized by community sentiment, were particularly receptive to nationalism. Moreover, the correlation translates fairly clearly into the political sphere. When true Christian democratic parties exist, as in Belgium and Catalonia, they also adopt a nationalist stance. There, the Catholic community is presented from the start as being national. In the absence of Christian democracy, nationalist groups sometimes assume this function directly. One example is the Basque Nationalist Party, whose original program was in fact based on defense of a national Catholic organicism. This substitutional capacity probably shows most clearly the extent to which Catholic communitarianization facilitates the shift to nationalism. The example of Italy confirms this hypothesis: in the northeast, small business owners formed part of the Christian democratic electorate. After Christian democracy collapsed, they began voting for the Northern League, which from then on represented the new means to defend the specificity of the "white areas" characterized by Catholicism.

A network of entrepreneurs—the second aspect of civil society—provides these regions with a particular economic base conducive to maintaining a communitarian spirit. Their economic fabric is made up of small- and medium-sized, family-style businesses (SMEs) that share the same spirit of personal initiative. This structuring into "human-size" units makes it easier to adapt quickly to technological innovations while preserving a degree of closeness in social relations, which are only marginally affected by class conflict. SMEs do not occupy the entire economic arena alone. In Flanders' small cities and urbanized rural areas, for instance, they share the stage with the strong presence of multinational corporations. Nevertheless, even in large companies, the culture of compromise and social cooperation remains very much alive.

Regional political authorities, moreover, make sure to preserve this internal cohesion as far as possible. This phenomenon is clear to see in Quebec, where the provincial government has set up a tight web of relations between the government, trade unions, development agencies and business. The aim is to coordinate economic activity by fostering interpenetration between trade union organizations, employer organizations, professional associations and government structures. The neo-corporatism that regulates relations between the various economic actors serves the political objective of national integration. Its implementation, however, is highly reliant on the powers devolved to regional authorities. For instance, the Generalitat of Catalonia, with limited powers in the economic sphere, can only act with caution, whereas the areas of responsibility allocated to Quebec and Flanders are broad enough in scope to pursue such a rationale.

As these civil societies are characterized by an aspiration to social harmony, encouraged by Catholicism, nationalism will be predominantly "bourgeois." It will not seek to revolutionize society and will prefer a pragmatic and legalistic approach to the national issue. Even in the Basque Country where "revolutionary nationalitarianism" enjoys considerable support—long represented by Batasuna, which took about 18% of the vote in regional elections until it was banned in 2003 on account of its ties to the armed ETA organization—the dominant nationalist current remains centrist, moderate and integrative.

While a global society is a complete civil society (showing organizational pluralism and intense economic activity), it is also a civic society, with a particular space for political expression. This public sphere is always anchored in a specific territory marked out by precise boundaries: for instance, Quebec province, the Flanders region or the autonomous community of Catalonia. It is manifested in the institutionalization of a specific system of government, usually with a legislative assembly elected by universal suffrage and an executive. An internal political scene can probably exist without it having its own institutions (such as in Scotland prior to the reestablishment of its parliament in 1999). However, in this eventuality, the nation, without specific representation, clearly has a limited capacity for action and suffers from a visibility deficit.

The institutionalization of power makes it possible to form a specific democratic space. The election of a "regional" parliament by the Flemings, Catalans and Quebecois creates a separate political arena with specific internal discussions and debates. This specificity is also starkly brought into focus by the existence of "regional nationalist" parties, in other words political groups that restrict their activity to the territory of the nation, without a state in whose name they mean to act.[18] The internal political scene can be occupied by a single party (the Parti Québécois) or, as is more frequently the case, by several parties representing various inclinations (in Catalonia, Convergence and Union, or CiU, the Republican Left of Catalonia; in the Basque country, the Basque Nationalist Party, Batasuna and its various incarnations, Aralar, Eusko Alkartasuna).

The case of Belgium is probably the one in which party regionalization has been carried the furthest: aside from regionalist groups (the New Flemish Alliance, the French-speaking Federal Democrats), Belgium's three political families are remarkable for their division on a linguistic basis. Socialists, Christian Democrats and Liberals are thus each represented by two parties: one in the north, the other in the south of the country. When new political movements such as the environmental and extreme right parties emerged in the 1980s, they materialized in distinct groups: one for the Dutch-speakers, the other for the francophones. Regionalist formations generally carry considerable weight in the regional political system. They often assume responsibility for public affairs and are even a lasting dominant force, as was CiU, in office in Catalonia continually from 1980 to 2003 before returning in 2010.

While these regionalist parties by definition do not have a national base statewide, they nevertheless strive increasingly to influence the central government and gain additional political advantages. This strategy can take on various forms. In Canada, the Quebecois sovereignists chose to bring the debate over the independence of the "Belle Province" to the very heart of the federal political system by forming the Bloc Québécois in the federal parliament in Ottawa. In close conjunction with the Parti Québécois in Quebec, the Bloc initiated the referendum campaign of 1995, in which the sovereignists were defeated by only a slim margin.[19]

Spain took a different route. As central governments in Madrid were unable to form an absolute majority between 1993 and 2000, regionalist parties (especially the CiU) shrewdly decided to use their parliamentary support as a bargaining chip. From 1993 to 1995, in exchange for backing Felipe González, the CiU thus obtained the automatic cession of 15% of income tax revenue to the autonomous communities. After José María Aznar's Partido Popular won in 1996, Jordi Pujol, president of the Generalitat of Catalonia, used the same tactic and this time managed to double the share that was ceded to the communities. There is obviously a strong paradox here. A central government led by a rightwing and notably "Spanish-minded" party gives up a portion of its resources in favor of autonomous communities, because it needs regionalist party support in the Cortes. Similarly, in Belgium, the Flemish nationalist Volksunie (People's Union) organization, chose to take part in the Belgium government on two occasions in order to accelerate the federalization of the state.

However, in a global society, nationalism is not limited to groups that explicitly advocate a nationalitarian project. It runs through the entire political spectrum. Even nationwide parties are obliged to take regionalist sentiment into account and, if not integrate it, at least position themselves with respect to it. The Socialist Party of Catalonia, which is federated to the Spanish Socialist Workers' Party, does not object to moderate Catalan nationalism; the local incarnation of the Communist Party, Initiative for Catalonia, clearly advertises a leftist nationalism and promotes the systematic use of Catalan in the public administration. In Quebec, even if the Liberal Party does not subscribe to the Parti Québécois' breakaway strategy, it is nonetheless strongly attached to preserving the distinct character of Quebecois society within a reformed federal structure. One might remember that the neonationalism of the 1960s rose out of the Liberal camp, and that the sovereignist leader René Lévesque came from its ranks.

In Flanders as well, the spread of nationalism has grown. For a long time nationalism was contained within a fairly narrow fringe of society, but the gradual consolidation of a homogeneous Flemish public space through language legislation and batavianization of the education system led the unitary Belgian political forces to make a series of adjustments that amounted to adopting a nationalist program, albeit nuanced. The Catholic Party, with a strong foothold in rural areas and smaller cities, was the first to take up some of the Flemish nationalist demands, but the Liberals and Socialists soon followed suit. Nationalism became widespread, now transcending party differences. While at first it was supported only by a nationalist political party representing, by definition, a mere fraction of the social body, it has become a horizon shared by all political forces. At this stage, nationalism can be considered fully actualized, for it has transformed into an across-the-board phenomenon, neither specifically left nor right, but both at once.

As Eric Hobsbawm writes, "Its very vagueness... gives [nationalism] a potentially universal support within its own community."[20] This vagueness is unquestionably valuable. For nationalism to be received broadly, it must not be associated with any particular social project. Such careful omission is only natural: nationalism seeks to preserve the greatest possible social consensus, and to do so, it must bring together the middle class and the working class, the rich and the poor, and the religious and the secular under the same banner. This is why it has no interest in promoting social reform: to do so would require emphasizing differences within a national body, the very cohesion of which is central to its program. The rare attempts to reconcile a nationalist rationale and a class rationale have always resulted in the clear subordination of class to the national endeavor. Thus socialist Zionism, which aspired to achieve both social and national revolution, ended up sacrificing the former on the altar of the latter. Ben-Gurion and his followers did not turn the Jews into a proletarian nation, but "nationalized" the working class by allowing it to be absorbed by its national mission.[21]

Although such lack of precision may be necessary, it is not enough to ensure the success of nationalism, which also owes its impact to its extreme simplicity. It rests on an elementary principle, autonomy, which since the eighteenth century has been at the heart of modernity. From the moment individuals aspire to determine themselves as freely as possible, it is only logical that members of a national group shaped by political entrepreneurs demand to be "masters at home," as did the Quebecois in the 1960s. Nationalism "takes," in a given society, precisely because it is weak in comprehension and broad in extension, to use terms borrowed from logic. Therein lies the key to its capacity for rallying a broad segment of the group to which it means to give voice.

A Quasi-State

The institutionalization of deliberative and governmental structures offers another highly valuable asset. It provides a true para-state apparatus that will play an increasingly significant role in citizens' lives and inevitably compete with the central state. That peripheral nationalisms adopt a protest stance against the state by no means implies that they reject the state as a principle of political organization. They simply intend to use it to their advantage by creating an alternative state structure. This yearning for a state is a feature of all protest nationalisms, even if it manifests itself with varying intensity.

The example of Quebec is particularly pertinent and is worth considering at length. After the Act of Union establishing United Canada in 1840, nationalism in Lower (French-speaking) Canada was expressed in a defensive model.[22] At the instigation of the Catholic Church, which was all powerful at the time, a survival strategy was put in place designed to preserve the established order: upholding of religious faith, preservation of family and parish structures, resistance to industrialization. Such traditional nationalism aimed to preserve the unity of all French Canadians, a pan-Canadian human group concentrated mainly in Quebec but present as a minority in the other provinces. Consequently, this cohesion necessarily relied on immaterial bonds such as religion and culture. It also called for a withdrawal of the political, which was all the easier as the state in question, being British, was considered the enemy. This survival nationalism was swept aside remarkably quickly in the 1960s to make way for a modern nationalism in which "the State of Quebec" became the major actor.

State power was consolidated in the face of two adversaries. The first was the Church, which was stripped of its role in education, social welfare and culture, ministerial departments being put in charge of these sectors. Secondly, to counter the power of large private corporations, owned by the anglophones, the State of Quebec turned itself into an economic entrepreneur, particularly in the field of hydroelectric power (establishment of Hydro-Québec, construction of the James Bay dams). In Quebec, nationalism would thus be embodied not by the virtually non-existent francophone middle class, but by a state technocracy convinced that "the national state was becoming the great instrument for the emancipation of the French-Canadian nation."[23] The state's preeminence necessarily implied assertion of its jurisdiction over a specific territory, in this case Quebec province. French Canadian nationalism could only enter the political sphere in the sole province where French Canadians were a majority. The consequences were twofold.

First of all, it meant loosening ties with French-speaking minorities outside of Quebec, which, in the event of secession, would find themselves orphaned in an overwhelmingly English-speaking Canada. Secondly, this break with the ethnic rationale valued by traditional nationalism went hand in hand with the assertion of territorialized nationalism. Short of resorting to ethnic cleansing or institutionalized discrimination, refocusing on territory requires redefining belonging. Nationalism must appeal to all citizens present within a given territory, including members of minority cultural groups. Thus, in Quebec, the affirmation of modern nationalism went together with an open definition of the Quebec nation to incorporate anglophones, allophones (third-language immigrants) and native peoples.

The politicization of nationalism renders inevitable the substitution of territory as its structuring principle in place of ethnic group and culture. As it matures and begins to issue political claims, nationalism is obliged to define a sovereign space that is bound to a territory with borders. In seeking to structure a polity, it must overcome purely cultural logic. However, abandoning a primordial definition of identity in favor of a civic definition is not enough to remove all obstacles.

The territorialization of nationalism does not always have the desired effect, as the outcome of the 30 October 1995 referendum showed: 95% of anglophones and allophones voted against Quebec's accession to sovereignty. This failure is easy to explain: Quebecois nationalism has little appeal for these two groups, as their political space of reference remains Canada from the Atlantic to the Pacific. English-speakers refuse to become a minority in a sovereign Quebec when they are part of the majority in Canada. As for the allophones, who are generally integrated into the anglophone community, their primary loyalty lies with Canada, the country to which they immigrated, not with Quebec, where they reside. Their perception is radically different from the francophone perspective, whose primary allegiance is to Quebec.

The same remark could be made with respect to Catalonia. There, too, Catalan nationalism, even though it takes care to consider all inhabitants of the autonomous community as Catalan, only has a marginal hold on "internal migrants," the Andalusians and Castilians settled in Catalonia, for whom

Spain remains the frame of reference. As long as the majority and the minorities continue to define themselves with respect to different political spaces, the latter's adherence to the nationalist project will remain tenuous. The repressed ethnic aspect thus may resurface with a vengeance.

The Parti Québécois leader, Jacques Parizeau, in conceding defeat on the evening of the second referendum, bitterly claimed his party had been beaten "by money and the ethnic vote." He was clearly accusing the anglophones and new immigrants of being "bad" Quebeckers who had prevented true Quebeckers (descendants of the French) from acceding to sovereignty. Even if nationalism tends to have a territorial rationale, its ethnic underpinnings are never totally erased. While some may lay the blame on the *maquetos* (non-Basque "foreigners"), others will disparage the *terroni* (the "yokels" of Mezzogiorno) and non-natives (mainlanders living in Corsica), just as still others will clamor that they want to "give France back to the French."

Fear of minority groups is likely to grow as the quasi-state consolidates its institutionalization. In the process it attempts to lay claim to as many powers as possible, while also reducing the spheres in which the central state can intervene. Although such extension of its prerogatives is obviously constrained by the constitutional provisions and laws governing the division of powers, regional institutions, in a deliberate strategy of national consolidation, will seek to accumulate as much power as they possibly can. In Flanders, the region's powers in economic and cultural matters have been brought under the same bodies (Parliament and the government), whereas different bodies exercise them on the French-speaking side. In Catalonia, the Generalitat exploited the ambiguities and loopholes in the Spanish Constitution and the statute of autonomy to increase the scope of its powers as much as possible, which only amplified its dispute with the state before the constitutional court in Madrid. For its own administration, it also instituted a new territorial unit (the *comarca*) in place of the traditional division into provinces.

The existence of a para-state political structure clearly facilitates the task of national integration. This is most apparent when it comes to language. Both Quebec and Catalonia have passed language legislation aiming to reassert that French and Catalan are the specific languages of these respective territories. Such legal provisions guarantee and stimulate the use of these languages in all areas of life (education, the workplace, the media, etc.). The political objective is not only to preserve but also to strengthen the national community, by enriching it with new speakers. Are these laws as repressive as some claim?

It should first be pointed out that the right of minority communities (English- and Spanish-speakers) to receive instruction in their own language is not in jeopardy. Criticizing such legislative measures in the name of formal equality and the central state's need to protect it is hypocritically to turn a blind eye to the fact that the more or less broad diffusion of a language stems partly from a political balance of power. How can anyone deny that had Quebec not established a language policy, the very future of a "distinct society in North America, embracing the full experience of modernity mainly in French"[24] would have been compromised? Without a language policy, new immigrants would very naturally and for utilitarian reasons have opted for English, further reinforcing the weight of the anglophone community, which in the area of Montreal is already considerable. French would not, of course, have disappeared overnight, but would gradually have been marginalized.

The precedent created by the former French colony of Louisiana, integrated into the United States in 1812, where the use of French suffered a rapid decline with the elimination of French schools and the mandatory use of English for official documents, shows that in the absence of any institutionalized protection, a minority language is bound if not to die out, then to be reduced to folklorization.[25] The law can thus legitimately protect a language to stem the process of gradual assimilation, as long as individual freedom of expression remains otherwise guaranteed. And such protection inevitably implies that the group in a minority at the state level (Quebecois in Canada, Catalans in Spain) retains the means to ensure the perpetuation of the language in the public sphere, particularly through the educational system. As Charles Taylor rightly remarked with regard to Quebec, "The aim is not only that francophones be served in French but that there still be francophones there in the next generation."[26] Language must be protected because it creates a certain type of social bond and ensures the long-term survival of a particular human group.

As an active agent in the national mobilization process, an autonomous regional power operates no differently than the state that encompasses it. It constantly seeks further to structure the society it is responsible for. And the place for such self-assertion is not only the domestic but, increasingly, the international stage.

Projection on the World Stage

Stateless nations increasingly tend to demonstrate their existence by presenting themselves as international actors in their own right and by striving to behave like sovereign states. The object of the exercise is also to use international recognition as an argument in favor of greater emancipation from the state that encompasses them. Ability to act on the international stage is of course variable. Whereas a recognized state that has a seat at the UN can establish or break off diplomatic ties with countries of its choice, depending on its political interests of the hour, stateless nations' room for maneuver is staked out by the constitution of the encompassing state and the powers it grants them. Their will to express themselves on the international stage will not, however, wane.

With its Commission for Foreign Affairs, Catalonia has deployed intense para-diplomatic activity that has led it to enter into bilateral accords with regional bodies such as the province of Buenos Aires, the state of Illinois and Wales. Between 1962 and 1992, Quebec, enjoying broader powers, concluded nearly 500 international agreements with sovereign states, primarily France and African countries, most of which were in the fields of education and science.[27] The prize for diplomatic activism, however, goes to Flanders, which, like the other federated entities that now make up Belgium, secured the rare power for a federal state of entering directly into international arrangements. It made full use of this new prerogative to sign cooperation agreements and treaties with several sovereign states (Chile, the Netherlands, Poland, Russia, etc.) as well as international organizations, with the clearly stated goal of endowing Flanders with its own foreign policy.

With the deepening of European political integration, Europe has become a major para-diplomatic issue.[28]

Whereas centralist nationalists, from the French Front National to the Austrian "Liberal Party" and the Danish People's Party, are readily anti-European, regionalist nationalists are usually staunch champions of Europe. Figures such as Alex Salmond, former leader of the Scottish National Party, Kris Peeters, former minister-president of Flanders and Artur Mas, president of the Generalitat of Catalonia vie with one another to make highly pro-European proclamations. Their motivation is obvious: they view European integration as the best means to diminish the powers of the central state and to strengthen regional powers. They espouse the slogan that Denis de Rougemont put forward in the 1960s of a Europe of regions, to describe the dual effect that construction of supranational bodies was supposed to produce: the gradual devaluation of the nation-state framework and the concomitant affirmation of the regions, viewed as both more effective and more "natural."

This hope is sustained by the institutional legitimacy acquired at regional level within Europe since the mid-1970s, with the establishment of the

European Regional Development Fund and the 1988 implementation of structural funds reform, earmarked for the most disadvantaged regions. This so-called cohesion policy increased the direct links between the Commission and regional bodies. But the regions have not only found themselves promoted to a technocratic space. With the Maastricht Treaty they have also obtained the beginnings of quasi-political recognition with the creation of a consultative assembly, the Committee of the Regions, made up of an impressive array of presidents of large regions and municipal officials. Lastly, the Maastricht Treaty also paved the way for national governments to be represented at the EU Council of Ministers by regional ministers when discussions touch on matters that have been transferred to them internally. This new procedure, however, only truly benefits those regions that already enjoy considerable autonomy within federal states.[29] In other countries, the game continues to be controlled for the most part by the central state, although to varying degrees. Unitary states remain the most averse to any regional interventionism.

The Europeanization of policy mobilizes infra-national actors as never before, but states are not irremediably weakened as a result. The changes in the state's role and capacity for action should be analyzed less in terms of retreat than in terms of restructuration.[30] Such redefinition of the state, however, obviously offers nationalist movements a new space within which to deploy.

Even when a region with a strong identity such as Catalonia cannot manage to achieve in Brussels the degree of emancipation from Spanish government oversight that it would like, it plays the European card to the utmost, to stress its international outlook while short-circuiting the central state as much as possible. The Generalitat of Catalonia, with a permanent office in Brussels since 1986, has a virtual embassy. It also seeks to stimulate interregional cooperation, whether at the transnational level (as part of the "four motors of Europe" network along with Baden-Württemberg, Lombardy and Rhône-Alpes) or at the crossborder level (under the Euroregion accord signed with Midi-Pyrénées and Languedoc-Roussillon, the Pyrenees Labor Community, the Mediterranean Arc). Jordi Pujol, president of the Generalitat de Catalonia from 1980 to 2003, was in fact for many years president of the Assembly of European Regions, which comprises over 200 European regions and whose goals are to foster interregional cooperation and strengthen regional representation within European institutions. The development of a genuine European para-diplomacy should serve to reinforce the assertiveness of powerful regions. European integration thus acts as a catalyst by offering peripheral nationalisms new opportunities, but it is not a direct cause.

Furthermore, while the process of European integration indubitably lends itself to instrumentalization by regions seeking greater autonomy, not all regions perceive Europe as an asset. In the Basque Country, in Ireland and in Corsica, underground organizations involved in armed struggle (ETA, IRA, FLNC Historic Channel) and their legal fronts (Batasuna and its different incarnations, Sinn Féin, Corsica Libera) are anti-European.[31] In keeping with "revolutionary" rhetoric and practices, these movements object to Europe for two reasons. First, the capitalist nature of European integration will only reinforce "foreign economic colonization." Second, its integration process, by strengthening cooperation and creating more ties of interdependence, will dilute national identities. Their ideal Europe is a mythical Europe, one of the people united in their mutual fraternity against market forces and technocrats.

Identity movements on the opposite side of the political spectrum, that is, on the right (Protestant unionists of Northern Ireland, Vlaams Belang), oddly share with their leftist counterparts a similar reticence toward Europe, which, by increasingly blurring national boundaries, contribute to erasing regional and local specificities. The battle waged by these conservative, sometimes straightforwardly reactionary, movements involves erecting impermeable barriers to preserve a collective identity supposedly under threat. Only advocates of a more civilized nationalism (the Basque Nationalist Party, the Social Democratic Labour Party in Northern Ireland, the Party of the Corsican Nation) see European integration as the best way to achieve their national aspirations, as it would limit state powers. Here again, the hope lies in increasing transfers of decision-making powers to the regions and in the institution of direct dialogue between regional bodies and officials in Brussels.

Not all regional actors, then, view European integration as an opportunity. Those that stand to gain the most from it display three characteristics: their nationalism is affirmed dispassionately, without resorting to violence and separatism; they have considerable economic clout; they operate within federal or highly decentralized structures. The Catalonia of Convergence and Union[32] and Flanders, dominated by the Christian Social Party, have had more room for maneuver in this subtle game than the Party of the Corsican Nation which, while asserting democratic nationalism, has only a limited political base and weak economic development platforms, or than Batasuna and its clones, entrenched in its intransigent and autistic nationalism.[33]

What do nationalitarian movements aspire to? Some may settle for broad autonomy within the existing state, but others are engaged in a truly separatist strategy with the goal of forming a new independent state. This is clearly the aim of integralist nationalism, which has a narrowly ethnic definition of the nation. Such intransigent nationalism can be promoted just as well through peaceful means (Vlaams Belang in Flanders or the Republican Left of Catalonia) as through armed struggle (Batasuna in the Basque Country). In other words, there is no relationship between the political agenda—to build a fully sovereign state—and the brand of mobilization put into action.

Ethnic nationalisms, however, do not hold the monopoly on separatism. Democratic nationalisms can also advocate this route, defending an open conception of national identity. They are engaged in a gradual, two-phase strategy. When in office, they strive to expand the powers devolved to their region or province. At election time, they do not lose sight of their ultimate goal of political separation, but try to achieve it through the ballot box. This is the rationale that twice (in 1980 and 1995) prompted the Parti Québécois to propose a referendum on Quebec's accession to sovereignty. It is equally the method pursued by the Scottish National Party. After winning a relative majority in 2007, it was handed an absolute majority four years later and decided to hold a referendum on independence in the fall of 2014, which it lost (44.7% voted yes; 55.3% no).

A major question remains, however: will moderate nationalitarian movements be satisfied with a self-determination that does not lead to independence? In other words, will the Flemish leaders of the Christian democratic CD&V party and the Catalan leaders of the CiU accept even a very broad autonomy as the ultimate solution? Officially, they never fail to claim that regional self-assertion within an increasingly federal Europe would suit them. But in reality, by demanding ever greater powers or the establishment of confederalism, they indeed seem to be pursuing a hidden agenda of independence. Yet such a perspective is in no way inevitable. It can be averted if modern states truly demonstrate an ability to rethink their internal functioning so as to take these demands positively into account.

PART TWO

MULTINATIONALITY

A CHALLENGE FOR THE STATE

5

THE IMPERFECT TRINITY

Democracy is often viewed as the perfect antidote to counter the rise of dissociative nationalism. The trouble is that even among those who claim to be democrats, conceptions of democracy vary. There is probably a common foundation with three pillars: representative government based on the free expression of popular sovereignty, a constitutional state that values pluralism, and strict adherence to fundamental civic and political rights. Yet, beyond this basic consensus, views differ considerably as to the content and purpose of democracy. Before examining how it is possible for a renewed liberalism to manage national differences within a single political unit, it is essential to explore the limits of the three principal approaches to democracy: the liberal approach (in its classic version), the republican approach and the multicultural approach.[1]

Individuals are the focus of both liberalism and republicanism and are deemed to be sufficiently effective to regulate diverging interests. There is thus no reason to take into account the logics of group affiliation in any way whatsoever. The public space belongs to all citizens and should not be appropriated, even in part, by groups representing a particularist agenda. However, this perspective can take two very different routes: one proceeds by avoidance, the other by substitution.

The first approach corresponds to that of liberal democracy, which accepts the autonomy of civil society and its internal diversity without providing for its institutionalization in the political system. A society's ethnic, religious and cultural plurality is both accepted *de facto* and disregarded *de jure*. The second perspective is that of republican democracy, which grants the state a central role unifying society around a single, undifferentiated citizenship. In this case, diversity is suppressed, if not openly combated, in order to promote the ideal of national unity.[2]

The Internal Contradictions of Liberalism

The liberal perspective, be it traditional (an extension of John Locke's thought) or innovative (following John Rawls),[3] rests on an atomistic conception of society as a collection of free and rational individuals. They are presumed to act as disengaged beings free from any *a priori* social, cultural or other determination and liable to choose freely the aims and values guiding their action. They are considered to be wrapped in a veil of ignorance, to use John Rawls' expression, as to their origin and place in society. Like individuals, political authority is supposed to be neutral regarding its ends. It should not defend any particular conception of the good but confine itself to protecting the fundamental rights of citizens and ensure that equal justice is applied to all.

Communitarian authors have heaped considerable criticism on this liberal conception.[4] Without reviewing the arguments of a rich and passionate debate, the supposed original neutrality thesis is particularly questionable. Although it is always theoretically possible to postulate that people are detached from any prior social bond, in reality things are reasonably different. In a liberal society, plenty of identity markers are certainly voluntary, but many identities remain givens: "people are born... with identities, male or female, for example, working class, Catholic or Jewish, black... and so on."[5] Some aspects of identity can probably be altered over the course of a person's existence (change of social class, conversion, naturalization). But people's identity structure will nevertheless continue to influence their choices to some extent, including in the political sphere.

This is particularly true in societies where the process of national integration has not managed to incorporate peripheral identities. In these often border regions, voters tend not to make up their minds according to a purely individual logic but rather on the basis of a particular identity they mean to defend, subsequently mobilizing around autonomist parties. For instance, nearly two-thirds of the Swedish minority in Finland systematically votes for the Swedish People's Party, which has thus taken on the role of representative for this Swedish-speaking population in its relations with the authorities in Helsinki.

When strategies of identity mobilization are robust, liberal individualism can do little to affect them. On the contrary, in societies wrought by intense national cleavages, the implementation of liberal democracy procedures only highlights the depths of the divisions. The international community has prided itself on two fairly recent "crisis resolutions," one in Bosnia and Herzegovina and the other in Northern Ireland. But aside from the fact that in the long run the viability of these peace settlements is far from guaranteed, their application flies in the face of liberal individualism. The Dayton Accords (1995), which put an end to the war in Bosnia, and the Good Friday Agreement in Northern Ireland (April 1998) both provided for general elections to be held in order to set up new democratic institutions. In both cases, however, voters gravitated to the various nationalist parties.

In Bosnia and Herzegovina, Muslims, Serbs and Croats overwhelmingly cast their vote for the Party of Democratic Action (Bosniak),[6] the Serb Democratic Party and the Croatian Democratic Community respectively, in other words for three nationalist groups. The reconfiguration of the political scene after the 2006 elections did not fundamentally alter the situation in the two entities that grew out of the Dayton Accords. In Republika Srpska (Serb), the nationalist Alliance of Independent Social Democrats (SNSD) is largely dominant. In the Federation of Bosnia and Herzegovina (Croatian-Bosniak), the Party for Bosnia and Herzegovina won a clear majority.[7] Similarly, in Northern Ireland, Catholics and Protestants voted for Irish nationalists and British unionists respectively. It was only within each camp that voters were distributed between moderates and radicals, the Catholic vote being divided between the Social Democratic and Labour Party and Sinn Féin, the Protestants between the Democratic Unionist Party and the Ulster Unionist Party. The Alliance Party, a non-sectarian group whose political message strives to bridge the divide between Catholic nationalism and Protestant unionism, has remained low in vote shares for the past twenty-five years.[8] In deeply divided societies, political mobilization thus mainly follows communitarian lines rather than being based on individual political choices.

While it is doubtful that people can totally detach themselves from their identity, it is just as unlikely that the state can be the neutral instrument that classical liberalism assumes to exist, disassociated from any cultural background. The nature of the ties between state and culture indisputably depends on the specific history of each state.[9] When the state is actively involved in defending a certain conception of the common good, the relationship between state and culture will be closer than if the state strives instead to ensure the autonomy of its citizens without deciding between various conceptions of the good. However, even the most liberal state will never be totally devoid of a cultural horizon.

The United States' brand of liberalism, even though it embraces exceptional cultural diversity, is not culturally neutral,[10] and nothing can erase the fact that the founding fathers were the descendants of British settlers whose mother tongue, English, became the language used in the public space. The Americanization of immigrants entailed anglicizing them, despite the increasingly multicultural nature of the United States. Such acculturation remains mandatory for new citizens. The procedure for acquiring US citizenship in fact requires applicants to speak English and to be familiar with the main political precepts on which the United States was founded. In other words, a recent Mexican immigrant who knows the United States Constitution perfectly but who only speaks Spanish cannot become a US citizen. This may be a textbook hypothesis, but it serves to point out that even in the United States, a paragon of liberal democracy, civic virtues are not enough to ensure membership in the national community.

The example of the United States highlights an essential point: adherence to common civic values (democracy, tolerance, equality, etc.) does not suffice to create a shared national identity. Acceptance of such political principles obviously contributes much to peaceful coexistence in a society, but it helps to understand neither the attachment some may have to other countries based on similar values nor separatist ambitions at work within a country whose citizens are nevertheless united by the same values. As the philosopher Wayne Norman wisely notes, Norwegians and Swedes share the same democratic values, but this convergence does not prompt anyone to question the split that took place in 1905 and demand the reunification of the two countries.[11] More generally speaking, diffusion of liberal democratic principles does not seem to be a catalyst for the world's unification. On the contrary, the similarity of value scales in no way offers a guarantee against the risks of state fragmentation. Thus, while the Quebecois in the 1950s were attached to highly conservative values, the wind of liberalization that swept through society in the 1960s led to a remarkable convergence of attitudes with the traditionally more liberal anglophones, both in terms of moral issues and regarding civil liberties and minority rights. Yet far from being a factor in appeasing the political divergences between Quebec and Ottawa, this convergence helped to sustain them.[12]

The existence of shared values is therefore not enough to understand how national unity is preserved or on the contrary why autonomist ambitions persist. Bavarians and Saxons coexist in Germany not because they share the same values but because they share a common German identity. French-speaking and English-speaking Quebeckers have trouble living together, even though their value systems have never been closer, because the feeling that they are sharing the same national Canadian experience is diminishing. The political career of former Canadian Prime Minister Pierre Elliott Trudeau offers an eloquent illustration that common values do not make a common identity.

Trudeau was a man who never hid his vociferous opposition to nationalism, which he considered to express primitive tribalism.[13] As it was based primarily on an emotional appeal, nationalism was dismissed as an element of cohesion, especially in a multination state. Only rational will could serve as a basis for the political pact. Yet this same man did precisely what in 1964 he had deemed to be an inadequate means to create a national bond in Canada: "invest... as much time, energy, and money as are required to prevent the country from breaking up. ... invest tax funds in such various enterprises as railways, radio and television, and the flag, the national anthem, education, arts councils, a film board... to link the country through a network of railways, highways, airlines, protect the national culture and economy by levying taxes and customs tariffs..."[14] There is no doubt that he departed from his initial principles and set about relentlessly strengthening national unity because he viewed the rise of Quebecois nationalism as a threat to Canada's survival.

The Canadian identity to be built rested on three main pillars: multiculturalism, made an official policy in 1971, bilingualism and the Charter of Rights and Freedoms. The Charter, which became part of the Constitution in 1982, is a central element of pan-Canadian nationalism. It may at first seem surprising, even perverse, to associate the term "nationalism" with a charter of rights stamped with the most classic version of liberal philosophy. The individualist perspective that runs through the text mainly emphasizes the two complementary principles of equality and freedom. But it is precisely because it is based on the protection of individual rights that the Charter cleverly conveys a specific national vision.

By setting forth uniform standards focusing on the fundamental rights of individuals, it makes Canada the only legitimate political space. Advocacy for individual rights should also serve to develop a primary national allegiance to Canada—or more precisely to the central state—among its citizens and qualify the attachment that some feel for sub-state entities, Quebec first of all. There is no doubt that by encouraging the idea of a single Canadian nation from the Atlantic to the Pacific, the federal authorities sought to reduce the appeal that identification with Quebec would have for francophones.[15] Contrary to those who view nationalism solely as a political force claiming to oppose the modern state in the name of cultural specificity,[16] the state itself is an eager producer of national identification, with cultural institutions fulfilling a significant role alongside school, the military and the law.[17]

However, the state's role as purveyor of nationalism in a liberal political context is doubly disguised. First, strengthening allegiance to the state is taken to be the expression of a legitimate national sentiment, patriotism, whereas conversely, challenging the state is invariably disqualified as the manifestation of a regressive force, nationalism. By this rhetorical trick, the true convergence between the two concrete forms of nationalism is thus camouflaged.

Second, the state is presented as organizing strictly egalitarian relations with all citizens. However, this all-embracing and abstract conception is well suited to the national needs of the majority group and the expectations of groups scattered throughout the territory: religious and linguistic minorities, immigrants and so on. It is much less satisfactory for territorialized groups that consider themselves nations in the full sense and view citizenship-based nationalism as a means of diluting their specific identity. This majority nationalism, beneath a veneer of universalism, may well be unconscious, but is nevertheless very real.[18]

Thus the English-speaking Canadians will deny that their allegiance to the central state has anything to do with their attachment to a specifically English Canadian culture. Such an assertion is untrue, for they often hold to be Canadian practices and realities that are specific to their linguistic group. It is nevertheless claimed in good faith, in that the anglophones are to a great extent unaware of their own national motivations. This blindness stems from the fact that "English-speaking Canadians have not had the same need to distinguish between allegiance to a linguistic community and allegiance to the truly pan-Canadian community. They could afford to run the two together because, as they were the majority, the distinctive character of their linguistic community was never threatened."[19]

This is an essential observation. The anglophones ardently embraced the project for a Canadian identity not because they subscribed more than the francophones to the liberal values contained in the Charter of Rights, but because this blanket conception of nationalism was consonant with their own interests. As long as the political frame of reference is the Canadian state as a whole, English-speakers, who make up the absolute majority of Canada's population, are assured of keeping the ultimate political power through the national institutions (Parliament, Supreme Court). Moreover, as long as the individualist rationale prevails, it renders void any generic measure aiming to protect a specific cultural identity such as Quebec's. Yet, the self-serving rationality that prompts a majority group to support state nationalism is rarely acknowledged openly. In general, its members camouflage it by posing as generous partisans of a national unity driven by sincere idealism and battling against dangerous, narrow-minded separatists.

The Canadian example is not unique. Prior to the division of Czechoslovakia in 1993, on the Czech side there was similar incomprehension with regard to Slovak nationalism, viewed as reactionary, and an identification with the federation as a whole, simply because for Czech elites, Czech interests and the federation's interests were one and the same.[20] This overlap explains the difficulty the Czechs had in assuming their independence after the separation with Slovakia. They had to explicitly define a national identity that until then had primarily been expressed through the central state. English-speaking Canada would undoubtedly face the same difficulty in the event of Quebec's secession. The central state's promotion of a national identity based on citizenship alone can hardly ward off such a prospect. The refusal to take into account Quebecois specificity at the institutional level, far from diminishing the lure of separatism, invariably contributes to intensifying it. In this regard, classical liberalism, by focusing solely on the legal equality of individuals, evades the issue of collective differences, but the backlash of such disregard is likely to be devastating.

The Republic Put to the Test of Plurality

Is the republic, so often invoked in France, the most apt form of government to come to terms with pluralism?[21]

An unequivocal "no" at first seems the obvious reply, and this even more clearly than in the case of liberal democracy. Liberalism is founded on what the philosopher Isaiah Berlin called "negative liberty," in other words freedom from external constraints so as to protect the individual's private sphere. It gives civil society broad autonomy with regard to the state and guarantees its natural plurality. On the other hand, republican democracy is based on positive liberty, in other words on active political participation in the public sphere through which emerges the general interest that the state is then supposed to guarantee. Unlike in the liberal model, the state does not have a limited role of arbiter. On the contrary, it intervenes actively to promote a particular form of civic life based on strong patriotic involvement.

By thus making citizenship the cornerstone of individual identity, constantly reactivating and mobilizing it against its "enemies" (aristocrats, European monarchies, the Catholic Church, etc.), civic republicanism is indeed, as Michael

Walzer has observed, "a left-wing version of communitarianism."[22] Citizenship became the alpha and omega of belonging to the nation, which implies two complementary aspects: equal rights and the confinement of particular identities to the private sphere. In other words, citizenship is theoretically a principle that transcends concrete attachments. For it to be fully realized in a classical republican framework, however, the public space requires considerable cultural homogenization. If true freedom consists of participating actively in political debates, mutual comprehension among citizens must be optimal, thereby requiring the formation of a uniform cultural base. It is thus hardly surprising that consolidation of the French republic in the late nineteenth century went hand in hand with an intensive effort of acculturation.

Some politicians and intellectuals are convinced that the republican model, based on a strong conception of national identity, has lost none of its virtue. While lamenting the withering of the republican ideal, Régis Debray considers that "the republic is not just one more political regime [but] an ideal and a struggle" that today is more valuable than ever because its aim in society "is to fulfill a universal function."[23]

This universalism should not be idealized. In the age of militant republicanism, in the 1900s, the relentless pursuit of political loyalty among civil servants involved putting into practice the motto "the functions of the Republic will be fulfilled only by republicans!" In an entirely different vein, this curiously mirrors the nationalist slogan "Give France back to the French."[24] By excluding practicing Catholics from the senior branches of the civil service, the state lost the very neutrality it claimed to embody. Some viewed these misguided policies as partly forgivable during the consolidation phase of the republican regime, but they endured in the three departments of Algeria where Muslims, who had an undeniable majority, were nevertheless deprived of citizenship until 1947. Even then, they were only granted "local citizenship" within the framework of a specific electoral college, which clearly conflicted with the principle of "one person, one vote." Indeed, a Muslim candidate had to win ten times more votes than a French candidate in the first college to become a member of the Algerian Assembly.[25]

Such two-tier citizenship, totally at odds with the democratic ideal, is completely unthinkable today. However, the effective universalization of such an ideal is far from providing an adequate response to the true diversity of modern societies. Formal equality among citizens does not prevent French citizens of Maghrebian or African origin from encountering countless obstacles to achieving a true presence on the political stage. Even though republican parties on both the right and the left have started to be more open to diversity, French citizens of immigrant background continue to have only a limited role in national elected assemblies. One might object that this is a temporary dysfunction that will vanish over time. That may be true. The fact remains that if citizenship does not give every member of the body politic a reasonable (not to say equal) opportunity to be able to represent the nation, it is necessarily an illusion. As an indirect consequence, this situation can only encourage communitarian demands, for instance reserved seats in elected assemblies.

Such snags in the republican ideal certainly do not call it entirely into question. They nevertheless serve to highlight the intrinsic limits of an overly abstract conception of citizenship. Past republican elites themselves, moreover, clearly realized that identification with the nation could not be purely civic in nature, and that it was essential to take the local level into account. Thus under the Third Republic were produced countless history and geography textbooks imparting to pupils information about smaller-level "heartlands" (*pays*, department, region), the underlying idea being that to feel an attachment to the national community, it first had to be shown toward local communities.

As it was too difficult to grasp, the French homeland was concretized by glorifying the local level: the beauty of its landscapes, its local specialties (food and wine), its local figures. This detour via local "heartlands" is of course an instrumentalist strategy. Its objective is never to promote regional cultures in themselves but always to underscore that primordial diversity is in fact harmoniously fulfilled in national unity. "The Russian-doll principle of building the nation makes each little land a miniature ideal of France, from its origins to the present day."[26] Even though they were involved in an ambitious task of national unification, the republicans thus were forced to admit, out of pragmatism, that citizenship as an abstraction had to be embodied if it were not to become evanescent.

This sentiment is reflected in the spontaneous perceptions of "ordinary citizens." The "usual" representations of citizenship show that individuals associate roles and qualities with citizenship very different from academic conceptions. While scholars discuss citizenship in terms of commitment to the body politic, the individual experience of citizenship accords little importance to politics.[27] Some people view themselves primarily as individuals, for whom the only legitimate horizon is humanity as a whole, and refer to their citizenship only insofar as they are caught up in a socio-political group in spite of themselves (scrupulous citizenship). Others, of particular interest here, claim an inherited citizenship perceived as inseparable from a specific French national identity. This "naturalist" conception is shared by the two groups that subscribe to inherited citizenship: "nationals" and "republicans." While the former tend to view France as an eternal entity with a time-honored history, and the latter emphasize the legacy of the French Revolution, the two currents converge around one and the same holistic vision. The citizen is considered a cell of the national body; his public-spiritedness is part of a communitarian project. Empirical research in this case fully corroborates previous remarks about the need for communalization: political association, based on a purely contractual version of citizenship, is not enough to form national bonds. It has to be rounded out by a process of communalization, in other words the emergence of a subjective sense of belonging to the nation.[28] For ordinary citizens, "the political conception of the nation is at once more nebulous, more vague, and much less widespread than the ethnic notion of nation."[29]

The need for communalization in fact contributed to a commemorative fervor that reached its height in France in 1996 with the state's decision to honor the 1500th anniversary of the baptism of Clovis. This event was intended as a "commemoration of origins, from Gaul to France," to use the very terms employed by the committee assembled for the occasion. In other words, the aim was to situate the Republic in the long term of history, in the course of which the national community was fashioned. Once again, national identity can hardly be reduced to the celebration of citizenship alone. The former looms larger than the latter and constitutes its condition of possibility. Citizenship is deployed in a space that is historically situated.

Beyond Jacobinism

Is this republic, not averse to situating itself in a millennial religious tradition, capable of meeting today's challenges?

The French Republic is obviously less in jeopardy than some claim, denouncing in alarmist tones the "wreckers of the republic" engaged in a colossal endeavor to dismantle it.[30] Despite the new obstacles it encounters, the republican system of integration continues to function fairly well. A thorough survey conducted by Michèle Tribalat thus shows that the assimilation of immigrants, defined as "the reduction of specificities through the mixing of populations and the convergence of behaviors," is very real. With the notable exception of the Turks, tempted by a strong communitarian pull, the integration of other immigrant groups in France occurs gradually and is manifested in a wide array of phenomena: mother tongues are replaced by the French language, traditional matrimonial practices are resorbed, mixed marriages see an increase, religious behaviors are adjusted, social practices become more open to French society.[31] This trend is nevertheless thwarted, particularly in the most socially disadvantaged strata, by strong communitarian withdrawal that keeps French society at a distance.[32]

While the republican model can thus hardly be called a failure, its effectiveness over the long term will depend highly on its ability to adapt. A return to hardcore republicanism that would revive French exceptionalism is a pipedream; such a remobilizing endeavor encounters a dual impediment.[33] First, the construction of an "integrated" national identity such as that set up by the Third Republic presupposes a strong state. Even though the state retains a stronger presence in France than in many other countries, economic globalization together with European unification diminishes its room for maneuver. Two institutions that have traditionally been central to manufacturing citizens have changed radically. Public education, which no longer enjoys a monopoly on the transmission of knowledge, is less a producer of citizens than of professionals. And the army, with the end of mandatory military service—once a real rite of passage—has ceased to be the great machine for manufacturing national sentiment that it once was.

Alongside this retreat of the state, citizens have gained in autonomy. More than anything, they seek to defend their individual freedom to act in the private sphere and no longer actively involve themselves in politics. Citizenship, understood as the exercise of political rights, has become a secondary dimension for modern individuals. As a result, classical republicanism, which requires citizens to be fully mobilized, becomes impracticable. In this context of an civil society autonomous with respect to the state, a return to the sources of republicanism, rooted in intransigent universalism and active citizenship, is a utopia out of step with the dominant ethos of contemporary societies in which the ideal of authenticity heightens the demand for recognition and nourishes a policy of valuing differences.[34]

In fact, the republican nation-state has had to learn to come to terms with social diversity out of pragmatism. While continuing to rely heavily on a rhetoric celebrating an abiding republican model, elites have learned to toy with ethnicity, even literally playing it up. The state thus plays an ever more active role in institutionalizing ethnicity via associations that act as intermediaries between groups and public authorities.[35] This phenomenon is evident in the political management of immigrant populations.[36] It is not absent among groups, such as the Jews, associated with the fate of the Republic from the very start. The state encourages them to organize, "whereas [their] potential structuring into a particularist group with a presence in the public space remains contrary to the principles of the nation-state as it has been built in France."[37]

Further adaptations can be found in recent institutional re-arrangements the state has undergone. Admittedly, the 1982 decentralization law and the deepening of regionalization in the 1980s were initiated primarily out of a concern for functional adjustment.[38] The technocratic inspiration behind the reforms is clearly manifest in the drawing of the boundaries between regions, leaving Brittany without the city of Nantes, the historical capital of the Dukes of Brittany, and Languedoc without Toulouse but adjoined to Roussillon. Even though the French regions were shaped from the top down, generally with little regard for history, they have nonetheless become meaningful administrative divisions. The region is not only a legitimate new institutional echelon but also and above all a space with its own specific identity toward which citizens express an increasingly pronounced attachment.[39] This "regional patriotism," which often involves promoting the region as a place of history and culture, expresses a need for proximity and roots in a specific land.

The demand for identity moreover explains the dazzling success of the *pays*, entities spawned by the 1995 Pasqua Law which are areas exhibiting "geographic, cultural, economic and social cohesion." This territorial division was greeted with extraordinary enthusiasm, as over 250 *pays* were thus constituted. It revived ancient administrative divisions, given that the *pagi* were small territorial units inventoried by the Romans, many of which endured until the age of monarchies, thus connecting them with a long stretch of history. Even the former provinces that the French Revolution wanted permanently to abolish by supplanting them with departments sometimes resurface surreptitiously. The Pyrénées-Atlantiques department is thus made up of two "*pays*" with very old roots, the Bearn and the Basque Country. For the latter, this stage was quite obviously an important step in the assertion of a distinctive identity. The "*pays*" corresponded quite precisely to the three historical Basque provinces north of the Pyrenees. Many local elected officials and figures in the business community would moreover like to see this *pays* simply become a Basque department.

The French republic has shown audacity especially at its periphery. Corsica has thus enjoyed special status since 1991, which carries considerable derogations of common law. A number of powers have been devolved to the regional assembly in a broad array of areas. A law passed in January 2002 expanded the range of powers transferred to the Corsican assembly and made it possible to adapt regulations to the "island's specificities."

The internal autonomy French Polynesia has enjoyed since 1984 was reinforced once in 1996 but again, especially, in 2004 by an organic law that arranged overall transfer of powers to the overseas territory, with the state retaining its sovereign powers (defense, foreign policy, security, protection of civil liberties, etc.). The assembly of French Polynesia is able to pass "laws of the *pays*" within the context of its specific remit.

Bolder still was the agreement on New Caledonia (1998). Its most crucial innovation was the institution of a citizenship specific to that territory and therefore distinct from French citizenship. The break from the republican principle of all-embracing citizenship is obvious. Furthermore, even though this differentiated citizenship includes all the archipelago's inhabitants on an equal footing, it nonetheless rests on the preliminary recognition of two human communities: the indigenous people (Kanaks) and the immigrants from continental France (Caldoches). By referring to a Kanak people, which "had developed its own civilization, with its traditions and languages," representatives of the French Republic have explicitly taken the identity issue into account. Kanak identity is made up of various distinguishing traits (customary law, language, specific relationship to the land) that will feature prominently in the public arena and have symbolic extensions (name of the country, flag, anthem, motto, etc.). This specificity will be translated at the institutional level into broad autonomy, with major transfers of power from the central state to the territory and even shared powers, particularly as regards international relations in the Pacific Rim.

The Nouméa Accord is a radical departure from the republican norm with its principled equality and its unitary perspective. It will institute—at least for a twenty-year period—a federative conception within the French Republic, as New Caledonia will become *de facto* an associated state of France. The innovation is hence significant and the temptation to forestall is likely to be great, as the status of New Caledonia is presented as a unique and transitional exception in a context of decolonization, prior to the territory's accession to full emancipation, in other words independence. But another, more general lesson can be drawn from the Nouméa Accord. It has to do with the urgency of setting aside the state's Jacobin culture once and for all, so as to reorganize the management of diversity within the republic.

The pragmatic compromises the Republic has accepted attests to the fact that political elites have realized that its unity no longer implies uniformity. However, as significant as these advances may be, and even if they indicate that the unitary nation-state is truly able to adapt, they do not call into question its deeper structure. First, legislative audacity has been confined, with the notable exception of Corsica, to the overseas territories, because the Constitution explicitly mentions "the peoples of overseas territories." These peoples—who are moreover components of the French people as well—thus have the right to a particular organization that takes into account their specific interests and has resulted in specific institutional configurations (Territorial Assembly, a local quasi-government), a specific set of powers and a particular legal system (legislative specialty, recognition of customary law).[40]

Second, while the state's political unity implies neither institutional uniformity—as attested by the regime of French overseas territories and collectivities[41] and specific territorial communities such as Corsica—nor legal uniformity—preservation of local law in Alsace-Moselle, for instance—it stands opposed to official recognition of any sort of infra-state pluralism.[42] In other words, the unitary ideology on which the republic is based is not called into question. The Constitutional Council's jurisprudence is perfectly coherent on this point. It is often forgotten that, in its landmark decision of 9 May 1991, the Council legitimated the establishment of a particular status for Corsica. It clearly admitted the government's right to give a territorial government special status adapted to its specificities.

On the other hand, it invalidated Article One of the bill, which stipulated: "The French Republic guarantees to the Corsican people, a living historical and cultural community and part of the French people, the rights to the preservation of its cultural identity and the defense of its specific economic and social interests." The ruling was made on the grounds that the French people, "made up of all French citizens regardless of origin, race or religion," was an "indivisible category." The constitutional judges thus defended a classical conception in keeping with traditional French public law, which associates the indivisibility of the republic and the unity of its people.

The same line of argument is contained in the 15 June 1999 ruling, which found the European Charter for Regional and Minority Languages to be contrary to the Constitution. There again, the implementation of mechanisms to ensure the protection and promotion of these languages was invalidated on the grounds that conferring "specific rights on groups of speakers within territories in which these languages are used" would undermine the principles of the indivisibility of the republic, equality before the law and the unity of the French people. The state's inviolable position thus remains one of official refusal to acknowledge any internal differentiation, the unitary state forming one body with a single people.

Such strict republican orthodoxy has the advantage of fitting in with a familiar continuity but the considerable drawback of ignoring the aspiration for recognition of these linguistic regionalisms. Taking such aspiration into account would require dissociating two concepts that are too often confused in French political culture: nation and people. These two terms, however, are not synonymous. The nation is above all a legal-administrative construction, a collective body, the receptacle of sovereignty,[43] whereas the people is a sociological group formed by a population that has specific characteristics (religion, culture, language, history, etc.). It is therefore perfectly possible to admit the unity of the political nation while recognizing several peoples.

Such is the case in Spain. Its constitution proclaims "the indissoluble unity of the Spanish Nation" while recognizing "the right to self-government of the nationalities and regions of which it is composed." Similarly, the United States, as a nation that passed a democratic constitution in 1787, is made up not of a single block but of a federation of different peoples moving within one and the same political space. While France officially remains faithful to the myth of a single and unified nation, those viewing it from the outside do not perceive it in this way. The Soviets considered that 85% of France was made up of French people, the remainder being Alsatians, Bretons and Corsicans. By the same token, many German publications that are in no way extremist view France as a patchwork of peoples (Occitan, Corsican, Basque, etc.). They define the Alsatians quite simply as a German minority, just like the Germans of the Volga and the Transylvanian Saxons in Romania.[44] In North American studies of France, authors frequently look through "ethnic glasses" to define the country as a union of different peoples and communities, like the United States.

Does this show incomprehension of intransigent republicanism, which, with regard to an enthroned state, sees only citizen-individuals united by political ties? This is probably so, at least in part. But such a decentered vision of France conceals a notable virtue: it unmasks the legal hypocrisy of a state that turns a deaf ear to any demand for public recognition of the country's cultural plurality even as it is itself actively engaged in the defense of a culture, as attest the measures to protect the French language and the systematic promotion of France's cultural exceptionalism in all international fora. The only way out of such an impasse that obstructs substantial reform is to rethink the republic and reject Jacobin rigidity in favor of Girondist flexibility.

The Illusions of Multiculturalism

Some doubt that cultural rights, the new generation of human rights,[45] can ever truly find their place in a republican system of government. They advocate establishing a multicultural democracy that maintains the universalist rule of law while recognizing broader cultural pluralism.[46]

First, a useful semantic clarification. Although the term "multiculturalism" is obviously in fashion, it has come to mean such a variety of things that its conceptual value is sharply diminished. Sometimes it refers to the mere acknowledgment that more and more cultures co-exist within our modern states, a phenomenon related in particular to migration processes. At other times it denotes public policies set up by governments to manage this diversity. Lastly, it is sometimes used to qualify an ideology according to which identities, whether sexual, ethnic or religious, should be politically mobilized, the public space being based on a dialogue between different cultures.[47]

In this last meaning of the term, multiculturalism implies far more than tolerance, in the sense of accepting other ways of thinking and acting. It requires the active promotion of differences, considered as a source of richness for the society as a whole and as a political imperative to build a true democratic space. Given that so-called liberal neutrality is an illusion that obscures the cultural imperialism of the dominant majority, social equality requires "mechanisms for the effective recognition and representation of the distinct voices and perspectives of those of its constituent groups that are oppressed or disadvantaged."[48]

Cultural pluralism involves instituting differentiated citizenship with a dual system of rights: general for all and specific for "minority groups" (women, the elderly, the disabled, homosexuals, workers, ethnic groups). It is only by promoting difference that equal inclusion of all groups into the game of politics can be achieved, the state ultimately becoming merely a regulatory body overseeing domestic social diversity. As Pierre-André Taguieff notes in this vein, "the idea of a multi-ethnic and pluricultural democracy, founded on the principle of equality among communities," can only come about "in a postnational space."[49] Indeed, if all cultures are considered equivalent, the state must remove itself from any national identity embracing all citizens. The only bond that unites them is their attachment to the rule of law and democracy. Yet, although shared political values (equality among citizens, respect for freedoms, etc.) are required for democracy to function smoothly, their very general nature makes them an unsuitable foundation for national identity even though the rationale of the modern territorialized state requires one.[50]

Arising from generous intentions, radical multiculturalism, based on the co-existence and efflorescence of cultures within the framework of a purely functional state, in return kindles particularly vigorous attempts at national remobilization. It is certainly not by chance that in the three countries in which it occupies a central role in public life, whether an official policy as in Australia and Canada or a practice of acknowledging differences as in the United States, radical multiculturalism has fostered the resurgence of conservative nationalisms. In these three countries a populist current has developed that claims to represent "ordinary common sense" in opposition to political and intellectual elites favoring the dangerous utopia of a multicultural society. The hostility these populist movements feel toward the increase in migratory flows carries an indisputably xenophobic dimension, but more than the phenomenon of migration itself, which is hard to criticize in immigrant societies, what they criticize is the multicultural handling of the phenomenon, in other words the lack of any prospect of national integration.

Symptomatically, Australia's populist party, which had its heyday in the late 1990s, is called "One Nation," thus clearly objecting to a state multiculturalism that it believes sustains ethnic fragmentation. Preston Manning, leader of the Reform Party of Canada, which subsequently merged with the new Conservative Party of Canada, expressed a similar idea: "Its federal politicians talk incessantly about English-Canadians, French-Canadians, aboriginal-Canadians, ethnic-Canadians, but rarely about 'Canadians, period.' It has become patently obvious in the dying days of the twentieth century that you cannot hold a nation together with hyphens."[51]

Two lessons can be drawn from populist mobilizations. The treatment they prescribe for handling increasing societal diversity—the reassertion of a strong, exclusive nationalism that suppresses out of hand all forms of secondary allegiance—not only contradicts liberal principles but also aims to restore a supposedly uniform national identity based on absolute anglo-conformity. By doing so, the sycophants of nationalism deliberately ignore the fact that cultural pluralization was itself an essential element in shaping a specific national sentiment. For former British dominions such as Canada and Australia, it thus facilitated the process of detachment from Great Britain. The multicultural nature of these societies was fully embraced by the state, thereby helping to make them distinct.

Does this mean that any undertaking to establish a shared public culture among citizens is reprehensible? The answer is no, for without a unifying perspective, the fact of living together becomes merely a product of chance (residence in the same place) whereas "a nation is a soul, a spiritual principle" that implies "the present-day consent, the will to perpetuate the value of the heritage that one has received in an undivided form."[52] Radical multiculturalism is thus on the wrong track when it claims to banish any principle of collective identity overarching various cultural attachments.

This strategy of erasing the national reference only leaves it open to being taken over, distorted and eventually monopolized by the most extremist political forces.[53] The horizon of convergence need not be one-dimensional, based on burying individuals and groups in the body national; it can perfectly well come to terms with a moderate multiculturalism in which complementary identities (religious, ethnic, etc.) are maintained. It is time to shake off the false alternative that pits exclusive nationalism against unbridled multiculturalism, and to work toward reconciling liberalism and nationalism, which is by no means utopian.[54]

Distinguishing Differences

In addition to its false image of the state as great organizer of cultural differences, the fundamentalist version of multiculturalism rests on another debatable assumption: that all cultures are treated in an identical manner. The radical perspective of democracy underlying "hardcore" multiculturalist ideology implies equal treatment of all groups with a particular culture. If that means that Corsicans, Jews, Kabyles and homosexuals warrant equal respect, the issue is inarguable. But does that mean that the policy of recognition advocated by Charles Taylor involves granting identical rights to groups that are different by nature?

The multiculturalist approach often tends to erase distinctions and put all minorities into one bag, whether they are national, religious, ethnic, sexual or other. This is a mistake, because the three main categories—social groups, ethnic minorities and national communities—have dissimilar historic trajectories. Their need for recognition will therefore be expressed in different ways. Responses to the grievances voiced by one group or another will obviously differ.

Social groups seek mainly to combat factual or legal discrimination and argue for measures to facilitate their participation in society. This demand will take on different forms depending on the case. For women, it may be policies favoring equal access to positions of political responsibility; for gays and lesbians, legislation on homosexual marriage or a similar arrangement (civil union); for the disabled, the use of quotas to facilitate their access to the job market.

The other two categories present a very different profile in that, unlike the former, the collective aspect takes on crucial importance for their future. It is certainly not absent for social groups (such as sexual minorities), but in their case it does not have the same structuring role. On the other hand, for Malian immigrants, orthodox Jews and the Catalans, the existence of a community through which they can express their shared values and interests is essential to their self-perpetuation. Does that justify lumping them all together? Of course not, for it is crucial, following Will Kymlicka, to distinguish poly-ethnicity from multinationality.[55]

The first term refers to the internal diversity of societies due to the rise in international migration, a constituent phenomenon of immigrant societies such as the United States which is now becoming widespread. In this category can be placed religious minorities for whom religion is a mark of ethnicity (Jews, Protestants and Catholics in Northern Ireland and Bosnian Muslims). Multinationality, on the other hand, refers to the co-existence of different historic communities with their own culture living within the same state, brought together by conquest or more or less voluntary consent.

Let us temporarily leave aside ethno-religious minorities to focus on immigrant communities and "nationalitarian groups" (national minorities and "stateless nations"). Their trajectories are very different. The first form gradually as migrants arrive voluntarily; the second emerge after being incorporated, often by force, into a larger political unit, for instance following a military defeat. The presence or absence of intentionality has decisive consequences on the demands that the two groups might express. By leaving their country of birth and their familiar cultural environment to settle permanently in another country, immigrants "were not only uprooted; they had uprooted themselves."[56] They knew that the price to pay was called integration. This adjustment obviously does not imply the immigrants' total alignment with the majority norm. On the other hand, it does require acceptance of the unit's social framework (language, legislation, etc.) and the adaptation of practices that might be at odds with the existing social code (for instance excision and polygamy).

Muslim communities in Europe thus cannot legitimately expect their religion to have the same place as in Islamic countries where it is almost always the official state religion. They need to find a *modus operandi* suited to their minority situation in secular societies historically influenced by Christianity. Moreover, accommodation is not a one-way process, because the host society also has a duty to be open to them. Their presence will thus inevitably have an effect on national identity, which they henceforth contribute to formulating. However, the burden of adaptation is not equally shared. It will always weigh more heavily on immigrant communities due to the fact that they are being assimilated into an existing social fabric.

Some retort that the reaffirmation of immigrant identities amounts to calling into question the integrative rationale implicit in the "migration contract." Although the temptation of communitarianism does exist, I would rather be inclined to consider that public displays of ethnicity—with attendant demands such as the modification of school curricula to take into account the cultural contributions of various groups—imply a review of the modes of integration rather than a negation of them. In other words, whereas in the first half of the twentieth century, integration required merging with the nation, today it operates in a more open framework in which a more diffuse national identity can perfectly well be reconciled with a more assertive ethnicity. This reorientation should not be interpreted as something negative. It does not mean that integration does not work as well as previously. In some regards, the opposite is true.

The evolution of French Jewry, which can be measured over the space of two centuries, is a case in point. In the nineteenth century it had opted for great discretion in public life and demonstrated fervent patriotism. Such assimilation, criticized harshly by some today, went hand in hand with the preservation of remarkable community cohesion.[57] Conversely, today, while the Jews have gained far greater presence in the public arena, and their various institutions in France (CRIF-Representative Council of Jewish Institutions, the Chief Rabbinate, the Central Consistory) staunchly defend community interests, integration in the host society has never been deeper (the most revealing indication is the steady rise in "mixed" marriages). This proves that identity visibility is in no way synonymous with general communitarian withdrawal.

The persistence of an integrative rationale that even the reassertion of the "right to be different" cannot hamper is perceived by some as an unbearable threat to minority cultures. They favor a rigid form of multiculturalism that would enable various cultures to be preserved, each in its own social space.[58] Aside from the fact that this absolute communitarianism is based on a romantic, and deceptive, view of cultures as primordial forms of authenticity, it has the enormous drawback of disregarding the hopes and expectations of immigrants themselves.

They doubtless want the state and the host society to respect their original culture—a legitimate demand—and that it be granted institutional representation. But they are much more reluctant to consider the meticulous preservation of their cultures a good thing. It is worth noting that the most vehement indictment of Canadian multiculturalism comes from a Trinidadian of Hindu origin, who moved at the age of eighteen to Toronto, the mecca of multiculturalism. Criticizing multiculturalism for its reified and exotic view of difference, Neil Bissoondath condemns it especially for hyping cultural diversity as the backbone of Canadian identity.[59] But cultivating difference is not enough to lend a minimum of coherence to the Canadian national projects and in this regard it complicates the task for new immigrants. They are encouraged to cherish their cultural heritage whereas they had precisely left their native country to broaden their horizons and integrate their new homeland. But the multiculturalist rhetoric renders problematic such integration, which requires acculturation, adjustment to another lifestyle and adherence to a common set of values.

His diatribe, which is also a remarkable plea for creative freedom, no doubt bears the mark of the rebellious spirit of his uncle, V.S. Naipaul, known for his often vehement criticism of anti-freedom traditions—but it also fairly accurately reflects the demand for national identity expressed by many new immigrants to Canada. Proof of this lies in their greater attachment to the pan-Canadian nationalism that developed in the 1980s around the Charter of Rights and Freedoms, national symbols (flag, national anthem, Canada Day celebration) and federal institutions. This phenomenon is not confined to Canada. In Great Britain as well, "the greatest psychological and political need for clarity about a common framework and national symbols comes from the minorities. For clarity about what makes us willingly bound into a single country relieves the pressure on minorities... to have to conform in all areas of social life, or in arbitrarily chosen areas, in order to rebut the charge of disloyalty."[60] More than multiculturalism, immigrant communities are eager for a patriotism they can rally around.

Furthermore, the community configurations of ethnic and national groups are not of the same nature. The former hinge on familal solidarity networks, associational structures and to a certain extent neighborhood territoriality. On the other hand, national groups often form global societies that have a complete social structure, their own institutions, a specific political space, a given territory and a particular culture.[61]

There are hence a number of elements that argue in favor of a clear distinction between polyethnicity and multinationality. As a result, the solutions policymakers will be bound to offer these two types of groups will be different.

While for the former, the primary objective remains integration into the host society—with the option of preserving identity particularisms—it is important above all to facilitate assimilation by combating all forms of discrimination (racial, religious, etc.) and by the temporary implementation of preferential treatment (affirmative action) so as better to observe the principle of equal opportunity.

Such measures also generally meet the needs of ethno-religious minorities. Thus, for diaspora Jews, the primary expectation has to do with scrupulous respect for their status as citizens and an unrelenting fight against manifestations of anti-Semitism. But the most devout among them are also eager to win occasional adjustments to better reconcile life in society and religious observance (for instance to be exempt from school on Saturdays). In the same vein, by granting Sikhs the right to wear their traditional turban and not be obliged to don regulation headwear in the Mounted Police, the Canadian authorities have adopted a measure that facilitated the community's integration.

An active policy of defense and promotion is not, however, always sufficient or appropriate for ethno-religious groups. For instance, had national sentiment been consolidated in the nineteenth century on a linguistic basis, the Serbo-Croatian-speaking Muslims could have participated in a secular national movement together with the Croats and the Serbs. If a unified nationalism of the South Slavs had prevailed, the Muslims could have defended their rights as a religious community within one and the same political space. But this evolution was hampered by the persistence of a strong link between the Serbian nation and orthodoxy and the rise of a Croatian nationalism revolving around Catholicism. That being the case, the Muslims really had no alternative other than to define themselves as a national community as well, a status that Tito's government finally granted them in 1968.[62]

In a similar vein, had emancipation of the Catholics been swifter and their social advancement not long been hobbled by the Protestants' grip on the Irish economy (particularly in Ulster), an integrative rationale based on equal rights might have managed to develop within the United Kingdom. Instead, the Protestant oligarchy's staunch resistance to any far-reaching reform led the Catholics down the path of an increasingly overt nationalism that involved a rift with London. In a context of nationalist competition or in a colonial situation, ethno-religious groups can thus engage in a process of "nationalization" and call for the same institutional autonomy, even independence, that national groups classically demand. But while ethnic groups with a religious basis can make such a shift toward nationalism, it is highly problematic for immigrant minorities.[63]

When a nationalist mobilization occurs, it takes place in the host country but for the benefit of the country of origin (such as the Kurds in Germany in favor of creating an independent Kurdistan in Turkey or the Sikhs in the United Kingdom fighting for the establishment of Khalistan in Indian Punjab).

Despite the structural difference between immigrant minorities and national groups, some politicians have nevertheless contrived, for more or less palatable motives, to erase all nuances and subsume them under the generic category of multiculturalism. Canada's promotion of multiculturalism from 1971 thus appeared to be motivated by the legitimate goal of taking into account increasing ethnic diversity. But behind these generous intentions, a narrower preoccupation seems to have presided over the state's celebration of multiculturalism: to forestall the Quebecois nationalist claim by drowning it in a big pool of multiculturalism. In other words, at work here is a strategic use of multiculturalism that former prime minister of Quebec René Lévesque had correctly perceived when he said, "Multiculturalism, really, is folklore. It is a 'red herring.' The notion was devised to obscure 'the Quebec business,' to give the impression that we are *all* ethnics and do not have to worry about special status for Quebec."[64] National groups are thus suspicious toward the multicultural project, which tends to grant the same degree of recognition to all ethnic minorities whereas they themselves wish to benefit from special treatment corresponding to their national specificity.

This pinpoints the weakness of state multiculturalism: its natural propensity to create a level playing field, expanding on the redistributive logic of the modern state. The same criticism also applies to liberal and republican projects which both rest on an isomorphic perception of individuals (whether as rights-holders or as citizens). By refusing to let go of this egalitarian logic, the three modes of democratic organization encounter obvious difficulties in attempting to differentiate situations sufficiently, and so in taking account of the specificity of national expressions. To do so necessarily implies greater openness to national plurality on the basis of a renewed liberalism.[65] A reorganization of the nation-state seems indispensable at the very least. In many cases, the aim should be to get beyond it and invent something new.

6

AUTONOMY WITHOUT TERRITORY

How do states meet demands for political recognition from nationalitarian movements? How can they accede to them within a democratic framework? This latter caveat is essential, as it naturally leads to dismissing as illegitimate any "solution" that would contradict the basic human rights acknowledged by any democratic society. The suppression of difference through violence must clearly be rejected. Mass extermination, ethnic cleansing and forced populations transfers are all morally and politically unacceptable—even if such criminal behavior has often been backed by authoritarian regimes (Saddam Hussein's Iraq, Milošević's Serbia, Rwanda under extremist Hutu domination, etc.). Excluding from the start such practices, which are contrary to the rule of law, how can modern democratic states manage national pluralism?

The basic aim is to guarantee the autonomy of national groups, in other words allow them to administer themselves within a common political framework. There are only two ways in which this autonomy can be exercised: either on an individual basis or a territorial basis.[1] In the first case, rights are attached to individuals who belong to a specific group. In the second, they are exercised within a particular geographic and administrative space to which the national group is historically linked and where it has a demographic majority. Let us start by examining the first scenario.[2]

The Constellation of National Minorities

In Central and Eastern Europe, considerable inventiveness is needed. It is hardly conceivable to devise a strategy to circumvent national sovereignty given that over the past two centuries, the entire history of these peoples has gravitated around this thorny and often painful issue. Sovereignty should be limited rather than suspended in order to meet the specific challenge of reconciling the central state's authority with the autonomous existence of national minorities.[3]

This configuration is related to the specific historical trajectory that the formation of modern states followed in an area marked for centuries by three empires: the Ottoman, Austro-Hungarian and Russian empires. Even if these imperial orders were structurally linked to a dominant religion (Sunni Islam, Catholicism, Orthodox Christianity), they brought together highly diverse peoples without this being perceived as a threat either by the imperial powers ensconced in a transcendent dynastic legitimacy or by the various subjected peoples who generally enjoyed broad autonomy to organize themselves within this space. With the rise of the principle of nationalities in the nineteenth century, this fine organization gradually crumbled and the disappearance of two empires (the Austro-Hungarian and Ottoman empire) led to the creation of a host of new states after the First World War.

But these proved difficult to consolidate, as most were intended as unitary states that would deploy a strong national integration strategy, while their social underpinnings remained imperial, in other words based on a heterogeneous population. For instance, in 1919 Romania managed to bring together within its borders most of the populations of Romanian stock, but this broad inclusion also meant incorporating sizeable minorities (Hungarians, Jews, Germans, etc.) that made up a quarter of the total population. In Poland, the situation was more delicate still because over 30% of the population was made up of Ukrainians, Jews, Belarussians, and so on. All these states had a chaotic existence during the interwar period, as the affirmation of these young states' nationalist projects, which were often exclusionary, encountered fierce determination on the part of minorities to preserve their autonomy.

The Second World War brought about a dramatic and terrible "simplification" of the national issue with the genocide of the Jews and then, after 1945, the expulsion of the Germans from Czechoslovakia and Poland, population transfers (Hungarian Slovaks for Slovakian Hungarians) and border modifications such as the shifting of Poland to the west, which "deprived" it of its Ukrainians, Lithuanians and Belarussians. Yet while the minority issue became less acute, it did not vanish.

The Kokoschka-like image in which the profusion of paint strokes made it difficult to perceive the overall composition, and which reflected the medley of states in Eastern Europe prior to 1945, had vanished. But it was not replaced by a Modigliani painting with little shading and clearly separate blocks of solid color corresponding rather accurately to the situation in Western Europe, where states had managed to structure fairly unified and distinct national identities.

After 1945, Eastern Europe found itself in an intermediary position, closer to a Kandinsky canvas, like that on the cover of this book, in which colors are bound by precise geometric shapes but with strong contrasts.[4] The richness of this palette remained imperceptible for forty years, however, covered as it was by the dull grey of socialist realism. Its extraordinary intensity would only burst forth after the demise of communism, unfortunately in violent and dark colors with the disintegration of the Yugoslav federation in 1991.

The wars in Yugoslavia that swept from Croatia through Bosnia and Herzegovina to Kosovo in the wake of the non-negotiated breakup of a mul-tination state and in a context of exacerbated nationalism were accompanied by mass population displacements as well as systematic slaughter. This belliger-ent fury, fueled by the hope of forming a new state for each former republic, "settled" the question of national minorities by physically eliminating them and forcing them out. Nevertheless, the never-ending agony of the Yugoslav peoples should not mask the fact that in the post-communist space, many states have been able to manage their internal diversity fairly smoothly in a context that was anything but favorable. It is no easy task to regain national sovereignty—even often establish it, as was the case of the string of states born from the ruins of the USSR—while recognizing minorities within a demo-cratic constitutional state to be built from the ground up.

Yet, even though during de-communization tensions ran high and armed confrontations did occur (in Moldavia and the Caucasus for instance), the result is less negative than one might have feared, the Yugoslav federation being the notable exception. Many potential conflicts simply, and happily, did not materialize because political leaders avoided overdramatizing certain situations.

Restraint, for example, was characteristic of the attitude in Budapest under the Socialists (1994–8) with respect to the fate of the Magyars in Romania under the neo-communist Ion Iliescu. The new states had to come to terms with their internal diversity, which they have done more or less successfully, even though nearly all of them adopted a rather highly centralized unitary form of state. Contrary to a general trend noticeable in Western Europe, regionalization in the East remains embryonic. Strong affirmation of the central state is consistent with the desire to emphasize the nation's indivisibility, following the French republican model, in hopes of curbing centrifugal tendencies. But the insistent reference to the "universal nation of citizens" is undermined by the characterization of these states as national states in which the majority "ethnic nation" has its state and the other groups form ethnic or national minorities[5] distinct in their language, religion and history.

The state's ethnicity is sometimes clearly affirmed, as in Croatia, in the constitution itself, at other times more implicitly. Officializing ethnicity is not anti-democratic in itself, and in Eastern Europe it is deployed in a democratic framework, as citizenship rights are granted to all and minorities enjoy specific rights (use of their own language specific schools, etc.). Nevertheless, even in an ethnic democracy, the association between the state and the principal nation often gives rise to a feeling of alienation from the state among minorities, even to friction and tension.

The preliminary condition to achieve a more or less stable balance is for the state to function in a truly democratic manner. That assumes that its political leaders, even those chosen in a context of free and fair elections, relinquish the populist temptation of presenting themselves as providential leaders embodying the will of the nation. Constant appeals to the "real people" invoked in a legendary fashion can only strain relations with national minorities who are only part of the "legal people" (the citizenry as a whole) while belonging to another "real people" (which generally resides in a neighboring country).

When Slovakia was led by the populist Vladimír Mečiar (1992–8), the prime minister never missed a chance to present himself as the authentic spokesman for the (elusive) people's will, generally paired with highly antagonistic rhetoric toward the 600,000 ethnic Hungarians living in the country (or 11% of the population). This aggressive populism reached a height during the summer of 1997 when Mečiar suggested simply swapping populations between Hungary and Slovakia. The victory of the opposition in September 1998 changed the course of events considerably. The new prime minister at the time made a noteworthy gesture in forming a broad coalition government that included ministers from the Magyar party of Slovakia. Significantly, the democratic rotation of power in Bucharest in 1996 that brought an end to Ion Iliescu's rule also went hand in hand with the inclusion of the Magyar Democratic Union of Romania in the new government coalition. Such practices are extremely positive because, by associating minority representatives with the exercise of power, they integrate the entire group into the political space of the state.

Deepening civic integration is an absolute necessity, but it cannot be the sole response in states defined as national (whereas sociologically they are plurinational): recognition of specific rights for minority groups is equally indispensable. The main question is of course how far to extend these rights, which most countries in "the other Europe" have defined through particular legislation. Generally, there are two types of specific rights: cultural and political. The former are the more extensive and revolve around teaching the minority language within a specific school system, its use in the public space, preservation of cultural identity through publications as well as radio and television programs. Naturally, acknowledging these rights only makes sense if the state itself sees to it that they are fulfilled, for instance by paying for the schools' operating costs and teacher training.

Emphasis on cultural rights is doubly justified. First, because in Eastern Europe, the cultural dimension played an essential role in the process of group identification, so much so that the term "nation" there refers first to the community of culture, not to the political community. The extreme importance of the cultural factor was, moreover, well perceived in the early twentieth century by Austrian Marxists like Otto Bauer and Karl Renner. It convinced them to suggest separating the state from the nation, the former holding sovereign political authority, the latter forming a distinct moral person, the carrier of cultural identity. Implementing this dissociation involves introducing the new principle of personality, by which individuals freely determine their national belonging, and consequently choose the language, schools and charity institutions that correspond to their identity interests. The state is thus no longer at one with the nation; rather, it accommodates a plurality of nations that are as many autonomous corporative structures, handling their educational and cultural affairs on a personal rather than a territorial basis.[6] Such national cultural autonomy, which has only been applied tentatively (Moravia in 1905–6, Estonia and Lithuania in the 1920s), has nevertheless received renewed emphasis in Hungary.[7]

Under legislation passed in 1993, Hungary recognizes thirteen national and ethnic minorities (Roma, Ukrainians, Germans and Greeks among others), which are administered by elected self-determining bodies in areas of competence devolved to them (education, culture). These bodies operate at both the local and the national level, thus institutionalizing true minority representation. Hungary offers its minorities (about 8% of a population of 10 million) generous protection assorted with a dual recognition that is fairly rare in Eastern Europe.

First, the constitution considers the minorities to be constitutive elements of the state. In other words, they are taken to be integral segments of the body politic in the same way as native-born Hungarians. Second, minorities have obtained collective rights, in other words the entire group holds rights that it exercises in the framework of an internal autonomy. Hungary is thus the exception that proves the rule. All neighboring countries have refused to grant minorities collective rights out of fear that such rights might be used to support secessionist or irredentist machinations.[8] These countries therefore do not recognize national minorities as such but only "individuals belonging to national minorities" who exercise their rights and freedoms "individually or collectively." The somewhat twisted phrasing, although it is used in most international documents, aims to emphasize that the only accepted rationale is on an individual basis.

The second reason that fully justifies insistence on cultural rights stems from the fact that in our advanced democracies they always appear as a new dimension of citizenship. After rights recognizing people in their irreducible individuality, then as members of a polity and finally as productive agents in society, many analysts today believe that citizenship needs to go a step further and include cultural rights, in other words those fostering the promotion of cultural references (languages, traditions, etc.) held to be essential in defining oneself.[9] As citizenship is no longer reduced to political participation, in post-industrial society it is essential to deepen democracy by placing the subject, with its personality and its culture, at the center of it.[10] Acknowledging the importance of cultural identity for both individuals and groups implies that the state works toward its fulfillment, while of course respecting citizens' fundamental rights.

As valuable as it is for minority groups to have an effective system for protecting their cultural identity, it is equally important to be extremely cautious in granting specific political rights. Establishing a "parliament of minorities" that would be elected by members of minorities inventoried on specific electoral rolls clearly goes against the democratic principle of unitary national representation. Such a measure resulting in division of the body politic should be rejected. Minorities should take part in the same election processes as the majority, as they are all part of the same political unit.

The general principle of freedom of speech and association naturally applies to minorities as well, which means not only that they have the right to campaign in and vote for national political parties, but also that they are free to establish political groups that defend their specific interests. Article 11 of the

Bulgarian constitution, which prohibits parties founded on "ethnic, racial or religious principles," runs counter to this concept, because it poses a potential threat to the freedom to organize of the 900,000 Bulgarian Turks, even if a liberal practice, upheld by the constitutional court, has allowed the Movement for Rights and Freedoms (MRF) to act as "representative" for the Turkish minority that comprises most of its electorate. Large minorities concentrated in a specific territory (such as the Hungarians in Romanian Transylvania or Bulgarian Turks in the Rhodope Mountains) are assured of having representatives in Parliament through their specific parties (UDMR, the MRF). The same is not true for minorities with a smaller population or which are geographically dispersed, such as the Poles, the Serbs and the Greeks in Hungary and Romania. In this case, it is perfectly legitimate to reserve seats for them in the legislature, as these two countries have done. Such an arrangement should perhaps be supplemented by a representative minority council, which the government would consult on all matters concerning them.

Lastly, even if national minorities cannot claim to have any systematic right to take part in the conduct of the state, their participation in government will necessarily be a positive signal of their political integration. The appointment of Magyar ministers to the Romanian cabinet that emerged from the 1996 democratic changeover of power subsequently became routine due to the fragmented political landscape. Thus the minority was associated with the state power structures and so given full legitimacy in the national political field. The same was true for the Turkish minority when the Movement for Rights and Freedoms became part of the governing coalition in Bulgaria between 2001 and 2009.[11]

But can the minority question be regulated at the domestic level alone? The priority given to protecting human rights after the Second World War, symbolized by the United Nations' passage of the Universal Declaration of Human Rights in December 1948, prompted international institutions to neglect the rights of groups, particularly of minorities. It was not until the collapse and disintegration of the Soviet empire and the rise of nationalism that international organizations, seeing the limits to the strictly individual approach, began to consider that to protect minority populations, these had to be granted specific rights. The three main declarations all date from the first half of the 1990s: the OSCE Copenhagen Declaration (June 1990), the UN Declaration on the Rights of Persons Belonging to National or Ethnic, Religious and Linguistic Minorities (December 1992) and the Council of Europe Framework Convention for the Protection of National Minorities

(February 1995). These declarations share two main characteristics. In substance, minorities have been guaranteed the right to express and develop their ethnic, linguistic and religious identity. At the same time, states have agreed to create the conditions conducive to promoting minority particularism, which supposes both positive action (encouraging the preservation of minorities through adequate means) and negative action (refraining from any sort of assimilation policy).

However, while such a plan may seem attractive on the surface, it suffers from an intrinsic limitation. On the whole it does little to put states under obligation. The OSCE and UN declarations, being political in nature, have only moral significance and are not legally binding. The case of the Framework Convention for the Protection of National Minorities differs in this regard, as it is a genuine multilateral legal instrument that consequently binds states to clearly outlined legal obligations. The Convention has two major stumbling blocks, however.

First, it contains only a statement of general objectives, leaving states to determine how these rights will be implemented in concrete terms via national legislation. Moreover, it does not provide for any judicial review but instead a loose political follow-up mechanism. International criminal law is gradually developing, giving jurisdiction to international tribunals (ICT for the former Yugoslavia, ICT for Rwanda, International Criminal Court) to try perpetrators of war crimes and crimes against humanity, further driving a wedge into the dogma of state sovereignty; in this context, the pusillanimity of the convention may seem a step backward. Except that, as one shrewd commentator has remarked, "There is a difference between the easy exercise of drafting an ideal instrument which has no chance of being ratified and the negotiation of a convention which will be accepted by the states and come into force, thus ensuring progress, albeit limited, in the protection of minorities."[12]

The convention that came into effect in early 1998 is a milestone, as it is the first multilateral norm pertaining to minorities. The fact that it was drafted with state participation and on the basis of their consent ensures it greater effectiveness. The precedent set by the League of Nations, whose international system of minority protection broke down because young states jealous of their newly acquired sovereignty were reluctant to honor obligations imposed on them, suggests that the Council of Europe method for seeking consensus is the right one. This European initiative provides a legal framework that is well suited to stabilizing relations between states.

Stability, moreover, was the key word of the pact adopted by OSCE representatives in March 1995, on a French initiative, in order to forestall the risks of imbalance growing out of nationalist tensions in Eastern Europe. Although it was basically a political agreement, the pact framed relations between the then fifteen European Union member countries, the three Baltic states and the six CEECs (Poland, Czech Republic, Slovakia, Hungary, Romania, Bulgaria). It had a beneficial effect on Hungary's relations with two of its neighbors, Slovakia and Romania, with which Budapest successively concluded treaties of good neighborliness and cooperation in 1995 and 1996.

These agreements combine recognition of border sanctity (a Hungarian concession, as the country had never really accepted the loss of territory resulting from the Trianon Treaty in 1920) and legal guarantees for the Magyar minority's cultural autonomy (a Slovak and Romanian concession, as these two countries had always been reluctant to commit to recognizing collective rights). Although these bilateral treaties did not solve all problems, their ratification nevertheless represents a normalization of minority issues.[13]

The treaties established a bilateral commission in charge of ensuring that the various clauses be honored, particularly those concerning national minorities, and stress the need for cooperation. They also underscore the national aspect of the state, which is held accountable not only for the fate of its citizens, but also for the members of the nation (in the ethno-cultural sense) who come under the political authority of neighboring states. This principle of responsibility is moreover often enshrined in the states' constitutions, as in Hungary, Croatia and Romania. Such constitutionalized scrutiny certainly tempers the states monopoly on sovereignty, but this should not be perceived as disturbing. It may result in excesses, as in 1990 when József Antall proclaimed himself prime minister of 15 million Hungarians—adding the Magyar minorities in neighboring states to the 10 million citizens of Hungary—and adopted an activist policy of defending Magyar minorities abroad. The conservative Viktor Orbán, elected in 2010, has gone much further by having a law passed that liberally grants Hungarian citizenship to Magyar-speakers in neighboring countries.[14] It should be noted that citizenship carries the right to take part in legislative elections in Hungary. As was foreseeable, the leaders of states sharing borders with Hungary scarcely appreciated this blatant interventionism. Slovakia, with a Magyar minority of 520,000 (10% of the total population) reacted immediately. After having considered the quasi-automatic revocation of Slovak nationality for anyone who took on another nationality, Slovak officials adopted a softer stance: only the holding of certain civil service positions (in the army or the police, for instance) is deemed incompatible with dual citizenship.

Clearly, the principle of scrutiny can lead to misplaced interference and disagreements if it is used to populist ends. Yet it would be unfair to criticize it out of hand, for if negotiated and ratified by bilateral treaties, it can on the contrary prove to be a useful tool. It gives the national minority greater assurance, knowing it can count on an external patron state, while placing the state where the minority holds citizenship under "critical observation," thereby hopefully encouraging it to honor democratic principles and avoid any authoritarian or discriminatory measure.

A Special Case: The Imperial Minorities

Leaving aside now the "old minorities," such as the Transylvanian Hungarians, to turn to the more recent minorities formed by 20 to 25 million Russian speakers who ended up in new states founded on the ruins of the USSR, we face a very different political configuration. Indeed, due to the collapse of the Soviet empire, Russians became a minority in spite of themselves, and these circumstances have had a considerable effect on their fate. In Ukraine, they were immediately given citizenship and were allowed to maintain a separate school system, just like other minority groups (Romanians, Poles, Hungarians, etc.). There is nothing surprising about this move. Kiev was the capital of the first Russian state and the fate of the two countries has been closely linked for centuries, creating a strong affinity between them.

The history of the three Baltic states is entirely different. Although they were independent after the Great War, the German-Soviet Pact of August 1939 put them under the control of the USSR, which, once the Second World War ended, undertook methodically to Sovietize them. This state of affairs persisted until they regained independence in the early 1990s, thus posing the delicate issue of the 2 million Russians, out of a total population of 8 million, who had migrated during the Soviet era.

Lithuania, where Russians and related peoples (Ukrainians, Belarussians) accounted for only 12% of the population, adopted a liberal policy similar to Ukraine's. Things were very different in Estonia and Latvia, where, respectively, ethnic Estonians made up 62% of the population and Latvians were just barely a majority (52%), with a mostly Russian "minority" population in both. Both countries passed a citizenship law reserving automatic citizenship for persons who held it in the interwar period and their descendants. The overwhelming majority of Russians who arrived after 1945 were thus not automatically granted citizenship. They instead must undergo a naturalization process requiring a period of residency and, especially, knowledge of the country's language, its political institutions and its constitution. Moreover, dual citizenship is not allowed. The goal of this policy—to avoid the mass naturalization of Russians—has been achieved, as approximately one-third of residents in the two countries had not obtained citizenship in the mid-1990s. These difficulties have undeniably encouraged some Russians to return to the Russian Federation, thus mechanically diminishing their proportion in the population as a whole (28% in Latvia and 25% in Estonia, whereas now the Latvians make up 58% and the Estonians 68% of their respective countries' population).[15]

This situation raises a very delicate question: does a state have the right to restrict access to citizenship on an ethnic basis for people legally living on its territory?[16] The answer obviously must take into account the context, in this case a dramatic one.

The Baltic states were subjected to forced and brutal incorporation into the Soviet Union under Stalin's rule. "Socially hostile elements," "bourgeois nationalists" and "counter-revolutionary kulaks" were transferred en masse to the Gulag. In the early 1950s, "in the special camps, 20% of the inmates were of Baltic origin. In total, 10% of the entire adult Baltic population was either deported or in a camp."[17] This merciless repression produced a demographic atrophy that was further accentuated by substantial Russian immigration, encouraged by the central authorities who were eager to accelerate the process of Russification. A gradual and implacable process of diluting Latvian and Estonian collective identities was patently at work.

In such conditions, independence was a providential lifesaver, returning control of their fate to the Baltic countries. They were thus able to stop their inexorable decline by enacting preservation measures, such as citizenship and language laws. The dangers they had faced were very real indeed, and "if radical 'ethnic protection' measures had not been taken urgently in 1991 to put a halt to the disappearance of the language, Russification in all likelihood would have continued and the breaking point would have soon been reached, resulting in the *de facto* disappearance of the Estonian and Latvian people."[18] Nowhere other than these two little Baltic republics has there been such fear for the very existence of the national community, so typical of Eastern Europe.[19] In a situation marked by an ancient historical trauma, the logic of "recovering the national identity" temporarily legitimates recourse to a restrictive definition of citizenship until the national identity can be stabilized.

For those who might object to such selective citizenship, viewing it as the privilege of an Eastern Europe that rebels against the idea of an egalitarian nation of citizens, it is probably worth remembering that republic-minded France went even further in the Nouméa Accord in 1998.

The Accord makes a distinction within the very body of French citizens, granting a specific citizenship to those who have settled permanently in New Caledonia. All those who arrived after 1988 are excluded from the benefits of Caledonian citizenship, hence the right to vote in provincial elections and referendums on self-determination (after a twenty-year period of residence, these people can, however, be incorporated into the electorate). Some French citizens in New Caledonia will thus be treated as foreign residents. This discrimination is justified in the preamble of the Nouméa Accord by the need to overcome the lasting traumatic effects of colonization, which presupposes giving substantial political power back to the original people. The electorate was thus restricted precisely to enable the Kanaks not to become even more of a minority—already they make up only 45% of the population—and to regain control of their destiny.

However, while access to citizenship for "non-nationals" can be limited in the event of historical reparation, the measure should not be permanent, or there is a risk of politically sidelining residents of the state instead of aiming to integrate them.

To this end, deprivation of citizenship, which prohibits foreign residents from choosing a parliament in which major national choices are decided, should be compensated by allowing them to take part in local elections where the issues, narrower in scope, affect the everyday lives of all inhabitants, whether citizens or not. Estonia has ventured down this path by granting the right to vote in municipal elections to all residents, including Russians. At the same time, social integration should be actively pursued, which is clearly not always the case. Latvian legislation (repealed in 1998), which tied the exercise of certain professions such as pharmacist, airplane pilot and even fireman to citizenship requirements, was patently discriminatory: the citizenship criterion merely intended to exclude Russians. Lastly, it is essential that provisions be made for a system of cultural autonomy for the new minority communities. But when such a mechanism exists, its application is sometimes limited, for instance in Estonia, to holders of citizenship (Finns, Swedes, Jews, etc.), thereby leaving the vast majority of Russian non-citizens completely by the wayside.

In the longer term, their total civic integration will become conceivable as the existential uncertainty about the nation's survival ebbs and collective self-confidence grows. After introducing "non-citizen passports," which already ensured their holders a degree of freedom of movement, Latvia decided to lighten restrictions on its citizenship law by removing age group quotas for naturalization and by introducing a degree of *jus soli* for children.[20] It also set up an integration program to accelerate the naturalization process. This program has borne fruit, as the proportion of non-citizens has been lowered to 20% (compared with 30% at the time of independence). However, for the integration process to be complete, not only must the state tone down its ethnic rationale, but minorities must also clearly demonstrate their will to integrate, for instance by learning the national language, even if they mainly use their native tongue on a daily basis.

What patently poses a problem for many Russians in both these Baltic republics, and explains the sluggish naturalization rate, particularly in the 1990s, is not so much the difficulty of mastering non-Slavic languages but the majority complex that has affected many of them. Having arrived during the period of the USSR's "grandeur," many saw themselves as part of the great Russian nation, whereas they have become mere residents of little Baltic states which, in their desire to ensure their hard-won independence, demand unequivocal support for the new national framework. In a way, it could be said that the Russians have had to learn to be a minority. This gradual learning process, combined with the Baltic peoples' growing confidence about their demographic consolidation, should eventually lead to normalizing the Russians' situation in these countries.

The system of cultural autonomy, possibly accompanied by territorial extensions in the form of specific districts, is suited to national minorities living in a country where the demographic majority group has its own state. It would appear inadequate, however, in cases where a society is more or less equally divided into two or more segments that have cohabited within the same state from the very start.

Consociation: A Delicate Transplant

A society subject to strong ideological and cultural dividing lines would seem at first glance doomed to chronic fragility. Yet, internal division is not necessarily a curse. If skillfully managed, it can even contribute to the social system's stability. The best example of this balance of opposites is without a doubt Switzerland: four national languages, two religions, four main political families, twenty-six cantons,[21] and yet unshakeable stability. The word explaining this miracle is consociation.[22]

The term, originally used to refer to the process by which the Netherlands was constituted through the voluntary alliance of provinces, today refers to a mode of managing societies characterized by deep social, ideological, religious and linguistic divisions and operates according to two principles.

The first principle is the recognition of large autonomy for the society's constituent groups. In the most accomplished consociations, such as the Netherlands and Belgium, each group, represented by specific political parties (Catholic, Socialist, Liberal, etc.), forms a world in itself with its trade unions, schools and universities, its hospitals and its communication networks. Individuals are thus essentially the responsibility of institutions administered by their segment. The state intervenes only to deal with subjects of common interest. Although such vertical segmentation does not characterize Switzerland, the cantonal and municipal framework indeed provides true community autonomy.

The second principle, which balances out the first, is permanent cooperation at the national level among elites of the various "subcultures." To avert the risk of division inherent in the strong compartmentalization between groups, their leaders together participate in formulating national policy, for instance in broad government coalitions. Switzerland certainly provides the most accomplished form of association among elites, as the federal executive relies on careful combinations of political affiliations, cantonal attachments, languages and religions. The blend of these two principles of autonomy and cooperation has enabled it to maintain great democratic stability and generally preserve national unity.

Consociations, however, make up a small club, mostly limited to Europe, and they owe their success to two main factors. First, strategies of compromise have been brought into play in situations where the major issue revolved around which social order to favor: traditional, liberal, or socialist-leaning. This ideological conflict basically pits the conservative, predominantly Catholic, religious segment against the liberal, secular end of the spectrum, originally "bourgeois individualist" in nature and then also socialist. The consociational rationale has proven fruitful because the two camps, rather than constantly striving to win a decisive but uncertain victory over their opponent, prefer to forge a compromise that preserves the autonomy of each segment within a political framework that all recognize as legitimate.

This second point is very important: when patriotism is shared in a common political allegiance, it takes the edge off ideological-religious cleavages. Consolidation of a national sentiment uniting Protestants and Catholics in the Netherlands in the seventeenth century explains why irredentist tendencies did not develop among the latter group in the two southern provinces where they were a majority. They did not ask to be united with Catholic Belgium but worked to strengthen their own institutions within the Dutch state.

Similarly, after the Sonderbund War that set conservative Catholic cantons in Switzerland against the rest of the confederation, the federal bond was renewed in 1848 so as to reconcile the cantons' sovereignty with the affirmation of national unity advocated by the radicals. By the same token, up until the 1950s in Belgium, Catholics and seculars independently managed entire segments of society such as education and healthcare, while their elites did their utmost to devise compromises and agreements without calling into question the unitary nature of the state.

The Belgian consociation later became paralyzed, and the reason for this loss of effectiveness is of particular interest here. It was brought on by the growing importance of the language difference between Dutch speakers and French speakers. Once secondary, it has now become a principal preoccupation. The good old political recipes based on compromise and consensus had become inoperative, because the very organization of political power was challenged. It was the state that needed an overhaul, leading to full federalization in 1993. The Belgian precedent offers an important lesson. With the rise of particular nationalist movements and the crumbling of an overarching loyalty to the state, consociationalism became largely ineffectual. As well suited as it may be to managing ideological, religious or social pluralism, it seems unable to contain conflicts of a national nature that tend to call into question the existing political framework.

Surprisingly, although its real effectiveness is far from obvious, a consociational solution was nevertheless chosen twice in the 1990s in circumstances of crisis resolution. The peace agreement for Northern Ireland is thus based on consociational mechanisms because it provides at once for proportional representation of political parties in the local assembly, a broad coalition (government portfolios are allocated in proportion to the votes obtained by each party) and an implicit right of veto, given that qualified majorities are required for all major decisions. Only this type of system, which gives each community comparable political weight, was likely to secure true popular legitimacy.[23]

Yet it has proven delicate to implement. Successful consociations have long since developed a culture of dispute settlement by compromise, defended by elites capable of overcoming communitarian divisions and joining forces on pragmatic bases. Such conditions do not exist in Northern Ireland, where the aim is to render a consociational system operational while Catholics and Protestants, engaged in intense political rivalry, still have strong mutual prejudices. For instance, the first Northern Irish government was not formed until November 1999, a year and a half after the semi-autonomous assembly was elected, due to prolonged disagreement between Republicans and Unionists over the issue of disarming the IRA. The issue was to poison the functioning of Northern Irish institutions until the IRA made its historic announcement in July 2005 that it had abandoned armed struggle. This sudden turnaround broke the deadlock and led to the withdrawal of the British Army from Northern Ireland and then the disarming of the Protestant paramilitary groups. Overall, demilitarization was the prerequisite for unblocking consociational mechanisms and forming a lasting bicommunal government bringing together two archrivals, the Democratic Unionist Party and Sinn Féin. The example of Northern Ireland is particularly instructive because it shows that to resolve a situation of extreme crisis, it is essential for the most radical elements to be convinced that the only alternative is power-sharing. By joining forces, the hardliners on both sides leave no room for even more extremist elements to torpedo the peace process.

The Dayton Accords of November 1995 set up a consociational arrangement in Bosnia and Herzegovina as well, but without satisfying the minimum requirements for it to function. More than three years of armed conflict, population displacement and ethnic cleansing during which nationalist hatreds were pushed to paroxysm hardly predisposed the political leaders of the three communities to cultivate a sense of compromise. This is nevertheless what they are theoretically compelled to achieve, because the new central institutions are based on an explicit ethnic distribution (tripartite state presidency, a parliamentary assembly with five representatives from each community, vice ministers not belonging to the same group as the ministers) and an implicit one (portfolios shared among the three communities). This parity and the existence of each group's right of veto risking a deadlock, a stalemate can only be avoided if there is a strong desire to cooperate.

Such will continues to be lacking. Neither the Croats, who have long sought to strengthen their virtual republic of Herzeg-Bosnia (within another entity, the Croat-Bosniak Federation), nor especially the Serbs, who have methodically consolidated their own republic (one of the two constitutive entities of Bosnia) have any real desire to bolster their common institutions. They have been much more eager to weaken them to preserve the existing partition. Despite some improvements, the central structures of Bosnia and Herzegovina thus remain empty shells that are kept alive for one reason only: to preserve the legal illusion of a Bosnian state that the international community is determined to safeguard for political motives.

By a bitter irony that speaks volumes about the spirit of accommodation prevalent in Bosnia and Herzegovina, many of the measures emphasizing the republic's unity (currency, passport, flag, license plates, identity card) have been imposed by the High Representative of the international community who plays a role of *de facto* governor. This individual must often resort to the special powers bestowed on him to invalidate controversial laws passed by the two federal entities or to remove refractory officials from office. Proof that the Bosnian state is standing on shaky ground, the Office of the High Representative, which was supposed to be dissolved in 2007, is still in existence.

Elections can certainly not be counted on to foster a shared civic space. On the surface, the vitality of democracy in Bosnia is bewildering. Voters are called to the polls every four years to choose the three representatives to the collegial presidency and the forty-two members of the assembly. At the same time, voters in the Croat-Bosniak Federation choose ninety-eight members of parliament, while voters in Republika Srpska elect eighty-three representatives as well as their president.

This democratic fervor is nevertheless largely deceptive. The Dayton Accords literally institutionalized ethnicity in two respects. First, the voters' choice is limited from the start because citizens in the Serb entity can only elect a Serb to the collegial presidency of Bosnia, while citizens of the Croat-Bosniak Federation necessarily choose a Croat and a Bosniak (Muslim). Second, the territorialization of ethnicity restricts eligibility requirements, because to be elected to the House of Peoples, one must be a citizen of the entity of one's ethnic group. A Serb from Sarajevo, for instance, is ineligible if he lives in Federation territory.[24] Such ethnicization of citizenship in fact encourages the communities to band together in their "ethnic" territory and clearly works against the restoration of a multination Bosnia.[25]

Furthermore, although "citizen" (non-ethnic) parties—especially on the Croat-Muslim side—have been gaining ground, nationalist groupings continue to occupy a large swathe of the political arena. The difficulty of building a unified democratic space contrasts with the robustness of centrifugal forces. While the Bosnian Serbs have developed special relations with Belgrade (creating a single market, freedom of movement of persons, close military and diplomatic cooperation), the Bosnian Croats have been granted the right to take part in elections, even presidential, that are held in Croatia. Only the Muslims, deprived of an outside protector, must resign themselves to live their political life entirely in their Bosniak reserve. This is the triumph of ghetto politics, in which "an individual's political allegiance to the state disappears behind communitarian identifications, the rule of law yields to identitarian conformism, the prescribed identity wins out over sovereignist claims that become devoid of meaning."[26] Such radical ethnicization of politics can only lead to a corruption of consociational democracy which, instead of encouraging dialogue and consultation, sustains communitarian withdrawal and general paralysis.

The consociational solution must clearly be used with care in a context of ethno-national antagonism. It too often risks maintaining immobilism and division. Only when trust can be established between the parties, often in exceptional circumstances (as in Northern Ireland since the mid-2000s), can consociation begin to function with relative effectiveness.

7

TERRITORIAL AUTONOMY

The second major method of managing national diversity is on a territorial basis, meaning that the autonomy granted to a given group is exercised within a delimited geographic and administrative space. Territorialization of autonomy can be achieved by different means depending on the type of state. It will be an exception in a unitary nation-state and the rule in a federal state.

Necessary Adjustments of the Nation-State

The notion of the nation-state implies that the state is an agent in instituting the nation, whose boundaries it shapes by suppressing "primary" identities (religious, regional, etc.) and diffusing a standardized cultural norm, its aim being to bring political unity in harmony with cultural unity.[1] Yet, this principle of social homogenization has always remained largely an ideal. In reality the culture/politics overlap remains very imperfect. Furthermore, building an all-encompassing national identity has proven to be much more difficult with the increasing democratization of contemporary societies.

In this general context, the traditional nation-state has not been exempt from a trend of reform involving institutional rearrangements. Unitary states in Europe have all undergone an *aggiornamento*.

Many have updated their institutions out of pragmatism, granting specific status locally to one or more groups that are in a minority at the state level but a majority in a given region. The central state thus does not call into question the overall organization of the territory, but it tolerates exceptions by allowing some areas to be at least partially governed by special rules and for them to exercise certain powers autonomously (usually in educational, cultural and economic matters). The oldest example is the Åland Islands, an archipelago in the Baltic Sea that is part of Finland but whose 28,000 Swedish-speaking inhabitants have enjoyed considerable autonomy since 1920. The local parliament has general legislative powers except in certain very limited areas (foreign affairs, the judiciary, state taxes). Similar rules apply to Greenland and the Faroe Islands, which come under Danish sovereignty. It is worth noting that these three island entities are members of the Nordic Council alongside the five member states (Norway, Sweden, Finland, Iceland, Denmark) that organize international cooperation in the Nordic region.

Such special statuses often apply to island situations as these raise very specific issues of an economic, fiscal and social nature.[2] France, moreover, primarily proved institutionally innovative in island territories (Corsica, New Caledonia, Polynesia).

Island particularism explains why Sicily and Sardinia are mentioned in the Italian constitution of 1947 as requiring special status. Three other areas of the peninsula—Friuli-Venezia Giulia, Trentino-Alto Adige and the Aosta Valley—also enjoy a measure of territorial autonomy to account for their historical and linguistic specificity. These five regions were granted various powers, but it is certainly significant that the broadest powers as well as considerable financial autonomy were granted to Trentino-Alto Adige, and within it, Bolzano province. This German-speaking Tyrolean province was annexed to Italy at the end of the First World War to reward it for fighting with the Allies.

German-speakers owe their autonomy to two favorable circumstances: first, a powerful regionalist party, the South Tyrolean People's Party (SVP), which garners over 80% of the vote in local elections and nearly two-thirds in legislative polls; second, the existence of a patron state, in this case Austria, which intervened actively to defend the former subjects of the Austro-Hungarian Empire. An Italian-Austrian agreement reached in 1969 put an end to a spate of attacks on property perpetrated by young SVP militants, exasperated by the limits Rome imposed on the province's autonomy. The new status in 1972, the result of an arrangement made with Austria, substantially increased this autonomy, which proves how heavily the active intervention of a patron state can weigh in preserving a strong system of protection in favor of national minorities.

Hence, even though French-speakers in the Aosta Valley, adjoined to Italy in 1860, are also largely represented by an autonomist party, the Valdostan

Union, their power of influence in Rome is more limited because France does not play the same role of external protector for them as Austria does for the South Tyroleans. This difference in attitude is probably the reflection of two distinct political cultures. The territorialized conception of the nation championed by France does not encourage it to engage in a specific policy toward communities at the fringes of France (French-speaking Switzerland, Wallonia and Brussels, Quebec) whereas Austria, due to a more cultural conception of the nation, deems it has a duty to intervene in favor of German-speakers beyond the borders of the former Habsburg Empire.

A unitary state can go further, however, in taking exceptions into account. It can make profound changes, not merely through functional regionalization as in France but by instituting an autonomous regime. This is exactly what the United Kingdom did under an initiative of Labour Prime Minister Tony Blair (1997–2007). He engaged in a policy of devolution involving the creation of regional assemblies in Wales, Scotland and Northern Ireland. The establishment of a local assembly in Cardiff and a regional parliament in Edinburgh gave two constitutive entities of Great Britain—Wales and Scotland—an institutional autonomy that they had lost when they were united with England in 1536 and 1707 respectively. The powers attributed to these new bodies should be accurately assessed. While for the Welsh Assembly they are fairly limited, they are more generous for the Scottish Parliament, which also has certain taxation powers. However, this controlled devolution should not mislead. In a country where the sovereignty of Parliament is literally dogma, Westminster has relinquished some of its powers in favor of regional assemblies elected for the first time in May 1999 and reelected every four years since. This devolution was meant to achieve two complementary objectives.

The first was to modernize the British state by instilling a measure of decentralization, thereby countering centralizing tendencies often deemed excessive and counterproductive to government action. The second aimed to forestall nationalist claims in Wales and Scotland by making room for specific political expression for the voters of these two nations. So far the wager has paid off, but the success is not certain to last, at least not in Scotland. In Wales, on the other hand, although the nationalist party, Plaid Cymru, exercises significant influence, the union with England made centuries ago and subsequent anglicization, especially in the south, make it unlikely that a strategy to break away from London will come to fruition. The plan for a Welsh assembly in fact nearly failed to win popular consent. There was a difference of only 6721 votes between the yes and no votes in the September 1997 referendum. Devolution has nonetheless unquestionably gained approval, as during another referendum in 2011, 63.5% of the voters agreed that the Welsh Assembly should pass laws in all twenty areas devolved to it.

The Scottish situation is different in that its collective identity has remained stronger, all the more as the union with England never obliterated a number of particularisms in the fields of education, the judiciary, the administration and religious practice (the Church of Scotland is Calvinist Presbyterian). The vibrancy of strong identity awareness explains the fact that the message of the Scottish National Party, which advocates outright independence for Scotland, has found persistent resonance, handing the party an absolute majority of 53.5% of the vote in May 2011 and giving it a landslide victory in Scotland in the 2015 UK general election (fifty-six of fifty-nine seats).[3] This sentiment would not have been enough in itself to give the SNP a sturdy electoral base had it not been for the weakening of the British identity with the end of its imperial ambitions and the discovery of oil in the North Sea, allowing the possibility of economic self-sufficiency for Scotland. These two factors gave the SNP's calls for sovereignty new credence.

The case of Northern Ireland is distinct yet again. The aim here is not only to give a "region" administrative autonomy but to put an end to a violent conflict between nationalists (Catholic) and unionists (Protestant) that arose out of a self-determination that remained incomplete because the partition of the island in 1921 had left a potential clash between Catholics (40%) and Protestants (60%) to fester in the six counties put under the British crown. For the first time since the start of the "Troubles" in 1969, the Good Friday Agreement in April 1998 offered the premises of a reasonable perspective of a solution to the crisis, despite the difficulties of implementing it.

The conflict between Protestants and Catholics in Northern Ireland is merely a facet of a broader conflict putting the two communities in opposition all over Ireland and beyond, in the entire United Kingdom. Because of these intertwining conflicts, any solution must be a comprehensive one that takes into account the three layers of conflict. This is precisely what the peace agreement is meant to do through its institutional mechanisms. In Northern Ireland, a semi-autonomous assembly with legislative and executive powers was elected. At the same time, two councils came into being. The first, the North/South Ministerial Council, brings together representatives from Northern Ireland and the Republic of Ireland to pursue cooperation in certain shared policy areas (transport, tourism, etc.). It is a means of signaling the unity of Ireland, a notion to which the Catholics are firmly attached. The second, the British/Irish Council, is made up of representatives of the Irish and British governments as well as delegates from "autonomous regions" (Northern Ireland, Scotland, Wales) and develops cooperation on the scale of the British Isles. It especially fulfills a demand on the part of Protestant Unionists to have an institution in which the entire United Kingdom participates. This three-stage structure is based on a principle of qualified sovereignty.

Given that nationalists and unionists have diametrically opposed views of who holds sovereignty in Northern Ireland, this essential issue has been temporarily left aside. On the one hand, London has repealed a law passed in 1920 that claimed its inalienable sovereignty over Ulster, while Dublin has repealed two articles of its constitution that mentioned the Irish government's jurisdiction over the entire island. On the other hand, the restoration of a regional assembly—its predecessor had ceased to function in 1972—gives local actors if not genuine sovereignty, at least responsibility in the conduct of Northern Ireland's affairs. At the same time, the establishment of cross-border institutions in charge of subjects of common interest—agriculture, the environment, etc.—is a means of blurring the border between north and south by promoting functional cooperation. Dodging the sovereignty question in this way may not provide a long-term solution, but in a situation in which demands clash head-on, such a method might foster the emergence of new and dispassionate approaches to settling a conflict in a deeply divided society.

With this devolution, the United Kingdom is no longer a unitary state, but nor is it a federal state. It is between the two, like Italy, which has gradually entered into a process of federalization that should make it possible to taken into account the desire for autonomy expressed by the Northern League.

The Mixed Virtues of Federalism

Federalism, contrary to the crude caricature that has been made of it in Bosnia and Herzegovina, can be a valuable tool for managing national differences.[4] The implosion of three federations (Czechoslovakia, USSR, Yugoslavia) in the early 1990s might give cause to doubt the merits of this organizing principle. But in all three cases, federalism had been implemented in an authoritarian context and was used merely as a tactic to give peoples who theoretically enjoyed equal rights only symbolic autonomy, true power resting with the party-state. To use Václav Havel's expression, the regimes were a form of federalized totalitarianism, which nevertheless produced some unanticipated effects.

The Soviet nationalities policy, for instance, which in Central Asia had the strategic aim of breaking up a Persian Islamic and Turkic-speaking area of civilization by literally inventing states (Uzbekistan, Turkmenistan, etc.), thus contributed to lending these national identities a certain degree of substance. Ethnologists and linguists participated in the effort to create a "scientific" justification for awarding these peoples their own Soviet republic in due form. Even though they were initially manufactured in this way, these nations gradually acquired their own relevancy.[5]

As for Yugoslavia, "at first a matter of pure form, the federal system eventually became real"[6] with the 1974 constitution that conferred considerable powers on the autonomous republics and provinces, to the detriment of the center, in the hope of thwarting centrifugal tendencies, particularly on the part of Croatia. We now know that far from taming nationalisms, these flourished even more with the deepening of institutional autonomy.

Does that mean that the very principle of federalization should be incriminated in the lead-up to war? I do not believe so. It is rather the context in which it took place that should be condemned, that is, within the framework of a communist ideocracy ruled by a single party and its rigid self-management, from both the political and the economic standpoint. This last dimension played a far more decisive role in the breakup of the country than what is often acknowledged. Economic solidarity between republics and provinces was increasingly difficult to accept for the richer republics (Slovenia and Croatia), which were reluctant to redistribute a portion of their resources to the poorer constituents (Kosovo, Macedonia, Bosnia). For the former, leaving the federation thus seemed to be a solution suited to their "economic nationalism."

If Yugoslavia's trajectory attests to the failure of federalism in an authoritarian context, Spain offers a fairly successful example of establishing a quasi-federal system[7] to accompany the return to democracy. There, it was essential to associate citizens' political freedom and the collective emancipation of the "historical nationalities" (Basque Country, Catalonia, Galicia). It would not have been possible to stabilize democracy on a purely republican rationale by rebuilding a civic space without recognizing national particularism. Indeed, the institution of a regime of self-administered regions has not sufficed to banish violence from the Basque Country, but the pursuit of bloody terrorist tactics cannot be attributed to actual dissatisfaction with a basically generous autonomous status. It is more due to the nature of Basque nationalism, which has never managed to shed a rationale of radical exclusion since it emerged under the leadership of Sabino Arana in the late nineteenth century.[8] With this exception, the Spanish solution has demonstrated enough flexibility to allow nationalitarian differences to express themselves while preserving a state framework.

As a system of government, federalism is based on a constitutionally defined separation of powers between the federal state and federated entities, each being sovereign in its devolved areas. Such shared sovereignty is organized by combining three standard principles: separation of powers among the different levels of government, the autonomy of the federated units, and their participation in the general conduct of the federal state (often via a second legislative chamber, such as the US Senate, the Swiss Council of States, or the Federal Councils in Germany and in Austria).[9] While a unitary state tends toward uniformity, a federal state is by definition based on the acceptance of internal plurality. This type of state organization, however, takes on two different forms that should be carefully distinguished.

First, however, it should be pointed out that federal states are a minority in the world. Out of the 193 UN member states, there are only twenty-five of them.[10] Many federal states—and especially the United States, historically the first—opted for federalism because it fit in with their philosophy of government. The fear of tyranny of the majority as much as of the dictatorship of a single person encouraged the constituent entities to view federalism as the ideal instrument to establish a vertical division of powers that would profitably supplement the horizontal separation between the executive, the legislative and the judicial branches. Moreover, federalism seemed particularly well suited to the very method by which these states were formed. For settlement countries (the United States, Brazil, Argentina, Australia, etc.), this type of organization seemed appropriate for large countries that had pioneer fronts and were formed by the successive annexation of territories as the frontier advanced. Federalism was also attractive to older countries such as Germany, formed by the voluntary aggregation of pre-existing entities (duchies, principalities, kingdoms). Political life was organized in such a way as to allow a national sovereignty to emerge while preserving local sovereignties.

In all these cases, however, federalism is based on the recognition of political entities (provinces, länder, states, etc.) that never correspond to specific ethnic, cultural or linguistic groups. As philosopher Will Kymlicka very aptly remarks, none of the fifty United States was deliberately connected to a national minority: Arizona is no more the state of the Navajo Indians than California and Texas have been singled out as states for Mexican Chicanos.[11] No state has been assigned to a specific group of immigrants (such as Minnesota for the Norwegians, or Wisconsin for the Germans), nor is any one state explicitly tied in with a particular religious group. Even though the Mormons made Salt Lake City their capital, Utah is not their state, any more than Pennsylvania is the state of the Quakers. The United States, like most federal states, opted for a form of territorial federalism in which the federated entities make up political units bringing together a body of undifferentiated citizens, just as the federal state brings together all sovereign peoples.

Sometimes, within some federations, a strong regional identity can be identified in a given federated entity, such as in the German Land of Bavaria or the Austrian Tyrol. According to de Tocqueville, federalism can only function where there are "not only nearly the same interests, the same origin, and the same language, but even the same degree of civilization."[12] But such "homogeneity of civilization" that the great historian mentions reduces federalism to a principle of territorial and political organization, whereas it can also be extremely useful as a tool for managing national diversity.[13]

This multination federalism provides a number of resources for organizing broad internal autonomy for federated entities with cultural specificities.[14] The federalization of Belgium in 1993, by strengthening the power of the regions (Flanders, Wallonia, Brussels) and of the Fleming, French and German-speaking communities, made possible a deep reform of the state, whose unitary organization was at odds with social and political evolutions. The dissociative federalism thus set up shrank the role of the central state while communities and regions saw their powers considerably augmented. Regions even won powers on the international scene, as they can conclude treaties with states as long as these pertain to the areas devolved to them by the constitution. By virtue of this partial international sovereignty, the Belgian federated entities participate directly in the revision of European treaties and the EU decision-making process.[15]

In Spain, the establishment of autonomous communities has given them considerable latitude that the "historical nationalities" in particular have put to good use. Since 1983 the Generalitat of Catalonia has embarked on a policy of linguistic normalization that has contributed to the remarkable expansion of Catalan in school. A more limited process of linguistic revival has also begun, following a Basque government initiative in education, radio and television broadcasting and within the regional administration. These policies, which aim to reverse the trend of castilianization intensified under Franco, would never have been possible without the considerable self-determination that Catalonia and the Basque Country enjoy within the Spanish multination state.

As for Canada, as soon as the confederation was established in 1867, the adoption of federalism has long facilitated cohabitation between the anglophone provinces and Quebec. The preservation of certain particularisms (civil law, educational system, Catholic religious institutions) in the mainly French-speaking province, made possible by federalism, was to some extent indispensable to make New France accept a political union resulting from its defeat at the hands of the English. This open federalism gave Quebec greater autonomy than the other provinces in certain policy areas (immigration, income taxation, pension plans, etc.).

That does not mean, however, that federalism is a magic formula that can curtail intensifying nationalist processes. In Belgium, for instance, constant separatist and populist pressure from the nationalist Vlaams Belang party has sustained a permanent game of one-upmanship among the Flemish political elite. Even the Flemish Christian Democrat Party (CD&V) under Yves Leterme's leadership did not hesitate to join forces in 2007 with a separatist party, the New Flemish Alliance, which in 2010 became Belgium's largest party. This situation would lead to an unprecedented government crisis that lasted a year and a half (541 days)—a world record—ending with the formation of a government led by the francophone Socialist Elio Di Rupo. This outcome was made possible by an agreement on an institutional reform that resulted in further transfers of power to the communities and regions (employment, health care, family allowances, etc.), greater fiscal autonomy,[16] and the transformation of the Senate into a chamber of federated entities.[17] This sixth reform of the state will increase the weight of the federated entities and eventually further compartmentalize the communities, thereby heightening the risk of the country's breakup. Essentially, the leaders of the two communities do not share the same perception of federalism. For the Flemings, it should above all allow the Flemish "nationality" to prosper and assert their region-community as a potential state. Conversely, most leaders of the French-speaking community have a utilitarian approach to federalism, which they view as an adequate institutional arrangement to protect the economic interests of Wallonia. To curb Flemish nationalism, tied to a strong cultural identity, the Walloons have tried to forge a collective counter-identity, but this attempt has remained largely unsuccessful due to lack of historic unity as well as a complex relationship with France.[18] The multination federalism advocated by the Flemings thus contrasts with a Walloon regional federalism. Rather than expend effort striving to find an unlikely convergence between these contrasting views of federalism, some suggest combining them into a specific institutional formula: asymmetrical federalism.

A Reformed Federalism?

The idea is simple: the aim is to give federated entities defending a specific conception of society rights and powers that other purely "territorial" and "administrative" entities would not enjoy. This solution has been recommended by many observers to renew Canada's federal pact, which has been in crisis for decades despite a remarkable succession of constitutional conferences, commissions and reports.[19]

In concrete terms, asymmetrical federalism goes much farther than merely awarding special powers in specific areas and on a generally pragmatic basis. This is already the situation in Quebec today. It amounts to transferring major legislative and budgetary powers from the central state solely to the nationalitarian federal entity. The other federated units that are merely decentralized regional structures would not benefit from such transfers. Quebec would thus obtain powers that Manitoba or British Columbia would be denied. This asymmetry would have the advantage of giving the Quebecois, officially recognized as a distinct nation[20]—in other words a mainly French-speaking society in an English-speaking North America—the means to preserve this specificity.

As appealing as it may be, in that it gives federated entities with a national base a particular form of recognition, asymmetrical federalism is not a perfect solution. First, it is difficult to set up. "Normal" federated entities are attached to the principle of equality between constituent units. While some specific powers may occasionally be granted here and there, resistance to instituting permanent asymmetry that would establish a status departing from ordinary law is strong. As for the central government, the tendency detected in most states based on aggregative federalism (Germany, the United States, Switzerland, etc.)[21] has been toward a strengthening of the political center and thus reducing existing dissymmetry. It is precisely in the name of an egalitarian conception of federalism and the need to stimulate a pan-Canadian national sentiment from the Atlantic to the Pacific that the nine other English-speaking provinces as well as the federal government in Ottawa have always refused the institution of asymmetrical federalism for Quebec.

Second, can asymmetrical federalism function harmoniously over the long term in a state entity? The example of Spain would tend to prove that it provokes a chain reaction of emulation and differentiation preventing the political system from truly achieving stability. By way of symbolic recognition for the strong cultural specificity of its historical nationalities, the Spanish constituent assembly put them on a fast track to full autonomy by immediately granting all of the powers provided by law. The other fourteen autonomous communities should have taken the slow road with a gradual rise in their autonomy. This differentiated mechanism aimed to establish an asymmetry between historical communities and ordinary regions.[22] Over time, however, the gap has narrowed considerably. Andalusia achieved autonomy through an accelerated procedure, while three other autonomous communities (Canaries, Valencia, Navarre) fairly quickly acquired powers similar to the "historical nationalities." Finally, in 1992, the ten communities with restricted autonomy won the transfer of thirty-two additional powers previously held by the central state (such as education, social services, environmental policy, etc.).

The process of equalizing conditions is the result of two factors. The first has to do with the central state's constant effort to take back with one hand what it granted with the other, in other words reducing the gap between the historical nationalities and the other communities. This goal should not be interpreted solely in terms of Machiavellian calculations. It also reflects the modern state's persistent concern for rationalizing its action by delegating identical powers to intermediary levels of government.

This tendency is reinforced by another factor: the mimetic effect that the historical nationalities' "privileged status" exercises on the other communities. The latter are in fact not satisfied with a second-rate autonomy and yearn to have the same powers as their elders. To deflect criticism from those who would justify preferential treatment of historical nationalities in the name of their strong identity, leaders of other autonomous communities have strived to cultivate a sense of regional attachment, drawing on the institutional apparatus now at their disposal. In Asturias as in Aragon, local dialects—*bable* and *fabla*—have been revived while Extremadura contrives to build its own identity on the legacy of the Conquistadors.

As a reaction, this tendency toward institutional equalization recurrently provokes demands on the part of the historical nationalities for the transfer of additional powers that benefit them alone, for they refuse to be put on the same level as "ordinary regions" such as Castile and León or Murcia. Oddly enough, the structural asymmetry between communities has managed to remain in place due to the weight of peripheral nationalisms in the Spanish legislature. In the 1990s, the political parties in office in Madrid, the socialist PSOE (1982–96), and then José María Aznar's Partido Popular (1996–2004), having only a relative majority in the Cortes, were forced to seek the legislative support of nationalist parties.

The Catalan Convergence and Union coalition exacted a heavy price for its support, winning a set of concessions, the most significant being the automatic assignment by the state of 30% of the income tax revenue to the autonomous communities. This provision of course mainly benefits the wealthier communities, such as Catalonia, and therefore reintroduces a regional imbalance, even if provisions are made for complex compensation mechanisms.

From 2004 to 2011, the Socialist José Luis Zapatero, who ended up heading a minority government, was once again obliged to seek support from nationalist parties on certain issues. In exchange, Catalonia won a new statute of autonomy in 2006, defining it as a nation in its preamble. This status reinforces its autonomy, even in certain sectors that fall under external relations.[23]

Finally, federalism, as much as it may respect specificities, is not enough to stave off clearly separatist nationalist dynamics. Theoretically, asymmetry should keep the federated entity within the federation by granting it additional autonomy. In practice, the opposite is to be feared, for a political reason that has been analyzed in depth with regard to Canada but which is also applicable to other cases.[24]

If considerable powers were devolved to Quebec alone, its political weight at the federal level would inevitably decline, because its representatives in the Parliament of Canada would no longer be able to vote on issues that fall exclusively to the National Assembly of Quebec. Such loss of parliamentary influence would result in a similar contraction of power at the government level and in the federal civil service. In that case, the additional autonomy won by the Quebecois, far from encouraging them to remain firmly tied to the Canadian federation, would push them to detach themselves further from a center where their presence would have shrunk considerably. In this regard, "massive devolution of exclusive powers to the government of Quebec alone would not dry up the sources of Quebec secessionism. On the contrary... extensive asymmetry would only be the last step before separation."[25] The pernicious effect of differentiated federalism does not, on the contrary, justify maintaining the status quo, but it highlights the fact that the risk of being caught between a rock and a hard place is real indeed and that the specter of the country's partition will not be vanquished by it.

For those who are convinced of the righteousness of their separatist cause, no form of asymmetry, however considerable, will ever replace the goal of total self-determination with the creation of an independent state. This has been seen to be true in Spain, where despite a highly favorable statute that gives the three Basque provinces virtual fiscal independence[26] and confers a broad scope of powers on the Basque police, kidnappings and deadly bomb attacks perpetrated by the ETA even in the Spanish capital did not cease after democracy was instituted. Indeed, they skyrocketed between 1995 and 1998 before the ETA declared a ceasefire, which was soon broken. It was not until autumn 2011 that the Basque organization announced a permanent ceasefire that might mean it is finally abandoning armed struggle. This situation is the consequence of two factors. First, the Spanish security forces' relentless fight against the ETA and the legal action taken against the various incarnations of Batasuna, its legal front banned in 2003, have dealt heavy blows to the independence movement. Furthermore, the 2009 regional elections produced a non-nationalist Basque government (a coalition of socialists and conservatives) for the first time since 1980, showing that the nationalists are no longer automatically handed the political leadership of the autonomous community.

What conclusion can be drawn as regards the advantage of federalism for multination states? The picture is clearly a mixed one. On one hand, "federalism seems the ideal mechanism for accommodating territorially defined national minorities." On the other, "unfortunately, though, it is no solution to national divisions within a multination state."[27]

Undeniable Success Stories

Federalism in fact is highly effective as long as internal divisions do not run too deep. This is primarily the case when a "plural nation" is based on cross-cutting cleavages, in other words multiple fractures that do not intersect, as in Switzerland. Federalism was introduced in 1848 as a solution of compromise after the short civil war pitting conservative Catholic cantons against liberal Protestant cantons.

This religious conflict did not map onto the cleavage between the two main linguistic groups, German-speaking and French-speaking, distributed across the two camps. Fribourgeois and Lucerners, although speaking different languages, shared the same attachment to Catholicism, while Genevans and Zurichers were attached to the Protestant reform. In other words, not all the Protestants were francophones, nor all the Catholics German-speakers, and vice versa. Furthermore, with the strengthening of modern political parties, all the Swiss are divided up into various political allegiances. Cantonal attachment also functions as a form of local citizenship that is more relevant than belonging to a linguistic group.

This abundance of cleavages has been an essential factor in the proper functioning of federalism. Political majorities are formed according to different configurations each time depending on the type of question posed. The secularization process has also helped to reduce the importance of the religious dimension, while the linguistic variable has gained in significance, fostering a binary logic between the French and German speakers. The clearest illustration of this phenomenon was the vote on Switzerland's adhesion to the European Economic Area, which came within a whisker of passing in 1992, the French-speaking cantons being largely in favor whereas the German-speaking cantons (plus Italian-speaking Ticino) were against. Despite the growing relevance of the linguistic factor, however, the persistence of other divisions continues to have a positive impact on the functioning of federalism.[28]

The second case to which federalism is particularly well suited pertains to situations where the state has to deal with regionalist claims that are not strictly speaking nationalist. There appears to be a subtle gradient leading from regionalism to nationalism, and yesterday's regionalism can be tomorrow's nationalism. Yet it is worth distinguishing between the two phenomena, not so much in terms of content (regionalist claims are not necessarily "poorer" and can also have a strong ethno-cultural dimension), but rather by their modes of political action. Regionalists will more readily accept the general political framework than nationalist currents do, the latter disputing the existing state order with greater ferocity.

India offers an example of a country where regionalism has in general been fairly well channeled.[29] The formula lies in the successful conversion of British territorial federalism, which disregarded the large cultural areas, into a multination federalism in the 1950s and 1960s. Six of the new federated states were created on the basis of regional languages: Andhra Pradesh (Telugu-speaking), Tamil Nadu (Tamil), Kerala (Malayalam), Karnataka (Kannada), Maharashtra (Marathi) and Gujarat (Gujarati). By creating administrative divisions on the basis of linguistic criteria, regionalist aspirations were given a territorial base. They were thus sufficiently legitimated to prevent them from being tempted to engage in confrontation with the central authorities. The strategy failed, however, in northern India with the Sikhs, and the creation in 1966 of a "federated Sikh state," Punjab, did nothing to prevent the rise of terrorist separatism. The reasons for this failure are complex and lie in New Delhi's inflexible policies, the political exploitation of Sikhism by the local elites and the support lavished on the most extremist movements by the Sikh diaspora in Canada and the United Kingdom. In this context of intense nationalist mobilization, where the demand for a sovereign state became unremitting, federalism seemed terribly uninspired and in any event incapable of stemming the growing politicization of Sikh identity.

On the other hand, with federalism, India again found a means of settling another type of identity claim satisfactorily: that of its indigenous peoples. The Indian tribal population has a dual particularity. First, regarding its origin: they are aboriginal peoples, inhabiting "ancestral lands" well before conquests and colonization took place, and they conserve the memory of their earliest presence. The second particularity is socio-economic in nature: the indigenous peoples have been subjected by more recent populations as well as the state to a systematic policy of dispossession and discrimination and have ended up totally marginalized economically and culturally. Restoring the dignity to which they legitimately aspire involves respecting their right to self-determination, which assumes that they be allowed to govern themselves. From this perspective, federalism would appear to be an appropriate solution to give the indigenous peoples substantial autonomy and equal representation in the existing political framework.

This is precisely what the central government of India did for the northeastern tribes by breaking up Assam, at the border of China and Burma, to form three new states (Nagaland, Mizoram, Meghalaya) on a tribal basis. In 2000, two new states were created in central India (Jharkhand, Chhattisgarh), also on a tribal basis, by re-dividing two existing federated states. The same principle was adopted by Canada, which since 1 April 1999 has a new territory—Nunavut—the land of the Inuit in the Canadian Arctic. The government in Ottawa redrew the federation's internal borders to enable 25,000 Inuit to manage their own affairs with an elected assembly and an executive. In both cases, federalism made it possible to honor the indigenous peoples' need for political recognition while maintaining a stable link with the federal center on which these peoples remain heavily dependent, particularly from a financial standpoint.

However, in deeply divided societies that are subject to strong nationalist mobilizations, federalism is only a precarious solution. In Belgium, federalization may have salvaged the state, but it has not put an end to centrifugal tendencies. Hardly had the federal reform of the state been completed when some Flemish officials demanded a confederal arrangement. One may as well say that such an outcome would mean the end of Belgium, as a confederation is a voluntary association of sovereign states with confederal institutions holding limited powers. Historically, in the United States as in Switzerland, confederalism was the precursor to federalism, in other words a deeper union. Reversing the terms of the equation would mean using confederalism as a means to ensure a "soft" secession. There is thus every reason to believe that such a confederalism of "repudiation" would be rejected by the party on which it would be imposed (Wallonia in Belgium, English-speaking Canada).

As appealing as the formulas of sovereignty-association or sovereignty-partnership may seem to the Quebecois nationalists because they combine political sovereignty for Quebec and preservation of an economic union with the rest of Canada,[30] they are on the whole rejected in English-speaking Canada, where the feeling is that if Quebec were to exit the federation, it would have to assume its responsibilities in full, and couldn't also count on a basically utilitarian association. To put it in more figurative language: once the marriage is dissolved, divorce cannot go together with cohabitation. When constant renegotiations of the federal pact fail, secession becomes a very real prospect.

8

THE SECESSIONIST TEMPTATION

Secession: the word is frightening as it immediately calls forth images of the terrible conflict between the southern Confederates and the northern Federalists that tore the United States apart between 1861 and 1865, immortalized by David Griffith in his film *The Birth of a Nation*. In the Civil War, the first military confrontation in the age of the masses, families fought against families. Due to the closeness of those involved in the clash, it was one of extreme violence. It meant unbinding what had been brought together, dissociating those who had been bound together, separating fellow citizens. This dramatic precedent has nourished considerable wariness toward any secessionist movement, automatically perceived as warmongering. The very nature of the modern state, for which territory is the natural and obvious anchor, makes it a god that jealously guards each and every scrap of its territory. This exclusive conception contrasts with those in vogue in empires and traditional monarchies.

Empires were based on a blueprint for civilization with a universal dimension. They pursued an expansionist process that was by definition resistant to territorial stability and in particular to the demarcation of fixed borders. Empires were encompassed by *limes* or *marches*, dependent principalities that were all highly mobile areas of transition. Monarchies during the feudal era remained trapped in a perspective of succession in which estate and kingdom tended to blend into one, the monarch disposing of portions of territory at will. Even when the inalienability of the crown estate was established (as in France with the Edict of Moulins in 1566), crown property could be ceded voluntarily, by the system of appanage, for the needs of war, or by force, after a military defeat.

It is doubtful that either empires or traditional monarchies ever gave land up readily, but at the same time such cessions did not cause the deep trauma that they invariably do today for states embodying a national ideology. When they must relinquish territory (as France did with Alsace-Moselle after 1870), this severance affects that nation at its very heart, for in a way it reduces its materiality. For empires and monarchies, the civilizing mission and dynastic principle serve as the main modes of legitimation and considerably diminish the negative impact of territorial amputation.

Conversely, because territory is the central element of nation-state legitimacy, nation-states are basically conservative and are moved to anger whenever the sanctity of their borders is threatened. Their leaders on the other hand seem far less particular when it comes to carving up empires. In scarcely more than a century, between the proclamation of Greece's independence in 1830 and the signing of peace treaties in 1920 in the wake of the First World War, the entire European continent east of a line running more or less from Bremen to Nice underwent unprecedented upheaval, with the emergence of a dozen new states.

Except for Italy and Germany, which achieved sovereignty in 1870 by a process of unification, all the other states created in this period came into being through the reverse process of breaking up two imperial structures, first the Ottoman Empire (Greece, Serbia, Bulgaria, Romania) and then Austria-Hungary (Poland, Czechoslovakia, Yugoslavia). The advent of these states was the result of clearly secessionist dynamics, as the aim was to break with the existing imperial order—to the point of bringing about the disappearance of a centuries-old state in the case of the Austro-Hungarian Empire. These separation processes, however, were looked upon with favor because they were undertaken in the name of peoples' freedom from despotism, of the oriental variety in Istanbul and the Catholic variety in Vienna. The dismantling of these empires was done according to a revolutionary principle, the self-determination of peoples.

The Ambiguities of the Principle of Self-Determination

An defining cause for nineteenth-century national movements, themselves stimulated by the ideology of national sovereignty embodied by the French Revolution, the idea of self-determination signifies each people freely choosing its political status. Behind its apparent simplicity, this principle raises huge difficulties in implementation, the most fearsome due to the undefined nature of the notion of "a people". As Ivor Jennings remarks regarding the principle of self-determination, "On the surface it seemed reasonable: let the people decide. It was in fact ridiculous because the people cannot decide until somebody decides who are the people."[1]

Should it have objective characteristics (language, history, religion, etc.)? If so, the Chuvash of Russia, the Hausa of West Africa as well as the indigenous peoples of the Americas can claim the right to self-determination, which implies, one might remember, the prospect of forming an independent state. Favoring instead a subjective definition of people as a gathering of individuals united by the desire to share a common destiny, is it justifiable to grant the right of self-determination to the people of Fiji, Cape Verde or Monaco and deny it for the Kurds and the Tibetans?

To shed at least some of the ambiguity, rules had to be defined to specify which peoples were eligible to embark on a process of self-determination. This notion of self-determination was the brainchild of US President Woodrow Wilson, who pictured its achievement through the "principle of nationalities." The aim was for peoples of Eastern Europe that could be identified by national criteria (language, history, etc.) to take their political destinies in hand. The new states were thus to correspond to peoples defined on an ethno-cultural basis. Wilson's famous "Fourteen Points," outlined in January 1918, left no doubt about this ethnic-based logic, as the reconstituted Polish state was to include "the territories inhabited by indisputably Polish populations" while "the frontiers of Italy should be drawn according to clearly recognizable lines of nationality." That was of course easier said than done, because the commingling of populations made it impossible to draw clear and precise lines of demarcation between them to match state with nationality.

Applying the principle of national self-determination in such a patchwork of peoples carried huge dangers that Wilson's own secretary of state, Robert Lansing, grasped immediately with remarkable prescience. In December 1918 he wrote in his diary, "There are certain phrases in the President's 'Fourteen Points' which I am sure will cause trouble in the future because their meaning and application have not been thought out.... When the President talks of 'self-determination' what unit has he in mind? Does he mean a race, a territorial area, or a community? Without a definite unit which is practical, application of this principle is dangerous to peace and stability... The phrase is simply loaded with dynamite. It will raise hopes which can never be realized. It will, I fear, cost thousands of lives."[2] Events would tragically prove this analysis to be premonitory. The new states (Poland, Romania, etc.) would invoke self-determination to assert their national exclusivism in the face of minorities on their territories, as would those defeated in the Great War (Hungary, Germany) engaged in irredentist strategies to recover their lost "nationals." Hitler's shameless manipulation of the principle of self-determination to justify his expansionist policies so as to include in the Reich ethnic Germans in Austria and Sudetenland would lead the international community to revise its interpretation of the doctrine after 1945.

At first merely a political principle, it has become a confirmed right mentioned in the Charter of the United Nations as well as in international declarations and conventions. Even if the exact legal implications of this right are far from clear, it has become a basic tenet of international law. At the same time, the promotion of self-determination was accompanied by a redefinition of its beneficiaries. To avoid the destabilizing effect of Nazi Germany's use of the principle in the lead-up to the Second World War, peoples' right to decide their own future is no longer recognized for nations (in the ethno-cultural sense) following Wilsonian logic, but only for peoples who have been deprived of free self-determination by colonialism.

Only peoples colonized by Western powers (with whom Palestinians under Israeli occupation and the Blacks of South Africa have been assimilated) can, in the eyes of the law, legitimately shake free from what is considered foreign political domination and form an independent state.[3] People entitled to self-determination are defined on a strictly territorial basis. For instance, it was not the Baoulé, Agni and Bété peoples who were allowed the right to self-determination to free themselves from French colonization, but the people of Côte d'Ivoire; in other words, all the colony's inhabitants. The principle of the sanctity of borders handed down from the colonial period is a natural consequence of the territorial definition of self-determination.

Between Wilson's "Fourteen Points" and the development of the UN legal arsenal, the basis for application of the self-determination principle has in fact shifted from ethnic and cultural identities to territorial boundaries.[4] It should also be pointed out that in international law, overseas colonies are not part of the national territory of the state that administers them. Their accession to independence thus cannot be interpreted as secession; rather it implies the restoration of a sovereign political capacity that the colonial power had usurped.

Furthermore, the right to self-determination is valid for a single use only. Once it has come into effect within the framework of the colonial administrative boundaries, it cannot be legally claimed by peoples that are part of an independent state seeking their own self-emancipation. Thus the right to secession is not recognized within constituted states, and such states are entitled to defend their territorial integrity, by force if necessary. This interdict explains the failure of the attempted secessions of Katanga (1960–3) and Biafra (1967–70) after most of the world's states refused to recognize them. Up until the early 1990s, the only victorious secession was that of East Pakistan in 1971, which owed its success to a particular geopolitical context (the province had been geographically separated from West Pakistan by 1,700 km since 1947) and specific political circumstances (Indian military support for the revolt).

The fact that international law opposes self-determination by secession[5] is not enough to quell separatist ambitions. These are expressed through violence the world over, in Senegalese Casamance, in the Kurdish regions of Turkey, in Corsica, and so on. The scenario is invariably the same: on one side are the separatists, who are involved in a strategy of armed struggle and/or terrorism, on the other is the state, which responds with crackdowns that are more or less subject to constitutional oversight and more rarely with offers to negotiate. It is not surprising that many secessionist movements involve armed clashes, as states are by nature fiercely determined to defend their sovereignty over the entire national territory.

Negotiate Secession?

Tipping into violence is in no way inevitable. Successful secessions exist: those that have been negotiated.

Domestic law rarely contains provisions for secession procedures because states live with the illusion that they will endure. How many constituent assemblies mention the nation's perpetuity in the preambles to their constitutions, without even envisaging that it could one day come apart? Some federal constitutions exceptionally carry a clause specifying the mechanisms for exiting the federation. This was the case of the Brezhnev constitution of 1977, which enshrined the republics' right to secede under certain conditions from the Soviet Union, defined as a multinational federal state. This right was of course purely theoretical in the age of communist totalitarianism, but its mere existence nevertheless lent legal legitimacy to the peaceful dissolution of the USSR in December 1991.

On the other hand, the invocation of this right by the four federated republics of Yugoslavia (Slovenia, Croatia, Bosnia, Macedonia) to justify their exit from the federation was entirely debatable from a legal standpoint.

While the preamble to the constitution of 1974 indeed mentioned "the right of each people to self-determination, including the right to secede," this basic principle needs to be interpreted in light of the articles of the constitution. Article 5 unambiguously stipulates, "the borders of the Socialist Federal Republic of Yugoslavia may not be altered without the consent of all the republics and autonomous provinces." By exiting the federation unilaterally, the four republics could well claim political legitimacy (declaration of sovereignty of parliaments, people's referendums in favor of independence) but certainly not legal justification.

The constitutional right to secede being an exception—today only Ethiopia and Saint Kitts and Nevis, an island state in the Caribbean, recognize this right—successful secession (smooth transition, good neighbor relations between successor states) will above all depend on the clear and unambiguous decision of all parties in favor of a peaceful negotiation process. While contractual secession processes are less frequent than those of a violent nature, they have a distinct advantage over the latter. They more easily achieve their objective, which is to split from the state. Whereas the Biafra rebellion was mercilessly crushed and many secessionist movements are sapped by an armed struggle that is as murderous as the outcome is uncertain,[6] some states have won independence without a drop of bloodshed.

In 1905, Norway put an end to the union it formed with Sweden in 1814 without meeting any opposition. A referendum in Norway nearly unanimously approved the breakup. The two governments subsequently negotiated the precise terms of the separation. Similarly, Iceland broke away from Denmark in 1944 after a referendum in which nearly 99% of voters approved the end of a union that had lasted for over five and a half centuries.

Referendum may theoretically seem to be a promising technique, as the people who supposedly want to secede are consulted democratically. When they come out overwhelmingly in favor of secession, as they did in the two Nordic countries, there are no grounds for dispute. Things are less clear when the issue is disputed, as it was in Montenegro. This former Yugoslav republic remained tied to Serbia when all the others had opted for independence. During the first decade of the 2000s, the separatist current gained strength, but it had a tough opponent to contend with. To settle the debate, the option of referendum was chosen, but the Montenegrin parliament, pressured by the European Union, passed a referendum law not only requiring that 50% of registered voters participate, but also that 55% of voters choose separation for it to take effect. In May 2006, 55.5% of voters answered "yes" to ending the union with Serbia.

Is it legitimate to require a qualified majority for secession, as was the case in Montenegro? I believe so, in that dissolution of the political bond in a state is a momentous decision in regard to which citizens should express their opinion clearly. The Canadian federal government adopted this stance by passing the Clarity Act in March 2000, following an opinion of the Supreme Court. Two principles stipulated in the law make it admissible: the clear wording of a question concerning secession and its scope, and the expression of a specific majority in favor of secession. These were included to avoid a repetition of the Quebec referendum of 1995, when in answer to the question of Quebec's accession to sovereignty, combined with an offer of partnership with Canada, 49.4% had answered "yes" and 50.6% "no."[7]

However, the way these principles are applied in law can hardly be deemed acceptable. The legislation leaves it up to the House of Commons in Ottawa to determine whether the referendum question is clear. In other words, the decision is placed in the hands of a political majority. It would have been ever so much more logical to entrust the power of such a verdict to a judicial authority such as the Supreme Court. Second, in the event a referendum is held, it is once again up to the House of Commons, following the vote, to decide whether a clear majority had expressed itself, but without the law stipulating what that entails. This amounts to giving the parliament the discretionary power of validating the outcome of a referendum, which hardly seems democratic.

With a proper framework, a referendum is a fully legitimate instrument of public consultation to conduct a peaceful secession or, more exceptionally, to endorse secession achieved by force of arms. A case in point can be found in South Sudan where, after a long armed struggle waged by the south against the north between 1983 and 2005, the peace agreement concluded in Nairobi made it possible to implement a staged process of dissociation that would lead to a referendum on self-determination for South Sudan. In January 2011, by an overwhelming majority, the South Sudanese chose independence, and in July of that year a new state came into being.

Yet there are equally cases in which the division of a state occurs smoothly by carefully circumventing the obstacle of referendum, as in Czechoslovakia. Unlike the fall of the communist regime in late 1989, accompanied by large-scale demonstrations, the country's division into two independent states in January 1993 owed little to mass mobilization, as it was the work of political elites who negotiated the split, taking care to avoid consulting the citizenry. The population, moreover, would certainly have opposed dissolution of the Czechoslovakian federation. In June 1990, only 6% favored this option. Two years later, despite a context of growing political polarization, only 16% approved this choice.

Yet the breakup took place anyway, peacefully, within an extremely short lapse of time. Even if endless and fruitless constitutional debates on reforming the federation had begun in the spring of 1990, the division of the country did not become a likely prospect until the June 1992 elections. It was organized in the space of six months. This very short time frame may seem surprising, but the swiftness of the secession no doubt guaranteed its success.[8]

Divorce, even when amicable, inevitably ushers in a time of anxiety and change, as the two partners give up their present certainty—certain even with the attendant difficulties—for future uncertainty. To ward off these fears and prevent them from enduring, a quick separation is preferable so that the divorce proceedings do not drag on. It also avoids persistent tensions and repeated pressures.

This is precisely the scenario that was adopted in the case of Czechoslovakia, and the absence of the people's direct involvement, as they were not consulted on the wisdom of the separation, undeniably helped make the procedure a smooth one. The federation's citizens had moved for decades within a common public arena and some were understandably attached to it. It would have been democratically appropriate for them to be approached. At the same time, opening a vast public debate followed by a referendum, amid a totally paralyzed political situation at the federal level (government deadlock, President Havel's resignation), would inevitably have blown the issues out of proportion, thus inflaming the situation. To prevent it from festering, the decision to put negotiations between the prime ministers of the two federated entities (Václav Klaus for the Czechs, Vladimír Mečiar for the Slovaks) on a fast track while observing the rules set out in the constitution—the federal parliament orchestrated its own demise by voting to dissolve the federation—proved to be the wisest solution.

Two essential factors facilitate secession by mutual consent. The first is a democratic-liberal context that encourages the search for negotiated compromises and precludes recourse to violence. In a state where repression is institutionalized and the ordinary form of government is authoritarian, it comes as no surprise that the state resorts to force to crush secessionist movements (Saddam Hussein's Iraq against the Kurds, Marxist-Leninist Ethiopia against Eritrea). On the other hand, when a country's political culture is firmly established on democratic foundations, there is theoretically no reason for secession not to be settled through negotiation, as are social conflicts and political disagreements. Imbued with a strong liberal tradition, Sweden took this route with Norway, and Denmark did the same with Iceland in 1944. Canada and Belgium are poised to continue in this vein in the event that Quebec and Flanders opt for separation.

This liberal legacy can be invoked only very indirectly in the case of Czechoslovakia, the successful separation of which was due to the second basic element: the gradual disintegration of the federal center, the only power that might have been in a position to stave off centrifugal tendencies. In the course of the two years leading up to the final split, the federal government had gradually grown weaker, whereas the power of the two federated republics became stronger. Symptomatic of this power shift was the growing influence of the Czech and the Slovak prime ministers—who would be the architects of separation—as the federal leaders watched their capacity for action shrink by the day. In a sense, the advent of two sovereign states in January 1993 was but the formalization of a dissociation of political spheres that was already well underway.

The growing deficiency of the political center was also a feature in the case of the Soviet Union and played a key role in the smooth division of the USSR into fifteen independent states. Viewed as a means to reform the socialist system and renew its effectiveness, *perestroïka* actually precipitated a wholesale crisis. It particularly kindled effervescence in the "peripheral nations," especially in the Baltic states and in the Caucasus. But the final blow to the communist autocracy came from Russia's return to front stage.

Far larger and more populated than all the other federated republics, Russia had the least autonomy in the Soviet system because many of "its" institutions (e.g. the Academy of Sciences, certain ministries, the Communist Party) were actually confounded with those of the federation in its entirety. By restoring Russia's sovereignty in June 1990, the Russian president, Boris Yeltsin, put an end to this anomaly, but as a result deprived the Soviet center of part of its institutional infrastructure. Soviet institutions were gradually drained of their substance, and when the center attempted to react, as in January 1991 when the Soviet special forces intervened in Latvia to put a stop to the republic's independence movement, it was too late. The failed coup of August 1991, fomented by rearguard communists, put an end once and for all to any hope of preserving the Soviet empire. The center, once so powerful, had disintegrated, paving the way for the USSR's gentle implosion. This retraction of the center is an essential element in explaining the peaceful nature of the crumbling of authoritarian states (or even their embarking on a democratic transition). Yugoslavia, however, provides a counter-example.

Here, too, the federation had been slipping into a crisis in the late 1980s, but unlike the USSR, where Russia, the centerpiece of the institutional framework, arose as an alternative to the Soviet center, Serbia did not choose to bypass or weaken the federal power. This was for two reasons.

First, the Serbs were overrepresented among the federal civil as well as military ruling elites. For utilitarian reasons, the Serbs thus had a strong attachment to the federation as a whole.[9] Second, among the constituent peoples of Yugoslavia, the Serb people was the most scattered throughout the national territory: 40% lived outside the Republic of Serbia. The Serbs thus viewed the federal state as the structure best suited to their situation of dispersal and considered the transformation of the federated republics into independent states to be a threat to the Serbian minorities beyond the Drina. Certain measures passed by Croatia (regarding the coat of arms, the language and the constitutional status of the Serbs) helped to sustain Serb anxieties that their president, Slobodan Milošević, was determined to exploit in his strategy of exacerbated nationalism. Far from leaving the federal center in a state of dereliction, the Serbs seized upon it as a means of combating centrifugal tendencies through war. The stage was set for the breakup of Tito's Yugoslavia to be achieved by violent means. Yugoslavia fits the classical model of contested secessions in which the desire for separation of a segment of the state's population meets with strong opposition.

Does that mean that unilateral secessions are necessarily debatable, even unlawful? Certainly not, and one line of argument in terms of ethics could provide useful insight into the discussion. Two distinct approaches have come to light.[10] For some, secession is an inalienable right belonging to any group in a given territory that is in a position to constitute a majority favoring separation from an established state. The right to secede is thus seen as a primary right that requires no justification whatsoever to be implemented. There is no need to invoke discrimination or a history of injustice. The group in question need not even claim a specific collective identity based on a common culture, language, or memory. The individuals that form such a group have the right to exit a given political association to form another in the name of their autonomy.

Many scholars challenge this ultraliberal conception and view secession instead solely as a remedial right that can only be exercised in a context of persistent iniquities. From this standpoint it emerges as a last resort when the political contract can abide no further revision. The philosopher Allen Buchanan, who has contributed extensively to renewing theoretical reflection on this issue, identified twelve arguments for the morality of secession, four of them truly decisive: systematically discriminatory resource allocation, flagrant political injustice (whether violation of political rights or the forced incorporation of a group into a state by annexation of its territory), serious threats to the group's culture, and mortal threats to its physical survival.[11]

Economicide, politicide, ethnocide, genocide: faced with these perils, any group has a moral right to secede. This more restrictive approach is, I believe, far more realistic than the previous one. Because any secession has momentous consequences (territorial alterations, establishment of new international boundaries, market splitting, redefinition of the contours of citizenship, etc.), and because many state breakups have been accompanied by massacres and violence, it is perfectly legitimate for such an event to take place within a carefully defined framework.

Secession should theoretically be implemented according to strict rules of procedure: prior negotiation of how to divide up state assets, public debt, guarantees for the minorities produced by secession; referendum, possibly with a qualified majority, if secession is disputed by the established state. But separation from the central state should also be justified by a particularly unfavorable political context. If such conditions are lacking, the risk of dissidence will be unduly multiplied, consequently having a destabilizing effect on the international system.

Secession: A Permanent Source of Instability?

Secession is not the magic solution some invoke, saying that if two peoples cannot manage to live together, all they have to do is part ways for everything to fall back into place. In reality, implementing dissociation is not always simpler than organizing association. It first raises the tricky question of how to divide the states spawned by the disintegration of a single political entity. Where should the borders be drawn?

The Arbitration Commission on Yugoslavia presided by the French lawyer Robert Badinter, after recognizing that the country was in the process of breaking apart, concluded that the boundaries between the federated entities should become international borders.[12] The principle of the sanctity of borders adopted in the context of decolonization was thus extended to the disintegration of sovereign states. The rationale behind this reasoning by analogy is clear: to find a means of regulating self-determination to prevent the advent of new states from producing more border disputes. The fact remains that the widespread application of the sanctity principle is far from self-evident, for two main reasons.

The first is that internal administrative boundaries are *ipso facto* turned into international borders. Should boundaries deemed legitimate in the domestic legal order recognized by all retain such legitimacy when the encompassing state comes apart? When the original political compact that bound citizens together is broken, why should the internal territorial division necessarily be maintained? Should it not be renegotiated? These questions cannot be given a straightforward answer and a distinction must be made. When administrative boundaries match long-standing historical boundaries, they acquire a strong presumption of legitimacy. This is the case regarding the border between Slovakia and the Czech lands as well as between Croatia and its neighbors, except in Eastern Slavonia.

Things are different when the administrative boundaries were drawn for strategic purposes, as when Tito invented the Republic of Macedonia in 1945 to restrict Serbia's territorial base. The same highly political logic prevailed in the Sovietization of Central Asia, the borders of which "[had] no rationality, whether geographic, economic or ethnic," but instead abided by a very clear Machiavellian principle: to ensure that "none of the new republics is really viable on its own, and thus capable of independence."[13] When borders are arbitrary and absurd to this extent, there is no reason why they should not be subject to a negotiated revision to make them consistent with a certain logic, whether in terms of function or of substance, taking into account historical factors, ethnic composition, and so on.

The second reason that application of the border sanctity principle to imploding states is debatable lies in an important theoretical contradiction. Progress toward secession generally is made in the name of a pre-political, historical-cultural identity. Claims to national self-determination of the Estonian, Slovenian or Armenian people are made because they are communities bound by a specific language, tradition and culture. Yet when it comes to defining the territorial basis of the nation, nationalist leaders readily put forward administrative boundaries, especially when these borders provide the state with a more comfortable territorial base.

Thus the Republic of Croatia was declared by virtue of "the millennial national identity of the Croatian nation," but the state's borders were not defined, to use Woodrow Wilson's expression, "along clearly recognizable lines of nationality." Instead, they simply coincided with the former boundaries of the Yugoslav republic. Its leaders invoked both national self-determination to justify separation from the common state and territorial self-determination to fix the borders of the breakaway state. Therein lay an inconsistency, which the rump state generally did not fail to point out when demanding that the borders be redrawn to include as many of its nationals as possible within its territory. If unable to achieve this end through mutual agreement, the state in question will resort to war without reservation.

This is precisely the route that Serbia went down by launching military operations—using the federal army—so that the Serb rebels in Krajina and Eastern Slavonia (Croatian regions bordering Bosnia) would wind up under Serbian authority. Seen from Belgrade, the aim was to impose Serb self-determination by force in these regions by uniting them to the motherland. The objective inevitably necessitated a radical and merciless conquest to bring about the ethnic homogenization of these territories, which involved the massacre and expulsion of Croats, the systematic destruction of villages, and so on. This tragic scenario was repeated with magnified violence in Bosnia due to the commingling of populations.[14] The conversion of internal boundaries into international borders in reality thus often proves to be a complex and painful process. It only happens smoothly if the secessionist state has strong ethnic homogeneity, in which case (in Slovenia, for instance) it can avoid both internal dissent fomented by the new national minorities and intervention by the rump state to protect them.

Slovenia, however, is exceptional, and most of the time new states are as multiethnic as the ones they broke away from, with the risk of provoking "secessions from secessions," as was the case with the Serbs in Croatia and Bosnia. The temptation is then great to do away with the rebel minority, especially if its members themselves have taken part in blameworthy abuses. This is what happened with the Serbs in Krajina, driven to flee before the Croatian offensive of August 1995. However, even if mass population expulsions and displacements are not inevitable—the dramatic turn taken by the breakup of the Yugoslav federation owes much to the Serbian government's cynical political exploitation of it—the sudden, almost overnight change in status that turns a former majority into a minority in the new political framework is a cause for apprehension that is not always unjustified as regards citizenship rights or access to employment.

To dissipate such fears, it is essential for the new state to grant specific rights to its minorities concerning the use of its language and a specific school system, for instance, and to energetically enforce them. The transformation is all the harder to accept if the new minority has a strong collective identity, such as the Serbs of Croatia, Orthodox Christians in a Catholic environment, who have always enjoyed considerable autonomy within the military borderlands (*krajina*), where they had been placed by the Habsburgs to protect the empire from the Turks.

That said, even if the conversion of internal boundaries into state borders has many serious drawbacks, it has one distinct advantage. It eliminates the need to draw a new border. Indeed, such an operation is never easy, even when it takes place in an atmosphere of good will. Where should the new frontier lie? If the criterion is ethnic, what cutoff point will be used to alter the border? Should there have been more than 75% of Serbs in the districts of Krajina for them to be united with Bosnia's Serb entity? Or would more than 50% have been enough? What about the Croats and other groups in these areas? Would they have been satisfied with minority status? Is a population swap the answer? Dividing up a territory in an area where people have lived together and mixed for centuries is impossible to achieve without unleashing violence, as the Bosnian ordeal made clear.

The partition of British India in August 1947 on the basis of the Two-Nation theory (one for Muslims, the other with a Hindu majority) offers another dreadful illustration. The commission in charge of drawing the borders decided on the following rule: all regions in which the population was over 50% Muslim would become part of Pakistan. This meant dividing up in particular two large states: Bengal to the east and Punjab to the west. Bengal, which had a very strong cultural specificity, was divided, placing its major city, Calcutta, under Indian sovereignty and cutting it off totally from its rural hinterland, now East Pakistan.

The division of Punjab was far more dramatic, as it completely shattered the cohesion of a society based on the cohabitation of three communities: Muslim, Hindu, and Sikh. The consequences of this absurd decision are well known: nearly 15 million refugees in both directions; at least 500,000 dead, victims of systematic killings or of exhaustion during forced marches; incalculable damage and pillage of property; women raped, and so on.[15] If only this horrendous human price had been the end of it—but this was not the case. Partition, which literally involves the carving up of a territory and the vivisection of a social unit, often perpetuates two types of problems.

The first is due to the demonstration effect secession can have on newly independent states.[16] These are not born "pure and innocent." They bear the stigmas of the original trauma. India, for instance, opted at first for an all-embracing definition of citizenship that included the Muslim minority (150 million strong today) that had not migrated to Pakistan. It thus chose to preserve the religious pluralism that had prevailed in British India. But this plan encountered increasing opposition from the Hindu nationalists[17] who in a way took hold of the two-nation theory initially advocated by the promoters of Pakistan, turning it against Indian Muslims: Pakistan, a Muslim state, now stands in opposition to a Hindu India.[18]

The feedback effect has been even more spectacular in the case of Pakistan. The new state was theoretically supposed to have a major asset in its "national" homogeneity, as the population was almost exclusively Muslim. Yet subsequent events showed that the idea of founding a nation on Islam was unrealistic. In 1971, East Pakistan, having a strong Bengali identity, seceded to create Bangladesh, but the domino effect did not stop there. Pakistan is still wrought by assertive regionalisms, even nationalisms (in Sindh, Balochistan, in Pashtun areas bordering Afghanistan), spurred by Punjabi domination of the state, as the Mohajirs (refugees who arrived with the 1947 partition) increasingly assert their own particularism.[19] Far from clarifying identity politics, partition merely further confused matters.

Similarly, after the disintegration of communist Yugoslavia, regionalism stirred in the formerly Italian peninsula of Istria in Croatia. At the same time, the new Republic of Yugoslavia,[20] unable to marshal support for a federating political agenda, found itself battling not only very active Albanian nationalism in Kosovo but the rise of autonomist sentiment among the Vojvodina Hungarians and, more worrisome for Belgrade, the increasingly clear assertion of Montenegrin nationalism, which ended up engaging in a successful secession process.

The second substantial problem raised by non-negotiated partitions and secessions is the fact that they often transform what was initially a domestic conflict arising from ethnic, religious or community strife into a confrontation between states. This change in the nature of the conflict is rarely a good thing. Suffice it to evoke the muted hostility between India and Pakistan since 1948, which has already led to three wars and perpetuates nagging armed tensions in Kashmir, all against a backdrop of a furious arms race and the nuclearization of the subcontinent, with the attendant risks of escalation and regional destabilization inherent in such a situation. The danger level of the conflict is rising because the two national groups now each have a state, with all that that implies in terms of the capacity to mobilize resources.

In a context of general crisis, the breakup of a state tends to favor the militarization of national conflicts and their entrenchment. Developments within the former Yugoslavia offer a tangible illustration of this law while innovating with regard to one essential aspect. The wars in Yugoslavia in fact were not only accompanied by classical internationalization of the conflict, with each party seeking military and political support from outside backers. They also induced a mysterious, multifaceted actor, "the international community," to intervene in various spheres (humanitarian, diplomatic, military, etc.) to guarantee the success of the national self-determination of peoples involved in dissociating themselves from a constituted state that was falling apart. That is the main point to be remembered here.

Secession and the Ethnicization of States

This attitude represents a radical change from the traditional stance taken by states, of great reluctance to back unilateral secession processes. While China and Russia resist such an evolution, Western states no longer have such scruples. It may be considered heartening to see it as a legitimate extension of the right to self-determination, which international law previously confined in large part to decolonization. Such newfound receptiveness, however, is offset by legal scruples that temper it, giving rise to increasing ambiguities and contradictions.

Thus, even though in Croatia's case its decision to exit the Yugoslav federation flowed from the Croatian people's desire for national emancipation, the "international community" officially recognized the right to self-determination for the people of the Republic of Croatia, in other words all citizens without distinction (Croats, Serbs, Muslims, Hungarians, etc.). The difference is an important one. First, it offered a means of skirting the fact that the largest minority, the Serbs (12%), who according to the Tito constitution were a constituent people of the republic on an equal footing with the Croats, rejected application of self-determination. Second, it took into account the previously mentioned concern for preserving Croatia's territorial integrity. National self-determination (in this case, for the Croats) thus lurked behind abstract sovereignist rhetoric (allusion to the citizenry and the territory of the republic).

The same ambiguity also reigned for a long time over Kosovo. The war waged by NATO against Yugoslavia in 1999—of questionable legality to say the least, as it was conducted without UN approval—was justified at the time by NATO Secretary-General Javier Solana, "as a moral duty... to stop an authoritarian regime from repressing its people in Europe at the end of the twentieth century." This intervention, once again, was a first, as a sovereign state was deliberately attacked in the name of the duty to interfere, because of a domestic policy issue. Diehard defenders of national sovereignty sharply criticized such an evolution, the principle behind which I personally find rather positive. Too many states have invoked the alibi of sovereignty simply to be able to perpetrate massacres at will. From this standpoint, it is no bad thing that states (or rather, their rulers) should be aware that they no long enjoy absolute impunity, but can be held accountable for their criminal acts.

At the end of the war, an international protectorate was set up with both a military presence (Kosovo Force, or KFOR, a NATO multinational armed force) and a civil authority (United Nations Interim Administration Mission in Kosovo, or UNMIK). Its mission was to engage a political process to determine the future status of Kosovo, taking into account the Rambouillet Accords of March 1999, rejected by the Serb party. The text provided for the establishment of "substantial autonomy for Kosovo," which was to take into account Yugoslavia's sovereignty and territorial integrity. Right from the start, the international community gave itself a mandate that was impossible to fulfill, for contradictions abound.

The first was logical in nature: how can one seriously invoke the magic words of "territorial integrity" regarding a country that has been bombarded for seventy-nine days and one of whose provinces is under a dual international protectorate? The second is political: even if military intervention was officially justified by the need to put a stop to Serb repression in Kosovo and the ensuing humanitarian catastrophe, it was also—and the Kosovars certainly interpreted it this way—an action in support of their long combat for self-determination.

Why was the Albanian population's aspiration to independence not granted right away? Certainly so as not to challenge unilaterally the international borders of a recognized country, even if it was perpetrating "ethnic cleansing" and repeatedly massacring civilians, as was the case of Yugoslavia under Milošević. Yet this intangibility of international borders did not work toward preserving the federation built by Tito—even though, constitutionally, the external borders couldn't be altered without consent of the constituent republics and autonomous provinces, thus making unilateral secession theoretically unlawful. The deadlock that gradually took hold of the federal institutions had probably made dissolution of the Yugoslav federation inevitable, but why recognize the right of peoples who had a republic, such as the Slovenes and the Croats, to shed a tattered federal bond and only half-heartedly grant it to the Albanians on the pretense that they merely had an autonomous province, even though its powers and rights were virtually identical to those of the six republics?[21]

Lastly, if the debate is posed in terms of a moral right to secession, the wait-and-see attitude of the "international community" becomes simply untenable.

The fetish of border sanctity leads to a paradox. The right of self-determination is recognized for Macedonians, who have a republic and a language codified thanks to Tito, and who resigned themselves to independence in 1991 because the Yugoslav federation was breaking up—but it is haggled over for Kosovars who, since their incorporation into Serbia in 1912, have never stopped campaigning in the name of nationhood to denounce that move. Yet if there were a people that could indisputably claim an ethical right to secede, it is indeed the Albanian people of Kosovo. Economically impoverished by massive layoffs in the civil service administrations and business, its culture has been endangered by school closings and strict control over means of communication and its political rights systematically violated. As if that were not enough, the Serbian authorities have launched into increasingly fierce repression, then undertaken wide-scale ethnic cleansing.[22]

In Kosovo, the international community invented "imitation" independence by making Kosovo look more and more like a sovereign state without it actually being one. The contradiction was untenable over the long term. Negotiations were held between the parties in 2006–7 in liaison with the Contact Group,[23] under the auspices of the US secretary-general's special envoy, the former Finnish president, Martti Ahtisaari. They came to naught, but the mediator nevertheless made his plan known, which drew the logical that the deadlock would endure. It was impossible to reintegrate Kosovo into Serbia, just as it could not be kept under international administration in the long term, and so the only realistic option left was independence under supervision.[24] In February 2008, Kosovo unilaterally declared its independence.[25]

This declaration officialized the province's secession, but it will not have full effect unless the UN member states consider it legitimate. Recognition by third parties is decisive for any new state, because it is tantamount to recognition of sovereignty. In this regard, for the moment Kosovo has only obtained partial recognition (by 111 countries in May 2015), which does not make it eligible for a seat at the UN, as China and Russia still do not recognize Kosovo's independence. Opponents to recognition include states that are viscerally attached to the principle of territorial integrity–many of them countries of the South—and those fearing that Kosovo could set a dangerous precedent justifying secessions in their own countries. The five EU states that have not recognized Kosovo (Cyprus, Greece, Spain, Romania, Slovakia) are in this category.

The mimetic effect of the Kosovo case should not be overstated, however. That the Kosovars obtained their own state does not mean that the Catalans or the Basques will follow suit.[26] Political reason should simply lead to admitting that at certain moments, some peoples can no longer live together. Establishing a border between two independent states then becomes the only way to quell hatred. Exceptional situations require exceptional solutions, even if that means deviating from the dogma of border sanctity.[27]

A contrario, that clearly means that the multiplication of states by division of existing political entities should not become the norm for settling national identity issues. Opposition to such a solution can be justified neither with the convenient taboo of sovereignty, too often used as an excuse to absolve reprehensible practices, nor by the concern to prevent an "anarchic" proliferation of states, which does not necessarily produce lasting instability.[28]

Instead, such reluctance is based on one fundamental consideration: that the spread of national self-determination through the creation of independent states for the Basques, the Flemings, and so on leads to promoting sovereign entities with strong "ethnic cohesion" and a pronounced identity base narrowing the political arena. The trend is indisputable in all recent dissociation processes, whether peaceful or violent. The Czech state has thus become mono-national since its separation with Slovakia. The departure of Slovaks and Slovakian Hungarians was the final act in a half-century's process of gradually removing all non-Czechs (Nazi extermination of the Jews, expulsion of the Germans from Sudetenland, transfer of Sub-Carpathian Ruthenia to Ukraine in 1945). "Of the multinational Czechoslovakia in the interwar period, there is nothing left but a nation-state of Czechs, as if we had undertaken ethnic cleansing."[29]

In the former USSR, the advent of new states also hastened the phenomenon of "ethnic unmixing." Russians of the Soviet empire left the peripheral republics (especially in the Caucasus and Central Asia) for Russia. The trend had begun some thirty years before with the emergence of a so-called indigenous national elite in the various republics, but it increased in scale after they achieved independence. While it is sometimes related to war, as in Georgia, and to the degradation of the economic situation, it more fundamentally flows from the consolidation of national states around the majority ethnic group. Even in cases where citizenship is granted liberally, as in Central Asia, state policies, starting with those promoting the use of the local language (Tajik, Uzbek, etc.) to the detriment of Russian, favor the group associated with the state and thus have helped to put members of these groups at the head of administration and business.[30]

Unfortunately, ethnic disentanglement often takes on violent forms, as it did in former Yugoslavia, which has lost its multinational character and yielded largely homogenous national states (or para-state entities as in Bosnia). In Croatia, the only significant Serb minority left resides in Eastern Slavonia, while in Bosnia, where the populations commingled to a greater degree, ethnic cleansing achieved its aim and now the three areas (Serb, Croat, Muslim) are each 90% homogenous. As for Serbia proper, its internal cohesion has grown with the influx of Serb refugees from Bosnia, Croatia and Kosovo. The latter has not escaped the process of homogenization, either. It was drained of half of its Albanian population during the NATO-instigated war. Serbs and Roma, subject to repeated acts of violence, also deserted it in large numbers, leaving it with a population that is 92% Albanian. The Serbs who have remained in Kosovo are confined either to the country's north, in an area *de facto* attached to Serbia (around Mitrovica), or in isolated enclaves, protected by international forces. The international community's ritual invocation of Kosovo's multinational character is therefore wishful thinking, but at the same time it is a necessary illusion. Serbs, even if in small numbers, must remain in an independent Kosovo to "prove" that the allied intervention indeed took place in the name of a universalistic and moral conception of democracy and not to foster the creation of an ethnically homogenous Kosovo. Only Macedonia escaped both civil war and "ethnic normalization," but there was serious alarm in 2001 with the development of an insurrection fueled by demands from the Albanian minority (at least 25% of the population). The crisis was defused by swift international diplomatic intervention, and a series of commitments were made to increase minority representation and rights: the number of Albanians within the state apparatus rose and Albanian was made an official language at the municipal level in towns with a large Albanian minority. Implementation of these reforms has nevertheless been slow and in many regards discord continues to smolder.

The tendency to seek congruence between a state and a historical community of culture has certain practical advantages, as democracy can more easily assert itself "by claiming to represent [a] body politic that takes the form of a community imagined as a national communion."[31] If the government and the governed are alike, sharing the same general culture and language, they will thus share common ground, making it easier to establish democracy. At the same time, this law of similitude leads to an intolerable contraction of the political space, which is then no longer the locus of face-to-face deliberation and dialogue discussed by Hannah Arendt, but the locus of closed groups and identity. The duplication of homogenous states then causes confusion between political community and "natural" community, and in that regard it signals a profound regression of the political.

Carried to the extreme, such a process inevitably requires the total reorganization of Europe on the basis of an ethnic federalism, with states that are homogenous from the standpoint of language and culture. This agenda, which is promoted by the new regionalist right in German-speaking countries,[32] would lead to a general ethnicization of international life that would be fundamentally anti-political. To avoid this danger, it seems far more desirable, insofar as it is possible, not to reduce people's national claims to the need for a state. In other words, to accommodate national diversity, an alternative to the nation-state would have to be invented in order not to remain trapped by the rationale that every group mobilized around a national base should have a state, a perspective that sustains the trend toward the proliferation of states.

CONCLUSION

THE FUTURE OF PLURALISM

A complex equation faces us in the twenty-first century. The strong aspirations for recognition embodied by nationalitarian movements cannot simply be ignored. Yet the proliferation of identity-based states would lastingly tarnish the pluralist ideal of democracy. Any solution will therefore involve looking beyond the nation-state, a perspective that requires reformulating two principles: the doctrine of self-determination and the congruence of culture and state. A clear path toward multinationality must be forged. This has become a tangible and necessary reality due to the increasing power of supranational entities, particularly in Europe.

Sovereignty without Independence

In practice, self-determination has been entirely reduced to the right to an independent state.

The state alone was thought to be able to realize the right of peoples to self-determination. This perception is highly simplistic, however, because paradoxically, "peoples' right to self-determination also means a people's right not to become a state," by organizing themselves autonomously within a multinational entity.[1]

International law does not restrict self-determination to gaining independence, because it prescribes the possibility of two other forms through which this principle can be implemented. With respect to decolonization, for example, it can occur either through integration into an existing state, or through association (with autonomous status) or any other political status freely determined by the people being emancipated from colonial rule.[2] These options remain valid on the condition that they result from a choice freely expressed by the populations concerned.

That means, *a contrario*, that the status of associated state, in which internal autonomy is paired with specific jurisdictional limits, particularly in military and diplomatic affairs, cannot be construed as a substitute for independence. This explains why the inclination among some Israelis to favor prolonging indefinitely the autonomous regime currently in effect, by which the Palestinian Authority has all the trappings of a state (executive, legislative and judicial bodies) but lacks the capacity to act in foreign policy or defense and has no control over its borders, should be categorically opposed. This position clearly runs counter to the Palestinian people's desire for full and complete independence. Permanent autonomy cannot be imposed on people as a means of maintaining control over them and perpetuating structural asymmetry. On the other hand, if such a relationship is based on explicit consent, it could perfectly well support self-determination, as illustrated by a number of micro-states in Europe and the Pacific.[3]

The fact that self-determination and independence are often considered synonymous is rooted in a confusion of the notions of sovereignty and independence. And yet it is crucial to distinguish between the two. The democratic revolutions in Eastern Europe were geared at the outset toward recovering sovereignty. First in the Baltic states, and later in Slovenia, Croatia and most of the other republics of the USSR, parliaments began by adopting declarations of sovereignty. This was a means of declaring that political authority lay henceforth with the various peoples in the federated states and not with the communist ideocracy. Regaining sovereignty in this case has been analyzed as entailing the restoration of democratic legitimacy, in which the original and ultimate political power is vested in the citizenry.[4]

Recovery of sovereignty did not logically imply, however, that the various republics were proclaiming their independence. Indeed, these initial moves could very well have been accompanied by a renegotiation of the federal pact by granting broad autonomy to the individual republics within a democratic framework. Matters played out differently, both because some participants clearly intended to pursue their quest for independence (the Baltic states, Slovenia and Croatia) and because the center, through lack of time or political will, proved incapable of instituting a democratic form of federalism. However, even if historically conditions were such that full independence was unavoidable, it did not inevitably follow from the restoration of national sovereignty.

Moreover, the functioning of federalism serves as a reminder of the important difference between sovereignty and independence. Switzerland has twenty-six cantons that are fully sovereign in their areas of jurisdiction, but only the Swiss confederation functions as an independent state on the international stage. This is also true of the Russian federation, whose twenty-one individual republics (Yakutia, Bashkiria, etc.) exercise broad sovereignty and have negotiated bilateral accords directly with the central authorities to define their rather considerable powers, including in external economic relations.[5] Nevertheless, these republics are not independent; in other words they are not subjects of international law.[6]

In each of these cases, sovereignty refers to two characteristics: political authority vested in the people and the federated entity's autonomy. Self-determination through sovereignty, frequently expressed through federal structures as well as specific rights granted to national minorities, will not always suffice to silence calls for separatism, as history has amply demonstrated. Still, it opens a promising avenue in many respects.

Article 3 of the 2007 United Nations Declaration on the Rights of Indigenous Peoples, for instance, mentions the right of indigenous peoples (who amount to roughly 370 million individuals) to "self-determination"—in other words, to "freely determine their political status and freely pursue their economic, social and cultural development."[7] The declaration describes a series of rights, including protection of indigenous cultures, rights to their lands, territories and natural resources, and participation in decisions affecting their lives. It was negotiated over a period of some twenty years because some states viewed it as a separatist threat. The text was ultimately adopted by an overwhelming majority, with four major governments—Australia, Canada, the United States and New Zealand—voting against it.[8]

It would be erroneous to fear the aspirations of the Canadian "First Nations," for example. Their goal is not to form independent political entities, but instead to exercise self-government within the areas where they are located in order to promote their cultures and have control over their lands, their resources and their economic development. Similarly, Jordi Pujol, the former president of the Generalitat of Catalonia, unceasingly reaffirmed that he intended to promote the "self-assertion" of his country while rejecting independence, which would necessarily involve a secession process.[9] By the same token, the Dalai Lama has claimed to be prepared to accept "genuine autonomy" for Tibet in the management of the region's affairs, with the exception of foreign affairs and defense, which would remain within the purview of the central Chinese government.[10]

These nationalist actors have sought sovereignty without attempting to gain political independence. The possibility should be acknowledged that they have resorted to double-speak, pretending to settle for broad autonomy for tactical reasons, in order to conceal deeper ambitions for independent states. Independence may remain an objective because achieving self-determination through sovereignty is limited to the domestic front, and it confers powers on a sub-state entity without granting it what nationalists most aspire to: international recognition.

There is some truth to this objection, but recent cases in which federated entities have acquired external sovereignty, in other words the ability to act internationally, cannot be disregarded. For example, after considerable reluctance owing to its Jacobin legal culture, France resigned itself to signing an accord for linguistic, cultural, educational and scientific cooperation in 1999 with the French Community of Belgium, which is now the only competent authority in this regard, replacing a federalized Belgian state that no longer has the capacity to intervene in this area. Similarly, the Russian constitution of 1993 grants the subjects of the Federation (in addition to the twenty-one republics, six territories, ten autonomous territories, one autonomous region, two cities of federal importance and forty-nine regions) the right to establish external international and economic relations in conjunction with the federal government.

Provisions of this nature grant powers to sub-state entities that are generally under the exclusive purview of independent states. The state's monopoly over international representation has been somewhat eroded, because most associated states (officially linked to an outside protector) have obtained the same international status enjoyed by independent states. The Marshall Islands, Palau and the Federated States of Micronesia—all three of which are associated with the United States—are members of the UN or other international institutions and can enter into international treaties in certain areas. This is also true of Monaco, Liechtenstein and San Marino, which are tied to France, Switzerland and Italy respectively. If the problem is approached from the opposite direction by examining independent states, it emerges that the group of those whose institutional apparatus has totally collapsed (Somalia, Liberia, etc.) is swelling dangerously, making their formal sovereignty seem a pure illusion. Beyond appearances and convenient certainties, the very idea of sovereignty needs to be revisited, as Bertrand Badie suggests, because it is "a doubtful concept" with complex origins that cannot currently claim to imply absolute, ultimate and unaltered power.[11] Next to the annihilated sovereignties of so many collapsed "independent" states, the sovereign powers of Flanders and Quebec seem far more robust.

Dissociating State and Nation

The theoretical distinction between self-determination through sovereignty and self-determination through independence is useful in another respect, because it makes it easier to dissociate between the civic and national community, in other words between politics and identity. The rule of congruence between culture and polity is in fact ill suited to most states throughout the world. In Eastern Europe, for example, the imposition of the nation-state model following 1918 was an endless source of problems, as Hannah Arendt had correctly pointed out.[12] This was a monumental mistake that fueled permanent instability within those countries and ultimately laid the groundwork for war. But because people appear to learn little from history, they continued to administer the same old remedies in the former Yugoslavia. It cannot be repeated often enough that in a space where entanglements are endless, brutal therapy is sometimes required. Population displacements and exchanges as well as massacres are the price to be paid if a nation-state is to triumph. Rather than lament this tragic reality once the irreparable harm is done, would it not make more sense to temper the nation-state logic by replacing it with a multination state model?

One appealing idea proposed by a number of scholars seeks to differentiate between the state, an agent of political unity and authority for organizing citizenship, and the nation, a historical community of culture.[13] Based on this distinction, it is entirely possible to imagine that the same political community can include multiple spaces of national attachment. Switzerland, where the federal political pact manages to transcend religious, cultural and linguistic pluralism, is one example of such co-existence among diverse national affiliations. The secret of the Swiss model's success resides in the fact that political integration has never required denying one's fundamental cultural identifications or local citizenship ties (to town and canton), which on the contrary have flourished by being granted explicit recognition.

This multinational model has demonstrated its effectiveness in plural societies, having been adopted in various forms in Spain, in Belgium and in Canada, entailing a variety of institutional mechanisms (federalism, regional or personal autonomy, etc.).[14] Although it has not proven able to absorb the most virulent forms of nationalism, it has partially subjugated and "civilized" them. Compared to the sad fate of the nation-state in the Balkans, Turkey and elsewhere, the multination state has a far better track record, and its "sins" are considerably easier to forgive. In a society deeply divided along national lines, the multination state appears well suited, if not ideal, as a means of enabling cohabitation.

Does this suggest that older states such as France and the United Kingdom, which are subject to far more limited nationalitarian pressures, can rest on their laurels and settle for managing the status quo? Clearly not. These states have in fact already initiated institutional reforms to address national plurality, and there is every indication that the trend will continue. Rather than struggling to combat it, it is in these nations' interest to support this trend, to prevent the situation from spinning out of control. The increasing diversification of societies makes the notion that a given state corresponds to a nation and a culture increasingly untenable. On the other hand, this makes the multination state an increasingly relevant concept, because by nature it is based on the expression of multiple identifications and is in harmony with the aspirations of modern individuals to refer simultaneously to several levels of attachment.

The autonomous status granted to Catalonia thus seems to meet the Catalans' expectations, many of whom (38%) define themselves as Spanish as much as they do as Catalan.[15] Along the same lines, there is no reason why deeper institutionalization of diversity in France, particularly by actively promoting the use of regional languages in the public space, should be perceived as a "de-Gallicization" when it takes nothing away but rather offers an additional asset.

Why strive to formulate things in terms of a zero sum game, as though gains on one side necessarily represent losses for the other? The dominant perception among citizens of multination states indicates on the contrary that this political model does not foster identity-based exclusivism. Instead, it corresponds to citizens' need for a dual identity. In a way, the question may be to recover, via the multination state, what was lost with the nineteenth-century multination empires. Naturally, it would be at once vain and foolhardy to resuscitate the imperial model that prospered in very different historical contexts than ours. Yet, without retrospectively idealizing a mode of political organization that plainly had serious deficiencies, it would be equally absurd to discredit it entirely. This sober assessment applies particularly to Austria-Hungary.

Clearly the Habsburg Empire, wavering between absolutism and liberalism and between power concentration and decentralization, was founded on a traditional political order increasingly out of step with deep social transformations and democratic aspirations. For centuries, however, the Empire was able to ensure the cohabitation of a mosaic of peoples. Some enjoyed considerable autonomy that was of particular benefit to the historic nations, which were entitled to their own state: Germans and Czechs in Bohemia, as well as Hungarians, Croats, Poles, and Italians.[16] Furthermore, although German was the principal language of culture and official power, the other vernaculars could be used both in the administration and in education. And indeed, "Austro-Hungarian" soldiers swore their allegiance to the Emperor in eleven different languages.

Following the Compromise of 1867, nationalist agitation swelled, especially among the Slavs of the South and in the Czech lands, but the Empire was not doomed to collapse due to some sort of implacable evolution. Even the Great War did not necessarily sound the death knell for the Empire, which for a long time continued to enjoy the loyalty of the vast majority of its subjects and was not initially slated by the Allies for dissolution.[17] The Empire began to dissolve due to both internal reasons and an ideological motive aptly identified by François Fejtö: the republicanization of Europe advocated by many French leaders involved the dismantling of Austria-Hungary, which was faulted for being both a monarchy and Catholic.[18]

The Ottoman Empire was similarly ill fated. Unlike its Austro-Hungarian counterpart, with its liberal philosophy, the Sublime Porte encouraged the preservation of a traditional, conservative order dominated by Islam. It would be an over-simplification, however, to dismiss the Ottoman imperial system by accusing it of Oriental despotism. "For nearly half a millennium the Ottomans ruled an empire as diverse as any in history. Remarkably, this poly-ethnic and multireligious society worked. Muslims, Christians, and Jews worshipped and studied side by side, enriching their distinct cultures."[19] The *millet* system, which ensured broad internal autonomy for the three religious communities (Greeks, Armenians, Jews), was fundamentally asymmetrical, no doubt, because tolerance toward minorities was enshrined in a legal framework that maintained Muslim supremacy out of principle, relegating Jews and Christians to the role of protégés (*dhimmi*).

Even if cohabitation among the various communities was not always idyllic, in accepting diverse identities, the imperial system had a clear virtue. Difference was in some respects a constitutive element of the empire, which was committed to achieving universality by uniting a wide variety of peoples. Furthermore, the empire did not adopt a univocal form, because identity references intersected instead of overlapping: "One could be Slavic, Muslim, or Catholic or Orthodox and speak a specific language such as Albanian, Romanian or Serbo-Croatian in everyday life, while at the elite level one could also use German, Russian, Hungarian, Turkish, Italian or French. Conversely, one could be Orthodox Christian but not Slavic, like the Greeks."[20]

The fall of the edifice was brought on primarily by the European powers' increasing interventionism and the influence of nationalism as an ideology.

With this new influence, people began to aspire to a new kind of dignity to replace the old tolerance, a shift that necessitated promoting the national principle above all else and simplifying the rules of identity politics. Unable to handle this transformation, which prompted Greeks, Bulgarians, Serbs, and other groups to define themselves in terms of nationhood instead of religion, the empire responded with a two-pronged policy that led it down a blind alley culminating in large-scale massacres. The first element of the response overtly asserted a form of pan-Islamism that was accompanied by severe repression against the Armenians (1894–6). The second element helped cobble together a Turkish nationalism to offset the nationalist agitation of the empire's Christians. This reversal was enacted with extraordinary violence toward the Armenians, who were victims of genocide in 1915. The record of the final years of the Ottoman Empire is indisputably horrific, but it would also be an error to overlook centuries of peaceful co-existence.

The fate of the third multination empire under the Czar also offers relevant insights. The empire ruled by the Romanovs earned its title as the "prison of nations" due to the intense oppression of nationalities. Yet this was not the result of a plurinational character, the empire being incapable of sustaining the cohabitation of diverse peoples. The empire ultimately dissolved because of the intolerable contradictions that characterized czarist policy as of 1825.

Up until the first quarter of the nineteenth century, the regime managed its multiethnic nature relatively well, even as it pursued a tremendous centuries-long campaign of expansion.[21] Russian policy was based on honoring the *status quo*, which meant preserving local political authorities. This explains the broad autonomy granted to the Kingdom of Poland and the Grand Principality of Finland. Such pragmatism was also reflected in the religious and linguistic domains, reminiscent of Ottoman policy in that regard. Tatar Islam existed side by side with German Lutheranism, Kalmuk Buddhism, Polish Catholicism and Judaism, with the Orthodox Church functioning as the dominant state religion (only the Uniates, viewed as traitors, were ill-treated from the start). In addition to Russian, the more widespread languages, including German, Polish, Romanian, and Swedish, were common within the administration and the education system. Armenian, Greek, Mongolian, Yiddish and Tatar were also present in the school system and in publications. The price of this religious and linguistic tolerance—the requirement of political loyalty to the ruling dynasty—was widely understood.

The system ceased to function smoothly from the moment that authorities were no longer satisfied by establishing legitimacy through imperial patriotism. Instead, they began to embrace a narrow, reactionary form of Russian nationalism. Reasoning in terms of a nation-state when the empire's social structure was patently multi-national was tantamount to heresy. Failure was all the more predictable in that national mobilization was driven by the autocracy. The state's recourse to violence was henceforth inevitable and included forced administrative integration to the west and the south (Poland, the Baltic states, and the Caucasus), massive Russification, and discrimination and pogroms against the Jews. Instead of curbing national identity movements, this policy of uniformization further strengthened them and reinforced their determination to break away from the imperial center. In attempting to behave like a nation-state when it was a hugely diverse multination empire, Czarist Russia precipitated its own downfall.

This discussion of empires is instructive, not because it intends to awaken nostalgia for restoration but because it underscores the fact that by dissociating state and nation, multination empires forged a path that merits re-examination.

Multinationhood: Gambling on Diversity

In 1862, Lord Acton, history professor at Cambridge, wrote that instead of the principle of unity, which holds that each state corresponds to a nation, he proposed the principle of diversity, "the co-existence of several nations under the same State is a test, as well as the best security of its freedom. It is also one of the chief instruments of civilization." In Acton's view, the unity principle on which the modern theory of nationality is based is both a source of despotism, because it fosters absolutism—the nation incarnate—*and* a cause of revolution, in that it maintains a constant nationalist insatiability. It is based on homogenization, which constitutes a fundamental denial of liberty because "By making the State and the nation commensurate with each other in theory, it reduces practically to a subject condition all other nationalities that may be within the boundary," and leads to an attempt "to neutralize, to absorb, or to expel them."[22]

Conversely, national diversity is "the foremost limit to the excessive power of the state... It provides against the servility which flourishes under the shadow of a single authority, by balancing interests, multiplying associations and giving to the subject the restraint and support of a combined opinion." The states that have come closest to perfection are those that "include various distinct nationalities without oppressing them." This form of diversity is the clearest manifestation of a free society. One would be hard-pressed to find more vibrant praise for the multination state. And this vision—according to which popular sovereignty, the greatest achievement of the democratic nation-state, blends with the noblest achievements of liberal empires—respect for ethnic and national plurality—is not sheer utopianism, because it has become the norm in such countries as Canada, Spain and Switzerland.

However, because these societies are based on considerable constitutive diversity, they run the significant risk of increasing internal compartmentalization, which closes each sub-unit in on itself and causes the political bond to atrophy. Opening up to diversity should therefore be compensated by the preservation of a shared public culture that can sustain a desire to cohabit within a multination state. This raises a major difficulty, however: the federating principle must be at once strong enough to act as a social cement and flexible enough to preserve the autonomy of the various sub-state entities. This ambitious, worthy agenda may resemble attempting to insert a square peg into a round hole, but it is a high and important calling.

The existence of shared values is often evoked as a prerequisite for binding a plurinational society together. How can these unifying values best be identified? Communitarians believe they should center on a shared conception of the good, that individuals should agree on the purpose of life in society and defend this substantive conception of the good life.[23] This vision, in which society is likened to an integrated organism, is both completely inconsistent with the complexity inherent in today's societies and at odds with liberal principles based on respect for individual autonomy and the diversity of approaches to the good. If this is unsuitable for the functioning of a modern state, it is even less appropriate in a pluralist state with highly diverse national components that differ considerably from one another and are eager to safeguard their collective identities.

But the idea of shared values can also be understood differently: as agreement about certain principles of justice, among which are respect for democratic procedures, acceptance of the rule of law, and equality and tolerance among citizens. While these liberal values are essential foundations for any democratic society, their general nature makes them unsuitable as the only federating bonds in a multi-nation state. Shared civic values are not a sufficient basis on which to forge a lasting national bond.[24]

Adherence to abstract political principles is not sufficient to hold a society together, which is why the constitutional patriotism proposed by Jürgen Habermas appears untenable.[25] In classic nation-states, political authorities constantly invoke history, language and culture in strategies to "nationalize the masses." Recourse to such tools is trickier in multination states due to internal cleavages, but they cannot dispense with a rallying perspective extending beyond adherence to universal legal standards.

Plurinational states may be able to find a partial binding agent in the acceptance of specific notions beyond the general principles that govern modern democratic communities. In Switzerland, for instance, the "neutrality—direct democracy—federalism" triad forms the basis for a political culture specific to the confederation with which the various linguistic communities identify. Similarly, federalism and the active promotion of human rights and peace (by participating in peacekeeping forces, for instance) are Canadian trademarks. This particularist reformulation of democratic norms, however, seems somewhat tenuous to fully legitimate the state framework.

At times, a true federating patriotism manages to emerge out of a shared history that somehow transcends linguistic, religious and cultural differences. This is obviously true in Switzerland, where the cantons' fight to preserve their independence from the greedy designs of powerful neighbors (France, the Habsburg Empire, Germany) nourished an affective attachment to the confederation that also involved a mythification of history. There is every reason to believe that William Tell never existed and that he never took part in the Rütli Oath (1291), the first alliance between three cantons, or stoically braved the cruel apple test imposed by the "Austrian occupant." But it actually matters little that Tell the hero is a legend or that the Swiss only half believe it. The William Tell epic, as glorified by Schiller and Rossini and amply promulgated in the schools, was the perfect symbol of a small rebellious people united by their love of freedom.

In many multination countries, however, history is more a source of mutual resentment and recrimination than a source of pride.[26] In Belgium, for example, King Leopold III decided to remain in his country after the German military victory in May 1940, while his government fled to London. His attitude fueled a long regime crisis after the war, with Flemings and francophones taking opposite stances. In the 1950 referendum that restored the king to the throne, 57% voted "yes," but although 72% of the Flemish voters answered in the affirmative, 52% of voters in Brussels and 58% of the Walloons cast a "no" vote. Only the king's abdication finally resolved the "royal question."

Armed conflict, which is often the catalyst for national solidarity—the rise in German nationalism after Napoleon's conquest is a case in point—frequently breeds division in plurinational states. This was the case during both world wars in Belgium and Canada.

In Belgium, the tactical support for Flemish nationalism provided by the German occupant in order to divide and rule caused deep bitterness among francophones after 1945. They accused Flemish activists of taking advantage of the country's weakness to further their separatist ambitions. Although the harsh sentences meted out to Flemish nationalists who collaborated appeased the francophones, they provoked resentment among the Flemings, who viewed them as an attempt to discredit their national movement. In Canada, when the country entered each of the two world wars, this unleashed a conscription crisis in Quebec, as the French Canadians felt that they were valued as canon fodder to defend the British Empire but that no one really cared about putting an end to their social and economic marginalization.[27] When antagonistic views of history take hold, they create strife rather than consensus and do more harm than good for the preservation of the bond of citizenship.

Conversely, the existence of a monarchy appears to provide a valuable stabilizing factor. The dynasty principle played a key role in consolidating political allegiance in the multination empires. It continues to fulfill a threefold function of cement, balance and mediation in divided societies such as Spain and Belgium. A socialist prime minister paid the greatest tribute to the Belgian monarchy by saying, "Belgium needs the monarchy like it needs bread!"[28] That a head of government who otherwise claimed to be fundamentally republican would say such a thing is surprising only on the surface.

In reality, in a divided country, monarchs are guarantors of national unity and embody the permanence of the state. Unlike presidents in a republican form of government, their legitimacy does not derive from the people, although the power vested in them, as in any constitutional monarchy, comes from the nation represented by the elected parliament. For this reason, they are able to act as symbols, wielding influence from the throne because they are above political quarrels. In some regards, the king is the only true Belgian, as he is above community cleavages. The institution of the monarchy clearly does not suffice to ensure the state's durability, but it is more an asset than a handicap in a multinational context.

The institution of monarchy probably also fulfills a unifying symbolic function in the former dominions, such as Australia[29] and Canada, in which the British sovereign remains the official head of state, although to a far more distant extent than in European constitutional monarchies such as Spain and Belgium. In the multination states of the Commonwealth, as well all those that are republics (Russia), more immaterial, intangible, federating principles are required to preserve the national bond.

Two elements—a redistributive welfare state and bilingualism—have shaped "Canadianness" and helped to distinguish Canada from its neighbor to the south, even if Canada and the United States share the same liberal democratic values. More subtly, even though francophones in Quebec and anglophones do not have the same interpretation of their common history, they have been shaped over the centuries by this shared experience.

Both groups have therefore contributed to building the Canadian national community and, in return, individual identities have been marked by this cohabitation within the same state. They have all nourished a "national conversation," in other words structured a public space for specific discussion on a point that matters to all, although to varying degrees. For decades, the Quebecois participated in building Canada by taking part in the country's economic boom as well as supplying a number of politicians to federal bodies. The Basques have similarly played an important role in Spain's economic development and have been among the most faithful partisans of monarchic traditionalism through Carlism.

This entire body of shared history leaves traces and helps forge a national *habitus*. This situation largely explains why, despite growing incomprehension, 40% of francophone Quebeckers voted "no" in the most recent referendum on sovereignty. Generally speaking, the state framework remains the dominant political reference, as Catalan voting behavior also attests. Despite the region's strong identity, 40% of the electorate does not go to the polls to elect representatives to the Catalonian parliament, whereas the abstention rate is only 30% for elections to the Spanish Congress of Deputies.[30]

Attachment to an "experienced" national space, however, does not remain stable, and the generational effect tends to reduce it. This is not because young people are by nature more nationalistic than their elders, but because the more powers the "constituent communities" (nationalities, provinces, etc.) obtain from the central state, the more these communities become the principal frames of reference and socialization. In Belgium, for instance, federalization has resulted in a greater lack of understanding between the Flemings and the francophones, as the two communities move more and more in two compartmentalized spheres. Flemish and francophone children go to different schools and do not watch the same television channels, and their parents do not read the same newspapers or even the same novels.[31] This kind of split does nothing to facilitate mutual comprehension, but if this were merely from a language standpoint, there would be less cause for concern. The same issues that interest every citizen can very well be tackled in different languages. The difficulty is that specifically national debates are often approached from different angles in the media, which actually tend to devote more attention to the communities and regions than to the country as a whole.

Finally, to function smoothly, a plurinational state should value plurality in its own right. "Our diversity has shaped our sense of ourselves," writes Jeremy Webber about Canada.[32] This axiom could easily be applied to other multination states. But nothing guarantees that this openness to differences will last, primarily because it is not always equally important to the various groups.

Thus, for many Canadians citizens, the country's two-nation foundation is an aspect of its singularity, and if Canada were deprived of Quebec, it would no longer truly be Canada but something else. That does not prevent attachment to "dual Canadianness" from being stronger among anglophones than among francophones, because the frame of reference for the former is Canada as a whole, bilingual at the federal level, whereas for the latter, their primary allegiance goes to Quebec province where French is the official language.[33] This divergence can only be overcome if different ways of belonging are recognized. An "old" anglophone Canadian or a recent immigrant from the Caribbean or elsewhere "might indeed feel Canadian as a bearer of individual rights in a multicultural mosaic."[34] On the other hand, for a Quebecois, an Inuit or member of an aboriginal group, such recognition falls short of the mark and would need to be deepened to take into account their specificity, which entails granting Quebec the status of a distinct society[35] and substantial autonomy to the First Nations. But this is in fact the problem, because one side denies the "profound diversity" of the other. In this context, the various partners can grow weary of a constant search for conciliation and balance between two opposing visions of diversity and may find it more expedient to part ways.

For those familiar with the French paradigm of a strong state, the multination state often appears fragile, but this fragility is highly relative. In the eyes of the Jacobinic state, which tightly frames civil society, there is something imperfect about the multination state. It is considered but "a collection of federated republics that would constantly fall prey to civil war," to borrow the words Robespierre used to stigmatize the Girondist republic as he stood before the Convention.[36] Yet this apparent weakness should rather be viewed as a great potential for flexibility and adaptability. A common public culture that is not too "padded," that is boiled down to fundamental political principles and certain ideals, such as a shared living experience and respect for diversity, is among the elements required to allow diverse nations to exercise broad autonomy.

For those who view the state as the supreme body that lays down the requirements of the general interest, the multination state will be seen as minimal and thus as a cause for concern. Others who are more accustomed to the complexity of its workings approach matters differently. For instance, in Belgium, for the philosopher of science Isabelle Stengers, "the undecidable nature of the future of the Belgian state is not a cause for panic."[37] Echoing her from the other side of the "community barrier," the great Flemish novelist Hugo Claus admitted to being "fairly pleased with this shapeless state as it can be seen to function today."[38] Finally, is not a "trimmed down" central state better suited to the post-national age, which is systematically described as an economic, social, and political retreat of the state?[39] Is it not better attuned to the powerful transformations in the political sphere, in which an integrative rationale tempers the nation-state framework?

The Postnational Question

In many respects, a state in which considerable powers are devolved to the regional level will be more willing to transfer others to a supranational level. It will view this redistribution of powers not as an unbearable alienation of sovereignty, but the application of a principle of political effectiveness, which holds that powers should be exercised at the most appropriate level. Thus, the fact that the "Europeanization" of a strong unitary state such as France arouses greater resistance than in a "meek" federal state such as Belgium is hardly surprising. Significantly, the Belgian elites consider the integration of Europe and its progress toward federalism to be a national goal, former prime minister Jean-Luc Dehaene not hesitating to take "European structures as part of Belgium's own [national] institutions."[40]

The fact that plurinational states are potentially more adaptable, making it easier for them to envisage something beyond the state, does not suggest that the era of postnationalism has arrived. New transnational phenomena and forms of integration indicate that "postnational" dynamics are at work. There is, however, still a long way to go before postnationalism can become a relevant political principle, even in a consolidating Europe. Postnationalism, as a European-wide projection of the constitutional patriotism Jürgen Habermas has proposed, refers "primarily to a non-nationalist motive of participation in a political community that is based solely on fundamental principles such as democracy and the rule of law."[41] In my view, it is unlikely to become a reality in the near future for two reasons.

The first reason relates to the very procedures of European integration, which for the moment have not made the emergence of a truly European public space possible. This development is an indispensable pre-condition for founding a common political culture. The codification of community law, the creation of the single market, the monetary union, the institution of a European citizenship and cooperation on internal security all demonstrate very well that regional integration is progressing and that complex processes for overcoming national logics are at work, but this is far from adequate to create a common public space.[42] If empirical proof were needed, it is provided regularly by the European elections: with an overall abstention rate of 55% across the Union, the European political community seems evanescent indeed.[43] Furthermore, even if certain elites already move in a European context, European civil society[44] remains embryonic to say the least, as the overwhelming majority of citizens in the twenty-eight member countries move exclusively or primarily within a national environment.

An additional factor to consider, even if the root causes lay partly in domestic politics, is that voters in two founding EU member states—France and the Netherlands—rejected the Constitutional Treaty in 2005 by referendum. This attests to genuine concern about the loss of national sovereignty inherent in an increasingly complex European project. The principled support that European integration continues to enjoy, although it varies from one country to the next, should therefore not be misinterpreted. It does not proceed either from a "European consciousness" or a post-national identification, but is explained by an array of strictly national interests.[45] The philosopher Jean-Marc Ferry, a talented advocate of postnationalism, himself admits that it is still in the project stage, and the European people are yet to be shaped through the development of participative democracy.[46] Will increased European-level exchanges and discussions suffice to create a shared political culture and build a unified public space?

This vision is steeped in an evolutionistic optimism that views the development of communications as a factor that increases interaction and obliterates local specificities in favor of a "superior" political community.[47] This causal link is, however, far from automatic, and cases abound where the flow of communication not only hasn't prevented the persistence of national particularisms, but has even stimulated them. There is therefore no guarantee that the formation of a communicational space in Europe will suffice to spawn a European populace.

Let us suppose, nevertheless, that such a guarantee does exist. Does this mean that postnationalism is certain to triumph? Nothing could be less certain, which leads to the second obstacle, which is related to its "hyperpolitical" nature, based solely on adherence to the values of democracy and the rule of law. At both the European level and within the national framework, constitutional patriotism is too loose a bond to alone ensure social cohesion and generate a feeling of belonging. Jean-Marc Ferry moreover acknowledges that it is impossible to make such political universalism the sole building block of European identity: "We roughly adhere to the same principles of representative democracy, the rule of law and human rights. But this adherence, which merely outlines the contours of a constitutional patriotism, grounds only a soft consensus with no great practical value."[48]

How can it be given sufficient depth to make it operative? The first solution would mean applying the nation-state solution to Europe, in other words constructing a super-state based on the nationalist principle of congruence between culture and politics. The ultimate goal would be for a European nation to emerge that would absorb the French, German and other nations just as France was built by "ingesting" the Occitans, Bretons, Savoyards and so on. In the 1950s, this reasoning guided those who believed that the European integration process, economic at the outset, would gradually spread to the political, social and cultural spheres, ultimately to result in the advent of a European state.[49] This scenario did not come about, as the European Union appeared as a *sui generis* configuration in which national governments, community institutions and informal networks permanently interact.[50] Because it is not a state, Europe does not have the same coercive powers of socialization and is not in a position to achieve the cultural homogenization, counterpart of political unity, toward which so many states have relentlessly strived. Still, even if a more substantial European power were to come into being, it would confront a frightfully difficult problem: what would serve as the foundation for this European culture?

A familiar triptych—Greek logos, Roman law, Judeo-Christian ethic—is often mentioned as the bedrock of European culture. To which it is easy to add the humanism of the Renaissance, the rationalism of the Enlightenment and the scientific method, as well as Romanticism, and a few other essential values such as fundamental rights and democracy. All of which is both much and yet very little.

Much, because the legacy is rich and impressive; little, because such a heritage in itself is not enough to sustain a culture. It is therefore imperative to forge an authentic European culture that extends beyond this patrimonial conception. The task is monumental. It would require the development of

European media, systematic promotion of plurilingualism and a complete overhaul of school curricula to Europeanize them. In short, Europe faces a prodigious cultural challenge that for the moment it has only very timidly taken on.[51]

Alongside the creation of a shared cultural substratum, the "nationalization" of Europe would also presuppose the emergence of a specifically European imaginary. But as Gilles Andréani notes, "if Europe has a history; it has no memory, in other words the mixture of historical truth and fiction, things remembered and forgotten, that brings together a human community around things done together in the past and the desire to do others in the future."[52] Creation of a shared memory will be difficult because there are at least as many motives for division as there are for unity,[53] and there is hence great temptation to manufacture a consensual European imaginary that would have little capacity to mobilize the population. It is clear that a European collective identity will emerge only following a long historical process, patient socialization and the strengthening of the political center. The rise of a European nation, which some federalist circles continue to believe possible, remains a utopian vision.

For this reason, the solution recommended by champions of postnationalism is as follows: connecting a form of constitutional patriotism at the European level with specific national cultural attachments. The aim would be to "combine [political unity] with national plurality, [to reconcile] the universality of the legal framework with the singularity of cultural identities."[54] European citizens would express their political will primarily through the Union, while their identity needs would be mediated by the member states. That this disjunction conflicts with the correspondence between political unity and cultural community prized by the nation-state is not an insurmountable handicap, as multination states are already at least partly based on this kind of differentiation.

It is considerably more doubtful, however, that allegiance to a European political center can completely dispense with a sense of European identification, however minimal. Further, if transfers of sovereignty to the Union continue, thus further devaluing the state framework as a political space, why should it remain relevant from a cultural standpoint? This situation would be immediately problematic for states such as France, where the political fulfills a major structuring role, and for those that have already relinquished the cultural aspect to infra-state entities, as multination states have done. There is every reason to believe that, although cultural identification may remain localized within state boundaries for small, fairly unified countries such as the Netherlands, Portugal and Ireland, for larger countries it will find expression primarily at the regional level.

For the time being, European institution-building has followed a contradictory trend. The various treaties concluded since the Maastricht Treaty in 1993 stipulate that the EU aims for "an ever closer union among European peoples" while respecting each member state's national identity. The implicit model is based on Jacques Delors' proposed federation of nation-states.[55] This formulation leaves something to be desired, as it associates the essentially pluralist federalist dimension with the essentially monistic nation-state dimension. In fact, to escape the European contradiction, the goal should be to build a multination federation[56] based on peoples and not on states. Multination states (as well as mononation federal states like Germany and Austria) are better equipped to reach this goal than classic nation-states, because they already largely depend on active recognition of plurality.

The postnational perspective does not eliminate the challenge of national pluralism. On the contrary, it lends it ever-greater intensity. Now, in Europe as elsewhere, the alternative is clear: to conceive and organize democratic multinationality, or else be resigned to the exponential multiplication of ethnic-based states. The first route does not guarantee rock-solid stability, but the second carries far greater risks, because it will not be devoid of violence.

APPENDIX

SUMMARY OF METHODS FOR
MANAGING NATIONAL DIVERSITY

		Systems of Regulation		
		Non-territorial		Territorial
		Consociation	*Personal/ Cultural Autonomy*	
Types of State	**Unitary**	Lebanon	Hungary	France Finland Denmark
	Regionalized			United Kingdom Italy
	Federal	Switzerland, Belgium Bosnia	Canada Belgium (Brussels)	Canada, Belgium, Spain, Switzerland Bosnia

This chart compares types of state and the systems for regulating national plurality discussed in Chapters 6 and 7. Some countries are found in more than one square because they combine several methods of managing diversity.

NOTES

FOREWORD

1. As Benedict Anderson noted, "Since World War II, every successful revolution has defined itself in national terms—the People's Republic of China, the Socialist Republic of Vietnam and so forth—and, in so doing, has grounded itself firmly in a territorial and social space inherited from the revolutionary past." *Imagined Communities: Reflections on the Origin and Spread of Nationalism*, London: Verso, 1983, p. 12.
2. Simon Dubnow, *Lettres sur le judaïsme ancien et nouveau*, Paris: Le Cerf, 1989, p. 150. Dubnow was murdered by a Latvian soldier in December 1941 during the Nazis' liquidation of the Riga ghetto.
3. See, among others, Ernest Gellner, *Nations and Nationalism*, Oxford: Blackwell, 1983; Anthony D. Smith, *National Identity*, London: Penguin Books, 1991; Benedict Anderson, op. cit.
4. The term was coined in the 1970s to designate left-leaning regionalisms that combined criticism of the nation-state with a denunciation of capitalism. I use it here in a broader sense, as a synonym for "dissociative nationalisms," as opposed to centralist nationalisms.

1. NATIONALISM AND GLOBALIZATION

1. 44.7% were in favor, 55.3% against. Alex Salmond resigned after the failure of the referendum. He was replaced by Nicola Sturgeon, the new SNP leader and Scotland's first female First Minister.
2. Generally speaking, in English, "Quebecois" refers to French-speaking inhabitants of Quebec, while "Quebecker" is used for all residents of Quebec, regardless of their principal language. In French, however, there is no such distinction and "Québécois" can refer either to all inhabitants, or only to French-speaking inhabitants, of Quebec.
3. Karl Marx and Frederick Engels, *Manifesto of the Communist Party*, Marxists Internet

Archive, 1987, 2000, 2010, https://www.marxists.org/archive/marx/works/download/pdf/Manifesto.pdf, p. 25, last accessed 10 December 2015.

4. See the group reflections collected by Guy Laforest and Douglas M. Brown (eds), *Integration and Fragmentation: The Paradox of the Late Twentieth Century*, Kingston, Ontario: Institute of Intergovernmental Relations, 1994.

5. The increasing geographic polarization of activity has been ably demonstrated by Pierre Veltz, *Mondialisation, villes et territoires. L'économie d'archipel* (2nd ed.), Paris: PUF, 2014.

6. E.J. Hobsbawm, *Nations and Nationalism Since 1780: Programme, Myth, Reality*, Cambridge: Cambridge University Press, 1990, p. 191.

7. Zaki Laidi raised this point, discussing the globalization of particularisms in *A World Without Meaning* [trans. June Burnham and Jenny Coulon], Oxford: Routledge, 1998, p. 59.

8. These figures are taken from Stéphane Dion's article, "Le nationalisme dans la convergence culturelle. Le Québec contemporain et le paradoxe de Tocqueville," in Raymond Hudon and Réjean Pelletier, *L'engagement intellectuel. Mélanges en l'honneur de Léon Dion*, Sainte-Foy: Presses de l'Université Laval, 1991, pp. 292–311.

9. Karl Deutsch, *Nationalism and Social Communication: An Inquiry into the Foundations of Nationality* (2nd ed.), Cambridge, MA: MIT Press, 1969.

10. C.E. Black, *The Dynamics of Modernization: A Study in Comparative History*, New York: Harper & Row, 1966, p. 174.

11. Michael Ignatieff, *Blood and Belonging: Journeys into the New Nationalism*, London: Vintage, 1994, p. 14.

12. Claude Lévi-Strauss, *Race and History*, Paris: UNESCO, 1952, p. 9.

13. Ibid.

14. Alexis de Tocqueville, *Democracy in America* [trans. Harvey C. Mansfield and Delba Winthrop], Chicago: University of Chicago Press, 2000, p. 395. The "Tocqueville paradox" was convincingly pointed out by Stéphane Dion, op. cit.

15. Ibid., p. 586.

16. Carlton Hayes, *The Historical Evolution of Moden Nationalism*, New York: Macmillan, 1931, pp. 234–236.

17. Jean-François Bayart, *The Illusion of Cultural Identity* [trans. Steven Rendall, Janet Roitman, Cynthia Schoch & Jonathan Derrick], London: Hurst, 2005, pp. 36–45.

18. The expression is borrowed from David Harvey, *The Condition of Postmodernity: An Enquiry into the Origins of Cultural Change*, Oxford: Blackwell, 1989, p. 278.

19. On questioning the principle of territoriality as federating the international scene, see Bertrand Badie, *La fin des territoires. Essai sur le désordre international et l'utilité sociale du respect*, Paris: Fayard, 1995.

20. Karl Marx, *Grundrisse* ("Outlines of the Critique of Political Economy"), 1857–61, https://www.marxists.org/archive/marx/works/1857/grundrisse/ch08.htm, last accessed 21 February 2015.

21. Kenichi Ohmae, *De l'État-nation aux États-régions*, Paris: Dunod, 1996.

22. The structural advantages of small countries in international competition (including a strong capacity for economic adjustment and export incentives) have been carefully analyzed by Peter J. Katzenstein, *Small States in World Markets: Industrial Policy in Europe*, Ithaca and London: Cornell University Press, 1985.

23. Michael Keating, "Nations without States: The accommodation of nationalism in the new state order," in Michael Keating and John McGarry (eds), *Minority Nationalism and the Changing International Order*, Oxford: Oxford University Press, 2001, pp. 19–43.

24. This validates Walker Connor's intuition when he claimed that "advances in communication and transportation tend also to increase the cultural awareness of the minorities by making their members more aware of the distinctions between themselves and others," in "Nation-Building or Nation-Destroying?" *World Politics*, vol. 24 (3), April 1972, p. 329.

2. THE NATION AS A COMMUNITY OF CULTURE

1. Ernest Gellner, *Nationalism*, London: Weidenfeld & Nicolson, 1997, pp. 1–4.

2. Claude Lévi-Strauss, *Race and History*, Paris: UNESCO, 1952, pp. 46–8.

3. Ernest Gellner, *Nations and Nationalism*, Oxford: Blackwell, 1983.

4. Regarding the mobilization of culture in forming nations, see Anne-Marie Thiesse, *La Création des identités nationales. Europe, XVIIIe-XXe siècle*, Paris: Seuil, 1999.

5. Bertrand Badie, *The Imported State: The Westernization of the Political Order* [trans. Claudia Royal], Stanford: Stanford University Press, 2000, p. 157.

6. Frantz Fanon, *The Wretched of the Earth* [trans. Richard Philcox], New York: Grove Press, 2004, p. 148.

7. Charles Taylor, *The Ethics of Authenticity*, Cambridge, MA: Harvard University Press, 1991, pp. 28ff.

8. Regarding this point, see Yael Tamir's discussion in *Liberal Nationalism*, Princeton: Princeton University Press, 1993.

9. Migration does not necessarily involve a change in cultural context. The founders of British settlement colonies in the United States, Canada, Australia and New Zealand, for instance, merely created an extension of their home country on another continent.

10. I borrow the distinction between these three deficiencies (political, social and cultural) from Andreas Kappeler (ed.), *The Formation of National Elites*, New York and Aldershot, Hants: New York University Press and Dartmouth, 1992, p. 1.

11. Michael Werner, "La Germanie de Tacite et l'originalité allemande," *Le Débat*, January–February 1994 (1), no. 78, pp. 43–61.

12. Gellner, op. cit., p. 61.

13. In the Ottoman Empire, the Turkish term "millet" referred to legally recognized

religious communities. There were three main *millets:* Greek Orthodox, Armenian and Jewish.

14. Hagen Schulze, *States, Nations and Nationalism: From the Middle Ages to the Present*, Oxford: Blackwell, 1996, p. 132.

15. For postnationalism, see the last chapter in this book.

16. Guy Laforest, "Herder, Kedourie et les errements de l'antinationalisme" in Guy Laforest, *De la prudence*, Montreal: Boréal, 1993, pp. 59–84.

17. For the history of Belgium, see Xavier Mabille, *Histoire politique de la Belgique. Facteurs et acteurs du changement*, Brussels: CRISP, 1986; Marie-Thérèse Bitsch, *Histoire de la Belgique*, Paris: Hatier *Nations d'Europe* series, 1992.

18. The Flemish example fully confirms Miroslav Hroch's theory regarding the importance of the cultural aspect in the emergent phase of nationalist movements among the smaller peoples of Europe. See Miroslav Hroch, *Social Preconditions of National Revival in Europe* [trans. Ben Fowkes], Cambridge: Cambridge University Press, 1985. Regarding the Flemish national movement, see Shepard Clough, *A History of the Flemish Movement in Belgium: A Study in Nationalism*, New York: Richard R. Smith, 1930.

19. See Gellner on the Ruritanian metaphor, op. cit., pp. 58–62.

20. Alain Finkielkraut uses this historical controversy as a point of departure to systematize the opposition between the German-style "genius-nation" and the French model of the "contract-nation" in his essay *The Defeat of the Mind* [trans. Judith Friedlander], New York: Columbia University Press, 1995.

21. Friedrich Meinecke, *Weltbürgertum und Nationalstaat. Studien zur Genesis des deutschen Nationalstaates*, Berlin and Munich: Oldenburg, 1915 (originally published in 1907).

22. Hans Kohn, *The Idea of Nationalism. A Study of its Origins and Background*, New York: Macmillan, 1946, p. 330.

23. Eugene Kamenka, "Political Nationalism. The Evolution of the Idea" in *Nationalism: The Nature and Evolution of an Idea*, London: Edward Arnold, 1976, pp. 3–20.

24. For a deconstruction of this opposition, see Alain Dieckhoff, "Beyond Conventional Wisdom: Cultural and Political Nationalism Revisited," in Alain Dieckhoff and Christophe Jaffrelot (eds), *Revisiting Nationalism: Theories and Processes*, London: Hurst, 2005, pp. 62–77.

25. Alain Renaut, "Logiques de la nation," in Gil Delannoi and Pierre-André Taguieff (eds), *Théories du nationalisme. Nation, nationalité, ethnicité*, Paris: Kimé, 1991, p. 36.

26. Louis Dumont, "Une variante nationale. Le peuple et la nation chez Herder et Fichte" in Dumont, *Essais sur l'individualisme. Une perspective anthropologique sur l'idéologie moderne*, Paris: Seuil, 1983, pp. 114–131.

27. Jenó Szúcs, *Les trois Europes*, Paris: L'Harmattan *Domaines danubiens* series, 1985.

28. Peter F. Sugar, Peter Hanák and Tibor Frank, *A History of Hungary*, Bloomington: Indiana University Press, 1990.

29. Although geographically located in Central Europe, the Slovaks are structurally part of Eastern Europe. Linguistic nationalism was promoted more than in the Czech lands, whereas political demands were voiced much later. For different reasons (geographic dispersal, linguistic babelization), the task of "cultural restoration" was also particularly intense among peoples such as the Jews deprived for centuries of political unity. For the undertaking of Hebraization, see Alain Dieckhoff, *The Invention of a Nation: Zionist Thought and the Making of Modern Israel*, London: Hurst, 2003, pp. 98–127.

30. These three stages have been analyzed in great detail by Hroch, op. cit.

3. CULTURE, A STATE AFFAIR

1. Ernest Gellner, *Nations and Nationalism*, Oxford: Blackwell, 1983, pp. 24–9.

2. Hagen Schulze, *States, Nations and Nationalism: From the Middle Ages to the Present*, Oxford: Blackwell, 1996, p. 139. It is well worth reading the fine pages the author devotes to the emergence of a national cultural awareness in Western Europe during the lower Middle Ages.

3. Benjamin Constant, "The Spirit of Conquest," in *Political Writings* [trans. Biancamaria Fontana], Cambridge: Cambridge University Press, 1988, p. 73.

4. Anderson has pinpointed the decisive role of a common cultural code—constantly reaffirmed through mass communications—in the development of national consciousness in his book *Imagined Communities: Reflections on the Origin and Spread of Nationalism*, New York: Verso, 2006 (revised ed.).

5. Jean-François Chanet, *L'École républicaine et les petites patries*, Paris: Aubier, 1996, pp. 203–283.

6. A number of accounts describe the decisive role of schoolteachers in the Gallicization process. See, for instance, Pierre Jakez Helias, *Le Cheval d'orgueil*, Paris: Plon, 1975: "Schoolteachers only speak French even though many of them spoke Breton when they were our age and still speak it at home. According to my parents, they have orders to do what they're doing. Orders from who? 'Guys in the government.' Who are they? The ones at the head of the Republic. So it's the Republic that wants to get rid of Breton? They don't wish any good on us" (p. 229).

7. Eugen Weber pointed out the use of colonial practices and references in the French provinces, in *Peasants into Frenchmen: The Modernization of Rural France, 1870–1914*, Stanford: Stanford University Press, 1976, pp. 485–496.

8. For an anthology of quotes that reveal attempts to eradicate the Catalan culture, see Josep M. Ainaud de Lasarte, *El llibre negre de Catalunya* ("The Black Book of Catalonia"), Barcelona: La Campana, 1995.

9. Hannah Arendt, *The Origins of Totalitarianism*, New York: Harcourt Brace Jovanovich, 1973, p. 299.

10. Gérard Noiriel, *La tyrannie du national. Le droit d'asile en Europe (1793–1993)*, Paris: Calmann-Lévy, 1991, pp. 83ff.

11. Jean-Jacques Rousseau, "Projet de constitution pour la Corse" in *Œuvres complètes, tome III*, Paris: Seuil, 1971, p. 498. Preserving a country's national specificity, according to Rousseau, goes hand in hand with an extremely stringent naturalization policy. While his proposed constitution for Corsica stipulated that any child born on the island would become a citizen, on the other hand, "the right of citizenship cannot be given to a foreigner; except once every fifty years if he should apply and be deemed worthy, or to the worthiest of the applicants" (p. 512).

12. Jean-Jacques Rousseau, "Considérations sur le gouvernement de Pologne," ibid., p. 533.

13. John Stuart Mill, "Considerations on Representative Government," in *Essays on Politics and Society*, Toronto: University of Toronto Press and London: Routledge and Kegan Paul, 1977, p. 547.

14. John Rawls, *Political Liberalism*, New York: Columbia University Press, 1993.

15. Will Kymlicka, *Multicultural Citizenship: A Liberal Theory of Minority Rights*, Oxford: Clarendon Press, 1995, p. 115.

16. Bronislaw Baczko, "Le calendrier républicain. Décréter l'éternité," in Pierre Nora (ed.), *Les lieux de mémoire, tome I*, Paris: Gallimard, 1984, pp. 37–84.

17. The Soweto riots broke out in 1976 after government attempts to introduce Afrikaans in schools.

18. Sociologist Sammy Smooha suggested the concept of ethnic democracy to describe Israel, in "Minority Status in an ethnic democracy: the status of the Arab Minority in Israel," *Ethnic and Racial Studies*, vol. 13 (3), July 1990, pp. 389–413. I believe it can be usefully extended to other cases.

19. For a detailed analysis of this ethno-democracy, see Alain Dieckhoff, "The Nation in Israel: Between Democracy and Ethnicity," in Haldun Gülalp (ed.), *Citizenship and Ethnic Conflict: Challenging the Nation-State* London: Routledge, 2005, pp. 83–98.

20. Cited by Claude Klein, *La démocratie d'Israël*, Paris: Seuil, 1997, p. 289. This translation: http://www.myjewishlearning.com/article/jewish-or-democratic-israels-former-top-judge-reflects-on-values/#, last accessed 15 December 2015.

21. See Marie-Paule Canapa, *Des États pluriethniques dans l'ex-Yougoslavie?* Paris: Cahiers du CERI, no. 7, 1993.

22. Riva Kastoryano, *La France, l'Allemagne et leurs immigrés: négocier l'identité*, Paris: Armand Colin, 1996.

23. Foreigners will have the right to become German citizens after eight years of residence in Germany, as opposed to fifteen years previously. Their children will be granted a German passport at birth, but between the ages of eighteen and twenty-three, they will have to choose between German nationality and that of their parents' original nationality. Contrary to the government's initial plan, the reform that was finally passed does not allow systematic attribution of dual citizenship.

24. In Sweden, the relationship between church and state has been in the process of revision for a number of years. Since 1 January 2000, the close link between the Lutheran Church and the state no longer exists. Norway followed suit in 2012.

25. Denis Lacorne, *La crise de l'identité américaine. Du melting-pot au multicultural-isme*, Paris: Fayard, 1997, pp. 335–6.

26. Ibid., p. 143.

27. Ibid., pp. 160–5.

28. The situation in the education system as well as changes in the legislation and regulations are outlined in Bernard Poignant's report to the prime minister, *Langues et cultures régionales*, Paris: La Documentation française, 1998.

29. Pierre Nora, "La nation-mémoire," in *Les lieux de mémoire, tome II*, Paris: Gallimard, 1986, p. 654.

30. This is even sometimes true of federal states. In Canada, after the passage of the 1931 Westminster Statute, which gave the dominion a fully independent government, consolidation of federal power soon manifested itself in the area of culture. The Canadian Broadcasting Corporation was explicitly created with the aim "to contribute to the development of national unity and provide for a continuing expression of Canadian identity." At the precise moment when the federal state was transforming into an interventionist welfare state, it also asserted itself as a cultural entrepreneur.

31. Gellner, op. cit., p. 13. See also pp. 35–43.

4. THE APPEAL OF NATIONALISM

1. Robert Lafont, *La Révolution régionaliste*, Paris: Gallimard, 1967.

2. For stimulating reflection on self-determination in Eastern Europe, see Stéphane Pierre-Caps, *La multination. L'avenir des minorités en Europe centrale et orientale*, Paris: Odile Jacob, 1995.

3. Ernest Gellner, *Nations and Nationalism*, Oxford: Blackwell, 1983, pp. 43–5.

4. Cameroon alone has approximately 230 ethnic groups.

5. Daniel-Louis Seiler, "La naissance des formations indépendantistes en Europe occidentale," in Christian Bidégaray (ed.), *Europe occidentale. Le mirage séparatiste*, Paris: Economica, 1997, p. 48.

6. Stein Rokkan, "Territories, Centres and Peripheries: Toward a geoethnic-geoeconomic-geopolitical model of differentiation within Western Europe," in Jean Gottmann (ed.), *Centre and Periphery: Spatial Variations in Politics*, London: SAGE, 1980, pp. 163–204.

7. Stein Rokkan's conceptual map of Europe was in particular revisited by Daniel-Louis Seiler, "Systèmes de partis et partis nationalistes," in Pierre Birnbaum (ed.), *Sociologie des nationalismes*, Paris: PUF, 1997, pp. 211–30.

8. In the National Assembly for Wales, the Welsh nationalist party Plaid Cymru won 21.7% of the vote in 2007 and 18% in 2011. In the Scottish Parliament, reinstated

in 1999 after having ceased to function for nearly three centuries, nationalists gar-
nered 32% of the vote in 2007 and 44.7% in 2011.

9. See for instance Michael Hechter's classic work, *Internal Colonialism: The Celtic Fringe in British National Development, 1536–1966*, London: Routledge and Kegan Paul, 1975.

10. The rational aspect of nationalist engagement has been pointed out by Michael Hechter and Margaret Levi, "A Rational Choice Approach to the Rise and Decline of Ethnoregional Political Parties" in Edward Tiryakian and Ronald Rogowski (eds), *New Nationalisms of the Developed West*, London and Boston: Allen & Unwin, 1985, pp. 128–46.

11. Ilvo Diamanti, who has devoted vital research to the League, analyzes this survey in detail in "Le Nord sans l'Italie," *Limes*, no. 1, 1996, pp. 257–71.

12. Data taken from Natascia Porcellato, "E la spaccatura del paese pesa sul 150° dell'Unità," in *Gli Italiani e lo Stato 2010*, http://www.demos.it/a00531.php, last accessed 7 March 2015.

13. I borrow the term "global society" from Simon Langlois who used it to describe the relations between Quebec and Canada: "Le choc de deux sociétés globales" in Louis Balthazar, Guy Laforest and Vincent Lemieux (eds), *Le Québec et la restructuration du Canada, 1980–1992*, Sillery: Septentrion, 1991, pp. 95–108.

14. Will Kymlicka, *Multicultural Citizenship: A Liberal Theory of Minority Rights*, Oxford: Clarendon Press, 1995, p. 76.

15. On the Scottish situation, see Jacques Leruez, *L'Écosse, une nation sans État*, Lille: Presses universitaires de Lille, 1983 and Michael Keating, *The Independence of Scotland: Self-government and the Shifting Politics of Union*, Oxford: Oxford University Press, 2009.

16. Montserrat Guibernau, *Nations Without States: Political Communities in a Global Age*, Cambridge: Polity, 1999; Michael Keating, *Plurinational Democracy: Stateless Nations in a Post-Sovereignty Era*, Oxford: Oxford University Press, 2001.

17. I borrow the distinction between civil and civic from Jean Leca, "Individualisme et citoyenneté," in Pierre Birnbaum and Jean Leca (eds), *Sur l'individualisme*, Paris: Presses de Sciences-Po, 1986, p. 174.

18. For a thorough presentation of regionalist parties, see Daniel-Louis Seiler, *Les partis autonomistes*, Paris, PUF, 1994, "Que sais-je?" series.

19. The May 2011 federal elections led to the collapse of the Bloc Québécois, which went from forty-nine members to four in the parliament in Ottawa following a massive voter shift to a social-democratic party, the New Democratic Party. The October 2015 federal elections further confirmed the weakness of the Bloc Québécois, which won only ten seats.

20. Eric Hobsbawm, *Nations and Nationalism Since 1780: Programme, Myth, Reality*, Cambridge: Cambridge University Press, 1990, p. 176.

21. See my discussion of this point in *The Invention of a Nation: Zionist Thought and*

the Making of Modern Israel, London: Hurst, 2003, pp. 92ff. See also Zeev Sternhell, *The Founding Myths of Israel: Nationalism, Socialism, and the Making of the Jewish State* [trans. David Maisel], Princeton: Princeton University Press, 1998.

22. In analyzing nationalism in Quebec, I follow Louis Balthazar's discussion in *Bilan du nationalisme au Québec*, Montreal: L'Hexagone, 1986.

23. Ibid., p. 133.

24. Guy Laforest, *De l'urgence*, Montreal: Boréal, 1995, p. 181.

25. Through an energetic campaign by citizens of Louisiana, supported by francophone institutions, French was restored as an official language in the 1970s.

26. Charles Taylor, *Reconciling the Solitudes: Essays on Canadian Federalism and Nationalism*, Montreal: McGill-Queen's University Press, 1993, p. 165.

27. Louis Bélanger, "L'espace international de l'État québécois dans l'après-guerre froide: vers une compression?" in Alain-G. Gagnon and Alain Noël, *L'espace québécois*, Montreal: Éditions Québec/Amérique, 1995, pp. 71–102.

28. Stéphane Paquin, *Paradiplomatie et relations internationales. Théorie des stratégies internationales des régions face à la mondialisation*, Brussels: Peter Lang, 2004.

29. Jean-Louis Quermonne, "L'Union Européenne: générateur ou catalyseur de la recomposition territoriale?" in Christian Bidégaray (ed.), *Europe occidentale. Le mirage séparatiste*, Paris: Economica, 1997, pp. 299–305. See also Liesbet Hooghe and Gary Marks, "Restructuration territoriale au sein de l'Union européenne: les pressions régionales" in Vincent Wright and Sabino Cassese (eds), *La recomposition de l'État en Europe*, Paris: La Découverte, 1996, pp. 207–26.

30. Vincent Wright and Sabino Cassese, "La restructuration des États en Europe occidentale," ibid., pp. 8–17.

31. See the special issue coordinated by Daniel Hermant, "Nationalismes et construction européenne," *Cultures et conflits*, no. 7, fall 1992.

32. Convergència split from the smaller, Christian Democrat Unió during the September 2015 regional elections and built a pro-independence alliance with the nationalist left (ERC).

33. Officially banned in Spain since 2003 due to its ties with the ETA, Batasuna has attempted to field candidates for election to the Basque Parliament under a variety of alternate names. These groups have generally been disqualified by the Spanish courts.

5. THE IMPERFECT TRINITY

1. This classification is based on the different ways of viewing relations between the private and the public sphere. Liberalism and republicanism both acknowledge this distinction, but whereas the former seeks to ensure the broadest possible autonomy for the private sphere, the latter has a clear tendency to value the public sphere and civic participation. As for multiculturalism, it radically challenges this canonical

division. The idea of a public space in which equal citizens all participate in fashioning the common good is a myth that masks true relationships of domination and exclusion. This situation can only be remedied if private identities, rather than being shunned, are fully involved in the public space.

2. For the distinction between liberalism and republicanism, see Alain Touraine, *Qu'est-ce que la démocratie?* Paris: Fayard, 1994. See also Guy Hermet, *La trahison démocratique. Populistes, républicains et démocrates*, Paris: Flammarion, 1998.

3. The early version of liberalism emphasizes toleration and adherence to pluralism. It should be distinguished from its contemporary reformulations, which focus more on redistributive policies aiming to benefit the less privileged members of society.

4. A thorough presentation of the controversy between liberals and communitarians can be found in André Berten, Pablo da Silveira and Hervé Pourtois, *Libéraux et communautariens*, Paris: PUF, 1997.

5. Michael Walzer, "The Communitarian Critique of Liberalism," *Political Theory*, vol. 18, no. 1., February 1990, p. 15.

6. The term "Bosniak" is synonymous with Muslim. The Bosniaks are thus members of the Muslim nation of Bosnia, formerly referred to simply as "Muslims." The term "Bosnian," on the other hand, refers to all the inhabitants of Bosnia and Herzegovina (including Serbs and Croats).

7. The 2010 elections brought about significant change with the victory of a non-nationalist party, the Social-Democratic Party (SDP), in the Bosniak-Croat federation. This win undeniably attests to the population's weariness regarding the endless deadlocks that nationalist groups inflict on the country.

8. John Crowley, "La pacification du politique en Irlande du Nord," *Critique internationale*, no. 1, 1998, pp. 35–42.

9. See the discussion regarding the relationship between state and culture in Chapter II, pp. 37–49.

10. Contrary to what Michael Walzer asserts in his otherwise very stimulating essay, *On Toleration*, New Haven: Yale University Press, 1997, pp. 55–56.

11. Wayne Norman, "The Ideology of Shared Values: A Myopic Vision of Unity in the Multi-nation State," in Joseph Carens, *Is Quebec Nationalism Just? Perspectives from Anglophone Canada*, Kingston and Montreal: McGill-Queen's University Press, 1995, pp. 137–157.

12. Regarding this paradoxical outcome, see Stéphane Dion, "Le nationalisme dans la convergence culturelle. Le Québec contemporain et le paradoxe de Tocqueville," in Raymond Hudon and Réjean Pelletier, *L'engagement intellectuel. Mélanges en l'honneur de Léon Dion*, Sainte-Foy: Presses de l'Université Laval, 1991, pp. 292–311.

13. For Trudeau's relationship to Canadian nationalism, I rely on the chapter "La culture politique canadienne et la Charte des droits et libertés" in Guy Laforest, *Trudeau et la fin d'un rêve canadien*, Sillery: Septentrion, 1992, pp. 173–205.

14. Pierre Elliott Trudeau, *Le fédéralisme et la société canadienne-française*, Paris: Robert Laffont, 1968, p. 204.

15. Laforest has carefully analyzed this strategic use of the Charter, op. cit.

16. John Breuilly, *Nationalism and the State*, Manchester: Manchester University Press, 1982, pp. 374ff.

17. For the national function of culture in Canada, see Joyce Zemans, "The Essential Role of National Cultural Institutions," in Kenneth McRoberts (ed.), *Beyond Quebec: Taking Stock of Canada*, Montreal: McGill-Queen's University Press, 1995, pp. 138–162.

18. Alain-G. Gagnon, André Lecours and Geneviève Nootens (eds), *Contemporary Majority Nationalism*, Montreal: McGill-Queen's University Press, 2011.

19. Jeremy Webber, *Reimagining Canada: Language, Culture, Community and the Canadian Constitution*, Kingston and Montreal: McGill-Queen's University Press, 1994, p. 210.

20. See Petr Pithart's analysis, "L'asymétrie de la séparation tchéco-slovaque," in Jacques Rupnik, *Le déchirement des nations*, Paris, Seuil, 1995, pp. 157–179.

21. I do not use the term "republic" in a purely descriptive sense to refer to a particular institutional regime, but as a genuine ideology based on the defense of the public interest, civic participation, separation of church and state, etc. See Claude Nicolet, *L'idée républicaine en France (1789–1924). Essai d'histoire critique*, Paris. Gallimard, 1982.

22. Michael Walzer, "Communauté, citoyenneté et jouissance des droits" in *Pluralisme et démocratie*, Paris, Éditions Esprit, pp. 167–181.

23. Régis Debray, *Que vive la République*, Paris: Odile Jacob, 1989, pp. 13 and 32.

24. Pierre Birnbaum, "La déchirure du lien étatique," in Noëlle Burgi (ed.), *Fractures de l'État-nation*, Paris: Kimé, 1994, p. 209.

25. Jean-Robert Henry, "L'identité imaginée par le droit. De l'Algérie coloniale à la construction européenne" in Denis-Constant Martin, *Cartes d'identité. Comment dit-on "nous" en politique?* Paris: Presses de Sciences Po, 1994, pp. 41–63.

26. Anne-Marie Thiesse, *Ils apprenaient la France. L'exaltation des régions dans le discours patriotique*, Paris: MSH, 1997, p. 60.

27. Sophie Duchesne, *Citoyenneté à la française*, Paris: Presses de Sciences Po, 1997.

28. See Chapter II, pp. 38–41.

29. Duchesne, op. cit., p. 307.

30. A caricatured example can be found in Christian Jelen's *Les casseurs de la République* (Paris: Plon, 1997) in which he depicts the French Republic as heaving its dying breath.

31. Michèle Tribalat, *Faire France. Une enquête sur les immigrés et leurs enfants*, Paris: La Découverte, 1995.

32. Regarding the phenomenon of territorial ethnic concentrations, see Michèle Tribalat, *Les yeux grands fermés. L'immigration en France*, Paris: Denoël, 2010,

pp. 143–82. On the question of communitarization among Muslims, see Gilles Kepel, *Banlieue de la République. Société, politique et religion à Clichy-sous-Bois et Montfermeil*, Paris: Gallimard, 2012.

33. For a thorough and inspired reflection on the evolution of French identity, see Pierre Birnbaum, *La France imaginée. Déclin des rêves unitaires?* Paris: Fayard, 1998.

34. Charles Taylor, *Multiculturalism and The Politics of Recognition*, Princeton: Princeton University Press, 1992.

35. Riva Kastoryano, *La France, l'Allemagne et leurs immigrés: négocier l'identité*, Paris: Armand Colin, 1996.

36. Vincent Geisser, *Ethnicité républicaine. Les élites d'origine maghrébine dans le système politique français*, Paris: Presses de Sciences Po, 1997.

37. Pierre Birnbaum, *Destins juifs. De la Révolution française à Carpentras*, Paris: Calmann-Lévy, 1995, p. 223.

38. Decentralization was constitutionalized by the 2003 constitutional revision granting local government a new set of powers: the principle of subsidiarity, legislative and regulatory experimentation, etc.

39. Élisabeth Dupoirier, "Les identités régionales" in Élisabeth Dupoirier, *Régions. La croisée des chemins. Perspectives françaises et enjeux européens*, Paris: Presses de Sciences Po, 1998, pp. 185–200.

40. Norbert Rouland, "Le statut juridique des autochtones de l'outre-mer français" in Norbert Rouland, Stéphane Pierré-Caps and Jacques Poumarède, *Droit des minorités et des peuples autochtones*, Paris: PUF, 1996, pp. 507–48.

41. France has five overseas territories: French Polynesia, Wallis and Futuna, Saint Pierre and Miquelon, Saint Barthélemy and Saint Martin.

42. Stéphane Pierré-Caps, "La France et les minorités," in Rouland, Pierré-Caps and Poumarède, op. cit., pp. 307–45.

43. Here I use the term nation in a purely political sense to refer to all of the citizens of a state. This meaning should be clearly distinguished from the socio-cultural definition that considers the nation as a global society, which makes it possible to apprehend instances of national pluralism within one and the same state. See the discussions in Chapter IV, pp. 69–70.

44. Yvonne Bollmann, "L'Alsace, une zone de dangers," *Limes*, no. 1, 1996, pp. 113–14.

45. The idea of cultural rights as a new generation of human rights (after civil, political and social rights) was put forward by Patrice Meyer-Bisch (ed.), *Les droits culturels. Une catégorie sous-développée de droits de l'homme*, Fribourg: Éditions Universitaires, 1993. Under his direction, the Institut interdisciplinaire d'éthique et des droits de l'homme (Interdisciplinary Institute of Ethics and Human Rights) at the University of Fribourg (Switzerland), has done a remarkable job of formalizing cultural rights (respect for cultural identity, participation in cultural life,

education and training, etc.). See its proposal for a declaration of cultural rights on its website, last accessed 31 December 2015: http://www.unifr.ch/iiedh

46. Michel Wieviorka (ed.), *Une société fragmentée? Le multiculturalisme en débat*, Paris: La Découverte, 1996; Alain Touraine, *Can We Live Together? Equality and Difference* [trans. David Macey], Stanford: Stanford University Press, 2000.

47. This classification is borrowed from Marco Martiniello's very useful clarification in *Sortir des ghettos culturels*, Paris: Presses de Sciences Po, 1997.

48. Iris Marion Young, *Justice and the Politics of Difference*, Princeton: Princeton University Press, 1990, p. 184.

49. Pierre-André Taguieff, *La République menacée*, Paris: Textuel, 1996, p. 72.

50. The breadth of this national identity is variable: it will be broader in a classical nation-state with a dominant, if not a shared, historical memory, a common language and perhaps the same religion. Conversely, it will be narrower in a plurinational state where more pronounced diversity makes it difficult to consolidate.

51. Quoted by Roger Gibbins, "Western Canada: The West Wants In" in McRoberts, op. cit., p. 57.

52. Ernest Renan, "What Is a Nation?" in Geoff Eley and Ronald Grigor Suny (eds), *Becoming National: A Reader*, New York and Oxford: Oxford University Press, 1996, pp. 41–55.

53. Pierre-André Taguieff pointed this out with regard to France when he wrote, "we must cease to allow the Front National a monopoly on the national idea." See op. cit., p. 59.

54. This blend of liberal toleration and "open nationalism" was largely dominant in Western Europe up until the last quarter of the nineteenth century, when extreme forms of nationalism came to the fore. The unleashing of violence these aroused tended to obscure the fact that liberalism and nationalism have not always been in conflict.

55. Will Kymlicka, *Multicultural Citizenship: A Liberal Theory of Minority Rights*, Oxford: Clarendon Press, 1995, pp. 10–33.

56. Michael Walzer, "Pluralism in Political Perspective," in *The Politics of Ethnicity*, Cambridge, MA: Harvard University Press, 1982, p. 9.

57. Phyllis Cohen Albert, "Ethnicité et solidarité chez les Juifs de France au XIXe siècle," *Pardès*, no. 3, 1986, pp. 29–53.

58. This is the case of Afrocentrism, a radical form of multiculturalism, which extols the African-American people and views African civilization as the axis of world history. From this standpoint, society cannot be based on universally accepted values (qualified as "Western"); it is no more than a juxtaposition of ethnic communities, each with its own view of the past and henceforth of the future. See Molefi Asante, *The Afrocentric Idea*, Philadelphia: Temple University Press, 1987. For a critique of Afrocentrism, see Denis Lacorne, *La crise de l'identité américaine. Du melting-pot au multiculturalisme*, Paris: Fayard, 1997, pp. 256–61.

59. Neil Bissoondath, *Selling Illusions: The Cult of Multiculturalism in Canada* (revised ed.), Toronto: Penguin Canada, 2002.

60. Tariq Modood, "Establishment, Multiculturalism and British Citizenship," *Political Quarterly*, vol. 65 (1), January 1994, p. 64.

61. Cf. supra pp. 68–74.

62. Paul Garde, *Vie et mort de la Yougoslavie*, Paris: Fayard, 1992, p. 144.

63. The only known case of a nationalist shift involves Afro-Americans, "involuntary immigrants" taken as slaves to the New World. The persistent social discrimination and pervasive racism attached to ethnicity sustained among some of them true nationalist aspirations defended by a group founded in the 1930s, The Nation of Islam. At first marginal, this movement, which advocated a break with white society and the creation of a separate black state, has managed under the leadership of Louis Farrakhan to exert growing ascendency over the Afro-American community in the United States. On this issue, see Gilles Kepel, *Allah in the West*, Stanford: Stanford University Press, 1997, pp. 44–75.

64. Cited by Neil Bissoondath, "A Question of Belonging," *Globe and Mail*, 28 January 1993.

65. This project has a certain affinity with the overhaul of liberal theory suggested by Sylvie Mesure and Alain Renaut, *Alter Ego. Les paradoxes de l'identité démocratique*, Paris: Aubier, 1999.

6. AUTONOMY WITHOUT TERRITORY

1. These two modes of managing national diversity are analyzed very thoroughly by Stéphane Pierré-Caps and Rainer Bauböck respectively in Alain Dieckhoff (ed.), *The Politics of Belonging. Nationalism, Liberalism, and Pluralism*, Paris & Lanham, Maryland: Lexington Books, 2004, pp. 221–81.

2. A table in the appendix compares the different types of states and modes of regulating national pluralism.

3. For a very thorough presentation of national minorities, see André Liebich, *Les minorités nationales en Europe centrale et orientale*, Geneva: Georg Éditeur, 1997.

4. I elaborate here on Ernest Gellner's suggestive image in *Nations and Nationalism*, Oxford: Blackwell, 1983, p. 139.

5. The distinction between the two types of minorities may seem arbitrary. That is one reason that many international documents associate them, as in the UN declaration of 1992 pertaining to the rights "of persons belonging to national or ethnic, religious and linguistic minorities." Yet it seems necessary to draw a boundary, albeit uncertain, between ethnic and national minorities. Ethnic minorities form restricted groups that are geographically isolated and concentrated, often in a doubly peripheral situation, such as the Pomaks (Bulgarian-speaking Muslim Slavs) or the Gagauz (Christianized Turks in Moldavia). National minorities are larger groups, often scattered over several countries, and are generally an extension of sovereign states. The

Hungarians scattered throughout Central Europe and the Balkans are in many respects the archetypal national minority.

6. For a synthetic presentation of national cultural autonomy as Karl Renner conceived it, see Stéphane Pierré-Caps, "Karl Renner, de l'État des nationalités à l'État mondial," *Revue d'Allemagne et des pays de langue allemande*, vol. 28 (2), April–June 1996, pp. 187–200. For Otto Bauer, see his book, *La question des nationalités et la social-démocratie*, Paris & Montreal: Arcantère Éditions, 1987.

7. Peter Kovacs, "La Hongrie et le phénomène de l'émergence des minorités" in Olivier Audeoud, Jean-Denis Mouton and Stéphane Pierré-Caps (eds), *L'État multinational et l'Europe*, Nancy: Presses Universitaires de Nancy, 1997.

8. The precedent set by the League of Nations, which had instituted a largely defective mechanism for protecting minorities, is often mentioned to justify refusing to grant group rights. Actually, the system set up fell apart because it was imposed on some states (the losers and the new states) through specific treaties, without the big winning countries (France, Italy) having to make any commitments. As for the specific rights granted the various minorities, they mainly pertained to the free use of their language. Minorities were only rarely granted recognition of a legal personality, and thus of collective rights. Regarding this point, see Pablo de Azcarate, *La Société des nations et la protection des minorités*, Geneva: The Carnegie Endowment for International Peace, 1969.

9. The American sociologist Talcott Parsons had already suggested adding cultural rights to the three dimensions of citizenship—civil, political and social. However, by this he mainly meant the general right to education so that a given population would have a basic shared culture. See *Social Systems and the Evolution of Action Theory*, New York: Free Press, 1977, pp. 334–40.

10. See Alain Touraine's theories, particularly in *Critique de la modernité*, Paris: Fayard, 1992; *Qu'est-ce que la démocratie?* Paris: Fayard, 1994.

11. For a stimulating parallel between the two countries, see Nadège Ragaru and Antonela Capelle-Pogăcean, "Les voix de l'appartenance: interpréter les votes 'ethniques' en Bulgarie et en Roumanie," *Critique internationale*, no. 53, October–December 2011, pp. 119–44.

12. Florence Benoît-Rohmer, *The Minority Question in Europe*, Strasbourg: Council of Europe Publishing, 1996, p. 51. This compilation contains a very thorough presentation of international systems to protect minorities.

13. For a complete and subtle assessment, see Antonela Capelle-Pogăcean, "Les relations hungaro-roumaines et la question des minorités magyares," *Études du CERI*, no. 12, 1996. See also her article, "Hongrie/Roumanie: rivalités et synergies dans la marche vers l'Europe," *Politique étrangère*, vol. 61 (4), 1996, pp. 853–66.

14. The law on citizenship is only one aspect of a much broader constitutional and legislative mechanism. A new fundamental law, starting with an invocation of God, came into effect in 2012. It makes clear reference to the Hungarian nation

as a single transnational nation and that "Hungary shall bear responsibility for the fate of Hungarians living beyond its borders." At the same time, the Parliament passed a series of organic laws and ordinary laws in a wide variety of areas (the courts, central bank, the media, etc.) that aim to reform the state by reinforcing the executive branch. Many of these provisions have been challenged before the Constitutional Court of Hungary and have elicited critical opinions from the European Commission for breaches of European treaties.

15. Regarding the phenomenon of Russian migration, see Dominique Arel, "Recensement et légitimation nationale en Russie et dans la zone postsoviétique," *Critique internationale*, no. 45, October–December 2009, pp. 32–4.

16. The restriction on access to citizenship is not purely ethnic, because the admittedly small number of Russians who were citizens of the two Baltic states in the interwar period automatically became citizens. Those who arrived after the Soviet annexation in 1940 do, however, fall under the law.

17. Nicolas Werth, "A State against Its People" in Stéphane Courtois et al., *The Black Book of Communism: Crimes, Terror, Repression* [trans. Jonathan Murphy], Cambridge, MA: Harvard University Press, 1999, p. 236.

18. Yves Plasseraud and Suzanne Pourchier, "États baltes: vers l'Europe," *Esprit*, no. 249, January 1999, p. 40. The above discussion also owes much to Yves Plasseraud's book, *Les États baltes*, Paris: Montchrestien, 1992.

19. István Bibó, *Misère des petits États d'Europe de l'Est* [trans. Gyorgy Kassai], Paris: L'Harmattan, 1986.

20. "Les Lettons font un pas vers l'Ouest," *Le Monde*, 15 October 1998.

21. Switzerland actually has twenty full cantons and six half-cantons, all having the same powers.

22. The consociational model was developed by Arendt Lijphart for the example of the Netherlands in *The Politics of Accommodation: Pluralism and Democracy in the Netherlands*, Berkeley: University of California, 1968. Lijphart later extended it to other countries, mainly in Europe (Belgium, Switzerland). See *Democracy in Plural Societies: A Comparative Exploration*, New Haven: Yale University Press, 1977. For an assessment of consociational functioning, see "Changement et continuité dans la théorie consociative," *Revue internationale de politique comparée*, vol. 4 (3), 1997.

23. On 22 May 1998 nearly 72% of the electorate in Northern Ireland voted in favor of the Good Friday Agreement.

24. Ronald C. Slye, "The Dayton Peace Agreement: Constitutionalism and Ethnicity," *Yale Journal of International Law*, vol. 21 (2), summer 1996, pp. 459–73.

25. The strict ethnic bipartition of the two entities making up Bosnia was softened in 2002 under pressure from the UN High Representative. The three constituent peoples of Bosnia and Herzegovina were acknowledged in their right to have representatives in the legislative, executive and judicial decision-making bodies of

both federated entities. This reform has, however, increased Bosnia's institutional complexity.

26. Bertrand Badie, *Un monde sans souveraineté. Les États entre ruse et responsabilité*, Paris: Fayard, 1999, p. 160.

7. TERRITORIAL AUTONOMY

1. Ernest Gellner, *Nations and Nationalism*, Oxford: Blackwell, 1983, p. 51.

2. Jean-Didier Hache (ed.), *Quel statut pour les îles d'Europe?* Paris, L'Harmattan, 2000.

3. Claude Barbanti, "Le Scottish National Party de 2007 à 2011: un parti toujours indépendantiste?" *Critique internationale*, no. 53, October–December 2011, pp. 103–17.

4. I will use the term "federalism" in the broad sense, describing federations, confederations and associations of states, rather than in the limited legal meaning.

5. This phenomenon is meticulously analyzed by Olivier Roy, *The New Central Asia: Geopolitics and the Creation of Nations*, London: I.B. Tauris, 2000.

6. Stevan Pavlowitch, "L'héritage titiste. Des mythes de Tito aux démons de la nation" in Jacques Rupnik (ed.), *De Sarajevo à Sarajevo. L'échec yougoslave*, Brussels: Complexe, 1992, p. 59.

7. The Spanish state's mode of organization borrows characteristic features of federalism (political and institutional autonomy of substate actors) but it is also tinged with French-style decentralization, Italian regionalism and even confederalism (for the Basque Country and Navarre). In any event, this *sui generis* system of autonomy makes Spain a multination state.

8. José Forné relates this nationalist intolerance to a quasi-racial essentialism and an obsession with pure lineage, in *Euskadi, nation et idéologie*, Paris: Éditions du CNRS, 1990.

9. See Claude Leclercq, *L'État fédéral*, Paris: Dalloz, 1997, pp. 33–39.

10. Among the twenty-five federal states, seven are located in Europe, seven in the Americas, five in Asia, four in Africa and two in Oceania.

11. Will Kymlicka, *Multicultural Citizenship: A Liberal Theory of Minority Rights*, Oxford: Clarendon Press, 1995, p. 28.

12. Alexis de Tocqueville, *Democracy in America* [trans. Harvey C. Mansfield and Delba Winthrop], Chicago: University of Chicago Press, 2000, p. 158.

13. I borrow the distinction between territorial and multinational federalism from Philip Resnick, "Toward a Multination Federalism: Asymmetrical and Confederal Alternatives," in F. Leslie Seidle (ed.), *Seeking a New Canadian Partnership: Asymmetrical and Confederal Options*, Montreal: Institute for Research on Public Policies, 1994, pp. 71–89.

14. Alain Gagnon and James Tully (eds), *Multinational Democracies*, Cambridge: Cambridge University Press, 2001; Michel Seymour and Alain Gagnon (eds),

Multinational Federalism: Problems and Prospects, Basingstoke: Palgrave Macmillan, 2012.

15. Françoise Massart-Piérard, "Les entités fédérées de Belgique, acteurs décisionnels au sein de l'Union européenne," *Politique et sociétés*, vol. 18 (1), 1999, pp. 3–40.

16. For a precise analysis of the financial implications of the projected reform, see Benoît Bayenet, *Etat de la question. Contexte des derniers accords institutionnels sur la 6ᵉᵐᵉ réforme de l'État et le financement des communautés et des régions*, Brussels: Institut Emile Vandervelde, 2011.

17. The francophone parties approved this agreement because it guarantees the financial transfers to Wallonia and the French community of Belgium while providing for the financing of Brussels.

18. Paul Tourret, "La quête identitaire wallone," *Hérodote*, no. 72/73, January–June 1994, pp. 58–75.

19. Among the considerations on the applicability of asymmetrical federalism to Canada, see Peter Leslie, "Asymmetry: Rejected, Conceded, Imposed" in Seidle, op. cit., pp. 37–69; Jeremy Webber, *Reimagining Canada: Language, Culture, Community, and the Canadian Constitution*, Kingston & Montreal: McGill-Queen's University Press, 1994, pp. 229–305; Will Kymlicka, *Finding Our Way: Rethinking Ethnocultural Relations in Canada*, Toronto: Oxford University Press, 1998, pp. 130–46.

20. In November 2006, the Canadian House of Commons almost unanimously passed a motion recognizing "that the Quebecois form a nation within a united Canada."

21. According to legal scholar Georges Scelle, aggregative federalism is based on the association of existing political units in order to form a larger political entity. He very usefully distinguishes it from disaggregative federalism based on the opposite principle, in other words the fragmentation of a united political entity into several federated entities (Belgium is a textbook case of this variety of federalism).

22. Francesc Morata, "La géométrie variable appliquée à l'État des autonomies: un bilan de la décentralisation politique en Espagne (1980–1995)," in Christian Bidégaray (ed.), *Europe occidentale. Le mirage séparatiste*, Paris: Economica, 1997, pp. 269–88.

23. Yolaine Cultiaux, "Le nouveau statut d'autonomie de la Catalogne: acte II de l'Etat des Autonomies," *Critique internationale*, vol. 37 (4), October–December 2007, pp. 23–35. In September 2010, the Spanish Constitutional Court invalidated part of the new status, provoking strong protest in Catalonia.

24. Stéphane Dion, "Le fédéralisme fortement asymétrique: improbable et indésirable" in F. Leslie Seidle, op. cit., pp. 133–52.

25. Ibid., p. 145.

26. Both the Basque Country and neighboring Navarre benefit from laws dating from the medieval period (*fueros*) that grant them the exorbitant privilege of being enti-

tled to levy most taxes, including on income. The two communities must transfer a portion of the tax revenue to the central state for its operating costs.

27. Kymlicka, op. cit., pp. 135–6.
28. For an analysis of the Swiss case, see Hanspeter Kriesi, "State Formation and Nation Building in the Swiss Case," in Hanspeter Kriesi et al. (eds), *Nation and National Identity: The European Experience in Perspective*, Zurich, Verlag Rügger, 1999, pp. 14–28.
29. The information concerning India has been drawn from the volume edited by Christophe Jaffrelot, *L'Inde contemporaine de 1950 à nos jours*, Paris: Fayard, 1996, pp. 199–280.
30. Regarding partnership, see Guy Laforest and Roger Gibbins (eds), *Beyond the Impasse: Toward Reconciliation*, Montreal: Institute for Research on Public Policy, 1998.

8. THE SECESSIONIST TEMPTATION

1. Ivor Jennings, *The Approach to Self-Government*, Cambridge: Cambridge University Press, 1956, p. 56.
2. Cited by Daniel Patrick Moynihan, *Pandaemonium: Ethnicity in International Politics*, Oxford: Oxford University Press, 1993, pp. 82–3.
3. Anna Michalska, "Rights of Peoples to Self-Determination in International Law" in William Twining (ed.), *Issues of Self-Determination*, Aberdeen: Aberdeen University Press, 1991, pp. 71–90.
4. Margaret Moore pointed out this transformation in "Introduction: The Self-Determination Principle and the Ethics of Secession," in Margaret Moore (ed.), *National Self-Determination and Secession*, Oxford: Oxford University Press, 1998, pp. 1–4.
5. Even though since the 1990s some twenty new states have come into being through fragmentation of a state, this has not led to a legal legitimation of secession.
6. The violent rebellion started by the Tamil Tigers in 1983 was finally crushed in 2009 by the Sri Lankan army. During the twenty-six years of conflict, between 80,000 and 100,000 people were killed.
7. The question asked of the Quebeckers in 1995 was worded as follows: "Do you agree that Quebec should become sovereign after having made a formal offer to Canada for a new economic and political partnership within the scope of the Bill respecting the future of Quebec and of the agreement signed on June 12, 1995 [an agreement between Quebecois nationalist leaders, A.D.]?" This question is far more convoluted than the one Montenegrin voters were asked in 2006: "Do you wish the Republic of Montenegro to become an independent state with full legal and international recognition?"
8. See Robert Young's comparative analysis of successful secessions in his edited book

The Secession of Quebec and the Future of Canada, Montreal: McGill-Queen's University Press, 1995, pp. 127–44.

9. This factor was also present in the Soviet case because Russians dominated the governing bodies of the USSR. Two other facts, however, explain why the Russians did not choose to save the federation: first, the decreasing numbers of Russians in leadership positions in the non-Russian republics, and second, the fact that the transfer of allegiance from the USSR to Russia did not challenge their imperial vision, as Russia remained a multination state, with its Tatars, Ingush, Siberian peoples, etc.

10. These two schools of thought and their arguments are well represented in the volume edited by Margaret Moore, op. cit. I borrow the distinction between secession as a primary right and as a remedial right from Allen Buchanan, "Theories of Secession," *Philosophy and Public Affairs*, vol. 26 (1), Winter 1997, pp. 31–61.

11. Allen Buchanan, *Secession: The Morality of Political Divorce, From Fort Sumter to Lithuania and Quebec*, Boulder, CO: Westview 1991.

12. For a detailed discussion of the commission's opinion, see Stéphane Pierré-Caps, *La multination. L'avenir des minorités en Europe centrale et orientale*, Paris: Odile Jacob, 1995, pp. 145–51.

13. Olivier Roy, *The New Central Asia: Geopolitics and the Creation of Nations*, London: I.B. Tauris, 2000, pp. 67–8.

14. Xavier Bougarel, *Bosnie. Anatomie d'un conflit*, Paris: La Découverte, 1996.

15. Jean-Alphonse Bernard, *De l'empire des Indes à la République indienne, de 1935 à nos jours*, Paris: Imprimerie nationale, 1994, pp. 97–103.

16. This phenomenon was pointed out by Donald Horowitz in *Ethnic Groups in Conflict*, Berkeley: University of California Press, 1985, p. 590.

17. With the 2014 electoral victory of Narendra Modi's nationalist Bharatiya Janata Party (BJP), the stress on *Hindutva* ("Hinduness") in India has clearly grown.

18. Regarding the Hindu nationalist attitude toward the Muslims, see Christophe Jaffrelot, *Les nationalistes hindous*, Paris: Presses de Sciences Po, 1993, pp. 405–12.

19. On all these issues, see Christophe Jaffrelot (ed.), *Le Pakistan, carrefour de tensions régionales*, Brussels: Complexe, 1999 and Christophe Jaffrelot, *The Pakistan Paradox: Instability and Resilience* [trans. Cynthia Schoch], London: Hurst, 2015.

20. The "second" Republic of Yugoslavia (1992–2006) was made up of Serbia and Montenegro.

21. Paul Garde, "Il faut donner au Kosovo la maîtrise de son destin," *Le Monde*, 4 October 1998.

22. Here can be identified Allen Buchanan's four main justifications for secession.

23. An informal group for diplomatic dialogue comprising Russia, the United States, Great Britain, Germany, France and Italy.

24. International Crisis Group report, "Kosovo: No Good Alternatives to the Ahtisaari

Plan," 14 May 2007. On the mediating role of the Finnish diplomat, see Milena Dieckhoff, *L'individu dans les relations internationales. Le cas du médiateur Martti Ahtisaari*, Paris: L'Harmattan, 2012.

25. Serbia took the matter before the International Court of Justice, which handed down an advisory opinion in which it stated that the declaration of independence did not violate international law. The decision, however, in no way implied that the Court recognized Kosovo as a state.

26. In practice, geopolitical considerations will always blunt the temptation to recognize a state. A state that plays an essential role in the regional or international balance of power will more easily command respect and be less vulnerable to foreign state intervention in favor of the secessionist movement. This is true of Turkey with the Kurds, of Russia with the Chechens and of China with the Tibetans and the Uigurs.

27. Paul Garde very aptly points out the particularities of Kosovo in his article, "Kosovo: missile intelligent et chausse-pied rouillé," *Politique internationale*, no. 84, Summer 1999, pp. 12–64.

28. Even if dissociation processes are sometimes achieved through war and thus have a negative impact on regional stability, once they are created nothing indicates that new states will, ineluctably and perpetually, be involved in clashes with neighbors on the grounds that their difference can only be expressed belligerently, "antagonism being these states' very substance" (a theory defended by Philippe Delmas, *Le bel avenir de la guerre*, Paris: Gallimard, 1995). In no way does the evolution of Slovenia, Slovakia and many other new states justify such a pessimistic assumption.

29. Petr Pithart, "L'asymétric de la séparation tchéco-slovaque," in Jacques Rupnik, *Le déchirement des nations*, Paris, Seuil, 1995, p. 175.

30. Regarding the phenomenon of "ethnic unmixing" in the USSR, see Rogers Brubaker, *Nationalism Reframed: Nationhood and the National Question in the New Europe*, Cambridge: Cambridge University Press, 1996, pp. 169–78. Regarding Central Asia, see Olivier Roy, op. cit., pp. 161–89.

31. Guy Hermet, *Le passage à la démocratie*, Paris: Presses de Sciences Po, 1996, p. 106.

32. Bruno Luverà, "L'internationale régionaliste entre masque et visage," *Limes*, no. 1, 1996, pp. 281–94.

CONCLUSION: THE FUTURE OF PLURALISM

1. Stéphane Pierré-Caps, *La multination. L'avenir des minorités en Europe centrale et orientale*, Paris: Odile Jacob, 1995, p. 152.

2. United Nations General Assembly, resolution 2625 (XXV), 24 October 1970. The 1964 union of the Zanzibar archipelago and Tanganyika to form Tanzania, and the association of the Cook Islands with New Zealand (which allows the Polynesian

archipelago considerable autonomy), both illustrate these two ways of materializing self-determination.

3. Monaco, San Marino and Liechtenstein in Europe; the Marshall Islands, Palau and the Federated States of Micronesia in the Pacific.

4. Joseph Krulic, "La revendication de souveraineté," *Pouvoirs*, no. 67, November 1993, pp. 21–32.

5. The most fully sovereign republic is Tatarstan. See Jean-Robert Raviot, "Le Tatarstan, une spécificité républicaine?" *Nouveaux mondes*, no. 7, Winter 1997, pp. 193–220.

6. Of all the republics in the federation, the situation in Chechnya is a different case. It was independent *de facto* after a twenty-month-long conflict with Russia (1994–6). Its final status was to be decided by 31 December 2001, but in September 1999, Russia unleashed another military offensive, which entailed particularly bloody battles with the Chechen independence fighters and did not spare civilians. The war, which had repercussions well beyond this Caucasian republic (hostage-taking, separatist attacks in Moscow) gradually subsided in the mid-2000s after the main independence leaders were eliminated and the pro-Russian president of Chechnya, Ramzan Kadyrov, undertook to "normalize" political relations.

7. Judith Zinsser, *Les peuples autochtones et le système des Nations Unies. Un nouveau partenariat*, Paris: Unesco, 1995. Isabelle Schulte-Tenckhoff, *La question des peuples autochtones*, Paris & Brussels: LGDJ & Bruylant, 1997. Stephen Allen and Alexandra Xanthaki (eds), *Reflections on the UN Declaration on the Rights of Indigenous Peoples*, Oxford: Hart Publishing, 2011.

8. These four finally ratified the declaration in 2009 and 2010.

9. See for instance the interview published in *Politique internationale*, no. 49, Fall 1990, p. 445.

10. *Politique internationale*, no. 72, Summer 1996, pp. 9–22.

11. Bertrand Badie, *Un monde sans souveraineté. Les États entre ruse et responsabilité*, Paris: Fayard, 1999

12. "It was even more doubtful whether it [this form of government] could be imported into an area which lacked the very conditions for the rise of nation-states: homogeneity of population and rootedness in the soil... 'One glance at the demographic map of Europe should be sufficient to show that the nation-state principle cannot be introduced into Eastern Europe.'" [quoting Kurt Tramples] in Hannah Arendt, *The Origins of Totalitarianism*, op. cit., p. 270.

13. Stéphane Pierré-Caps has described in detail the origin and characteristics of the multination state in his book, *La multination. L'avenir des minorités en Europe centrale et orientale*, Paris: Odile Jacob, 1995, pp. 223–316. See also Christophe Parent's remarkable essay on the multination state, *Le concept d'État fédéral multinational. Essai sur l'union des peuples*, Brussels: Peter Lang, 2011. One can also refer to Juan Linz, "State building and nation building," *European Review*, vol. 1,

(4,) October 1993, pp. 355–69 and Pierre Kende, "Quelle alternative à l'État-nation?" *Esprit*, no. 10, October 1991, pp. 23–30. See also Alain Gagnon and James Tully (eds), *Multinational Democracies*, Cambridge: Cambridge University Press, 2001.

14. Daniel Elazar, *Exploring Federalism*, Tuscaloosa: University of Alabama Press, 1987; Ruth Lapidot, *Autonomy: Flexible Solutions to Ethnic Conflicts*, Washington, D.C.: United States Institute of Peace Press, 1996; John Coakley, "Approaches to the Resolution of Ethnic Conflict: The Strategy of Non-territorial Autonomy," *International Political Science Review*, vol. 15 (3), 1994, pp. 297–314.

15. Annual opinion survey published by the Institute of Social and Political Sciences in Barcelona, *Sondeig d'opinió Catalunya, 2011*, Barcelona: ICPS, 2011, p. 36. About the same percentage favors Catalan identity. On the other hand, the proportion of those who define themselves primarily as Spanish has decreased considerably since the mid-1990s, to only 12%.

16. For more information, see Jean Bérenger, *L'Autriche-Hongrie (1815–1918)*, Paris: Armand Colin, 1998.

17. Point 10 put forward by President Wilson simply provided for greater latitude in the autonomous development of the people of the Double Monarchy, which in any event followed the drift of federalization that Vienna had begun to invoke, however belatedly.

18. The "conspiracy theory" mentioned by François Fejtö, seeing the alliance between Czech political leaders (Beneš, Masaryk) and French republican rulers heavily backed by the Freemasons as the decisive factor precipitating the fall of Austria-Hungary, seems excessive, however. See *Requiem pour un empire défunt. Histoire de la destruction de l'Autriche-Hongrie*, Paris: Lieu Commun, 1988.

19. Benjamin Braude and Bernard Lewis (eds), *Christians and Jews in the Ottoman Empire: The Functioning of a Plural Society*, New York: Holmes & Meier, 1982, p. 1.

20. Georges Corm, *L'Europe et l'Orient. De la balkanisation à la libanisation: histoire d'une modernité inaccomplie*, Paris: La Découverte, 1991, p. 51.

21. Here I rely on Andreas Kappeler, *La Russie Empire multiethnique* [trans. Guy Imart], Paris: Institut d'études slaves, 1994.

22. Lord Acton, "Nationality," in Gopal Balakrishnan (ed.), *Mapping the Nation*, London: Verso, 1996, pp. 30–6.

23. Will Kymlicka distinguishes between two forms of social unity, one based on the common good, the other on shared political values, in *Multicultural Citizenship: A Liberal Theory of Minority Rights*, Oxford: Clarendon Press, 1995, pp. 92 and 187–91.

24. Wayne Norman, "The Ideology of Shared Values: A Myopic Vision of Unity in the Multi-Nation State," in Joseph Carens, *Is Quebec Nationalism Just? Perspectives from Anglophone Canada*, Kingston and Montreal: McGill-Queen's University Press, 1995.

25. Jürgen Habermas, *The Inclusion of the Other: Studies in Political Theory*, Cambridge, MA: MIT Press, 2000, pp. 105–63.

26. This point is made by Kymlicka in *Multicultural Citizenship*, op. cit., p. 189.

27. Over 70% of the voters in Quebec opposed conscription in the April 1942 referendum.

28. Cited by Pol Vandromme, "Un rempart et un recours," *Le Monde des débats*, February 1994.

29. In November 1999, Australian voters clearly rejected the establishment of a republic.

30. Average abstention rate calculated on the basis of four national and regional elections held between 1999 and 2011.

31. Wilfried Dewachter, "La Belgique d'aujourd'hui comme société politique," in Alain Dieckhoff (ed.), *Belgique. La force de la désunion*, Brussels: Complexe, 1996, pp. 105–42.

32. Jeremy Webber, *Reimagining Canada: Language, Culture, Community, and the Canadian Constitution*, Kingston & Montreal: McGill-Queen's University Press, 1994, p. 31.

33. Kenneth McRoberts, "In Search of Canada Beyond Quebec," in Kenneth McRoberts (ed.), *Beyond Quebec: Taking Stock of Canada*, Montreal: McGill-Queen's University Press, 1995, p. 6.

34. Charles Taylor, "Shared and Divergent Values," in *Reconciling the Solitudes: Essays on Canadian Federalism and Nationalism*, Montreal: McGill-Queen's University Press, 1993, pp. 182–3.

35. Following the 1995 referendum, the federal government tabled a motion before the House of Commons recognizing Quebec as a distinct society. This motion is purely declarative and has no legal effect.

36. Cited by Laurence Cornu, "Fédéralistes! et pourquoi?" in François Furet and Mona Ozouf (eds), *La Gironde et les Girondins*, Paris: Payot, 1991, p. 270.

37. *Le Monde*, 9 September 1997.

38. *Le Monde*, 28 October 1997.

39. Jean-Marie Guéhenno, *La fin de la démocratie*, Paris: Flammarion, 1993.

40. *Le Monde*, 1 November 1996. On the so-called Europeanization of Belgium, see Emmanuelle Dardenne, "Entre réalités et idéalisme européens: le compromis belge," in Pascal Delwit, Jean-Michel De Waele and Paul Magnette (eds), *Gouverner la Belgique. Clivages et compromis dans une société complexe*, Paris: PUF, 1999, pp. 275–305.

41. Jean-Marc Ferry, "Quel patriotisme au-delà des nationalismes? Réflexion sur les fondements motivationnels d'une citoyenneté européenne," in Pierre Birnbaum (ed.), *Sociologie des nationalismes*, Paris: PUF, 1997, p. 436.

42. For a critique of this notion as applied to the case of Europe, see Andy Smith, "L'"espace public européen': une vue (trop) aérienne," *Critique internationale*, vol. 2 (1), Winter 1999, pp. 169–80.

43. Average voter turnout among the six founding states hovers around 45%. It is much lower in the twelve countries that joined the EU during the first decade of the 2000s, less than 30%. Large discrepancies exist, however, among newcomers: Malta stands out regularly for its civic-mindedness (with a turnout of nearly 80%) and Slovakia is just the opposite (less than 20%).

44. I borrow the term from Victor Pérez-Diaz, "La Cité européenne," *Critique internationale*, vol. 1, Fall 1998, pp. 101–26.

45. Mathieu Deflem and Fred Pampel, "The Myth of Post-National Identity: Popular Support for European Unification," *Social Forces*, vol. 75 (1), September 1996, pp. 119–43.

46. Ferry, op. cit., pp. 442–3.

47. Karl Deutsch, *Nationalism and Social Communication: An Inquiry into the Foundations of Nationality*, Cambridge, MA: MIT Press, 1969.

48. Jean-Marc Ferry, "The European State," in Riva Kastoryano (ed), *An Identity for Europe. The Relevance of Multiculturalism in EU Construction*, New York: Palgrave Macmillan, 2009, p. 188.

49. Ernst Haas, *The Uniting of Europe*, Stanford: Stanford University Press, 1958.

50. Christian Lequesne, "The European Union: how to deal with a strange animal," in Marie-Claude Smouts (ed.), *The New International Relations: Theory and Practice*, London: Hurst, 2001, pp. 55–72.

51. Jean-Marie Domenach, *Europe, le défi culturel*, Paris: La Découverte, 1990.

52. Gilles Andréani, "L'Europe des incertitudes," *Commentaire*, no. 85, Spring 1999, p. 30.

53. Jean-Marc Ferry suggests a radical path for forging a shared European identity by overcoming antagonistic national memories and forming a community of history. He thus proposes commemorating 8 May 1945 as the date of Europe's liberation. See *La question de l'Etat européen*, Paris: Gallimard, 2000, p. 160.

54. Jean-Marc Ferry, "The European State," in Kastoryano (ed.), op. cit., p. 182.

55. For a succinct presentation of this idea, see Gaëtane Ricard-Nihoul, *Pour une Fédération européenne d'États-nations. La vision de Jacques Delors revisitée*, Brussels: Larcier, 2012.

56. For an in-depth analysis of the concept of federation, see Olivier Beaud, *Théorie de la Fédération*, Paris: PUF, 2009.

INDEX

NAMES

NOTIONS AND THEMES